DATE			
JUN 23 1989			

CHOMSKY'S SYSTEM OF IDEAS

Chomsky's System of Ideas

FRED D'AGOSTINO

CLARENDON PRESS · OXFORD

1986

Oxford University Press, Walton Street, Oxford OX2 6DP

Oxford New York Toronto
Delhi Bombay Calcutta Madras Karachi
Kuala Lumpur Singapore Hong Kong Tokyo
Nairobi Dar es Salaam Cape Town
Melbourne Auckland

and associated companies in
Beirut Berlin Ibadan Nicosia

Oxford is a trade mark of Oxford University Press

Published in the United States
by Oxford University Press, New York

British Library Cataloguing in Publication Data

D'Agostino, Fred
Chomsky's system of ideas.
1. Chomsky, Noam — Contributions in linguistics
2. Linguistics
I. Title
410'.92'4   P85.C47
ISBN 0-19-824765-6

Library of Congress Cataloging in Publication Data

D'Agostino, Fred.
Chomsky's system of ideas.
Bibliography: p.
Includes index.
1. Chomsky, Noam.   2. Linguistics.   I. Title.
P85.C47D3 1986   410'.92'4   85-21624
ISBN 0-19-824765-6

Set by Grestun Graphics, Abingdon, Oxon
Printed in Great Britain
at the University Press, Oxford
by David Stanford
Printer to the University

This book is dedicated to
MY FATHER AND MOTHER

PREFACE

I HERE intend to discuss six important philosophical doctrines on which Chomsky's well-known and influential account of language is based. In the Introduction, I identify Chomsky's *subjectivistic* claim that the properties of any human language must be those 'that are given to it by the innate mental processes of the organism that has invented it' as the fundamental metaphysical notion on which the unity of his system of philosophical ideas in fact depends. In Chapter One, I consider and defend Chomsky's *individualistic* claim that linguistics is 'a subfield of psychology'. In Chapter Two, I consider and reject Chomsky's *mentalistic* claim that language users 'know' the grammars of their languages. I also there consider and defend Chomsky's *rationalist* claim that human language learning is mediated by innate mental schemata which define the range of possible human linguistic experience. In Chapter Three, I consider and defend Chomsky's *intellectualist* claim that linguistic phenomena are rule-guided, rather than law-governed. And in Chapter Four, I consider and defend Chomsky's *limitationist* account of human creativity, according to which there are biologically determined limits on the kinds of systems of beliefs or aesthetically significant objects which human beings can construct or find intelligible.

In each of these chapters, I will be particularly concerned not merely to rehearse or even to explicate Chomsky's own views on these matters. I will be concerned, rather, to consider in some detail critical arguments which bear on the cogency and acceptability of Chomsky's views. Although these views now constitute one of the orthodox accounts of human cognitive phenomena, no orthodoxy is ever well served by those who merely accept it in an uncritical way. We can, I think, best appreciate the merits of the currently dominant Chomskian account of human nature by seriously considering the criticisms which it has provoked. This is what I hope to do here.

I also believe that it is useful to try to show how the debate about Chomsky's views is related to debates in other domains of philosophical concern, and to debates which predate the development of Chomsky's system of ideas. I will, then, here try to show how some of the leading ideas of Chomsky's system are related to ideas which have been of interest to philosophers working in other areas and at earlier times. I do so not merely as a matter of historical interest, but because I believe, as Chomsky himself does, that we can often better understand contemporary philosophical thinking if we can trace it to its origins in earlier versions of the perennial problems with which it is concerned. And the problems with which Chomsky has been concerned are, as I hope to show, problems which have been of perennial philosophical interest.

The other thing which I hope to show is that Chomsky's various philosophical views tend to form a more or less coherent system of ideas. Chomsky's work, in other words, has a fundamental underlying unity. It does not consist merely of unrelated doctrines about a variety of human phenomena, but constitutes a unified account of the human condition, which I hope to explicate.

FRED D'AGOSTINO

August 1985

ACKNOWLEDGEMENTS

MY deepest intellectual debts are to my friends John Watkins and Geoffrey Sampson, both of whom have encouraged me in many ways and have, in particular, criticized versions of the work reported here in a friendly and constructive but searching fashion. Without their help and good advice, I would no doubt still be wandering aimlessly in the maze of Chomsky's system of ideas.

I would like to thank J. J. C. Smart and Noam Chomsky for helpful comments on the work reported in Chapter Four. Their advice led to many improvements in the material presented there.

I would also like to thank Mitzi Parkins for her skilful and efficient production of the final typescript version of this material.

Much of the material presented here has appeared elsewhere in a preliminary form. The bulk of Chapter One appeared as 'Individualism and Collectivism: The Case of Language', *Philosophy of the Social Sciences* ix (1978). Material presented in Section 6 of that chapter was outlined in my review of J. J. Katz, 'Language and Other Abstract Objects', *Australasian Journal of Philosophy* lxi (1983). The material presented in Chapter Two was outlined in my review article 'Knowledge of Language', *British Journal for the Philosophy of Science* xxviii (1977). The bulk of Chapter Four appeared as 'Chomsky on Creativity', *Synthese* lviii (1984), pp. 85-117 (copyright © by D. Reidel Publishing Company). Some of the material from Section 7 of that chapter is drawn from my review article 'Language, Creativity and Freedom', *Philosophy of the Social Sciences* xiv (1984). I am happy gratefully to acknowledge the kindness of the editors and publishers of these journals in permitting me to use this material in the preparation of this book.

CONTENTS

Contents

INTRODUCTION

CHOMSKY'S SUBJECTIVISM

In the past twenty-five years, linguistic research, especially in the United States, has increasingly come to be dominated by a theoretical and methodological perspective first sketched by Noam Chomsky in his book *Syntactic Structures*. Many commentators have suggested that Chomsky's account of language has had a revolutionary impact on linguistics.[1] Although I will mainly be concerned here to consider a number of philosophically interesting doctrines associated with Chomsky's account of language, I may perhaps first briefly indicate how Chomsky's contributions to linguistics have in fact revolutionized that discipline.

There are a number of ways in which one might proceed in this regard. One might, for instance, try to show that Chomsky's account of language is, with respect to some set of methodological standards, superior to the 'structuralist' account which it has displaced. To do so would be to provide a rational reconstruction of Chomsky's revolution in linguistics. To do so would be to show that those linguists who came to prefer Chomsky's account of language to the structuralist account were rationally warranted in doing so.[2] Alternatively, one might attempt, in a more playful spirit, to indicate the dependence of Chomsky's revolution on rhetorical excess, equivocation, and methodological short-cuts.[3] Or one might take a sociological

---

[1] See for instance J. Lyons, *Noam Chomsky*, London, 1970; J. Searle, 'Chomsky's Revolution in Linguistics', reprinted in G. Harman, ed., *On Noam Chomsky*, Garden City, 1974; and E. Bach, 'Structural Linguistics and the Philosophy of Science', *Diogenes* xxxi (1965).

[2] For the 'rationalist' claim that accounts of scientific revolutions ought to provide rational reconstructions in this sense, see I. Lakatos, 'Falsification and the Methodology of Scientific Research Programmes', in I. Lakatos and A. Musgrave, eds., *Criticism and the Growth of Knowledge*, Cambridge, 1970.

[3] For the 'anarchistic' claim that scientific revolutions depend for their success on these kinds of irrational factors, see P. Feyerabend, *Against Method*, London, 1975.

approach and attempt to identify the social and psychological pressures within the community of linguists which facilitated acceptance of Chomsky's revolutionary claims about language.[4]

I prefer, however, to proceed in a rather different and much less ambitious way. I will try instead to identify the leading or pivotal *metaphysical* idea on which Chomsky's revolutionary account of language depends. On the Popperian view adopted here, a metaphysical idea is typically embodied in a statement which, because of its distinctive logical form, is not subject to empirical refutation. Descartes's mechanistic picture of the natural world is a metaphysical idea in this sense. It can be taken to be embodied in the untestable claim that every natural process has its basis in a 'clockwork' mechanism. Although untestable, metaphysical claims of this kind can be inconsistent with testable empirical theories. It is for this reason that they can influence scientific thinking. A scientist who accepted Cartesian mechanism would, for instance, reject Newtonian gravitational theory, which postulates non-mechanistic 'action at a distance', and would try instead to construct a theory of gravitational phenomena which is consistent with Descartes's mechanistic world-view.[5]

My inspiration here is Watkins's discussion of the influential role which metaphysical ideas can play in the development of scientific theories. Since I am interested in demonstrating the unity or coherence of the philosophical ideas associated with Chomsky's account of language, this approach is indicated in this context. As Watkins has pointed out, metaphysical ideas are ideally 'suited to act as organizing principles at the center of a system whose parts have a mutual affinity because they all come under the same central [metaphysical] influence'.[6] In short, I will here try to isolate that metaphysical idea in terms of which the unity of Chomsky's system of ideas can be exhibited.

    [4] For a 'sociologistic' account of scientific revolutions, see T. Kuhn, *The Structure of Scientific Revolutions*, Chicago, 1970.
    [5] See J. Watkins, 'Confirmable and Influential Metaphysics', *Mind* lxvii (1958), pp. 350–1.
    [6] Ibid., p. 360.

I will proceed in a heuristic fashion in attempting to isolate what Watkins might call the 'metaphysical component' of Chomsky's account of language.[7] That is, I will try to show how Chomsky's characteristic metaphysical claims about language in fact emerged from his reflections on certain empirical linguistic phenomena.

In his earliest extensive discussion of the foundations of linguistics, Chomsky drew attention to a fact about language which he later called 'the central fact to which any significant linguistic theory must address itself'.[8] In that earlier discussion, Chomsky noted that the typical language user 'has observed [only] a certain limited set of utterances of his language', but can, 'on the basis of this finite linguistic experience, . . . produce an indefinite number of new utterances which are immediately acceptable to other members of his speech community'.[9] Chomsky later used the phrase 'the "creative" aspect of language' to refer to the characteristic he had so described.[10] Following Chomsky, I will say that language users who produce (or understand) sentences which are new to their experience manifest their linguistic *productivity*.[11] In effect, the problem of explaining linguistic productivity provided the context within which Chomsky's characteristic metaphysical claims about human language were developed.

We can reconstruct in the following way the relation between the phenomenon of linguistic productivity and the metaphysical component of Chomsky's account of language.

Modern linguists have tended to suppose that linguistic productivity is to be explained by assuming that language users produce (and understand) novel sentences by way of *analogy*

---

[7] For a characterization of the 'metaphysical components' of scientific theories, see J. Watkins, 'Metaphysics and the Advancement of Science', *British Journal for the Philosophy of Science* xxvi (1975).

[8] N. Chomsky, *Current Issues in Linguistic Theory*, The Hague, 1964, p. 7.

[9] N. Chomsky, *The Logical Structure of Linguistic Theory*, New York, 1975, p. 61.

[10] Chomsky, *Current Issues*, p. 15.

[11] See N. Chomsky, *Language and Mind*, New York, 1972, p. 92 n. 21.

with sentences with which they are familiar.[12] In opposition to this fairly widespread notion, Chomsky pointed out that such an explanation is vacuous unless the relevant notion of analogy is given some substantive content. This is so, in particular, because there will always be some ways in which novel word sequences which are not grammatical are nevertheless analogically similar to familiar grammatical sentences (and vice versa). [13] For this reason, Chomsky rejected analogical explanations of linguistic productivity and instead proposed to explain this aspect of language in the following way. A language can be thought of as a set of sentences, some of which will be 'familiar' to any given language user and some of which will be unfamiliar. A grammar can be thought of as a recursive definition of this (entire) set. We can then explain the productivity of language by assuming that language users employ a mentally represented counterpart of the linguist's grammar in producing (and understanding) the sentences of their language, both novel and familiar.[14] On Chomsky's account, then, language users are able to produce (and understand) sentences which are new to their experience because they are able to employ a grammar which provides semantic and phonetic interpretations for all of the sentences of their language.

The metaphysical implications of Chomsky's solution to the problem of linguistic productivity now follow more or less directly. In particular, it follows from Chomsky's proposal that a grammar of a language is, in effect, a theory about the psychological basis for language use. A grammar is, on this account, a theory of the mental states underlying the processes involved in the production and interpretation of utterances. And this suggests, in turn, a *subjectivistic* view of language, according to which language users give linguistic entities the properties which they have, and according to which the scientific identification

---

[12] For examples of this approach to the problem of linguistic creativity, see L. Bloomfield, *Language*, London, 1935, p. 275; C. Hockett, *A Course in Modern Linguistics*, New York, 1958, pp. 304 and 425 ff; and W. V. Quine, *Word and Object*, Cambridge, 1960, p. 9.

[13] See N. Chomsky, *Cartesian Linguistics*, New York, 1966, pp. 12–13.

[14] See Chomsky, *Language and Mind*, p. 100.

and explanation of these properties is, in effect, a psychological enterprise.

On this account, then, languages are subjectively constituted entities in a strong sense which distinguishes them from atoms and organisms and inanimate objects of familiar kinds. Our knowledge of atoms, for instance, is representational. Atoms exist and have the properties which they do have independently of our beliefs about them. Our beliefs about atoms record our attempts to *represent* these independently existing entities and their properties. According to linguistic subjectivism, however, languages, unlike atoms, do not exist and do not have properties independently of our (largely unconscious) beliefs about them. A language has the properties we believe it to have, then, not because these beliefs are accurately representational. It has these properties because our beliefs about its properties *constitute* it as an entity which has just the properties we believe it to have. On this account, in effect, a language is merely a reified non-entity; only the (largely unconscious) beliefs of language users are 'real'. As Chomsky says, a language 'has no existence apart from its mental representation' by its users, and its properties 'must be those that are given to it by the innate mental processes of the organism that has invented it and that invents it anew with each succeeding generation'.[15]

This subjectivistic account of linguistics is radically at variance with those objectivistic and instrumentalist accounts which were characteristic of much pre-Chomskian linguistics. An objectivistic account of linguistics construes languages as (possibly abstract) objects, the properties of which are not entirely determined by their users, as these properties are held to be by linguistic subjectivists such as Chomsky. According to instrumentalist accounts of linguistics, the goal of linguistic research is simply the construction of convenient recursive definitions of the sets of sentences which constitute the various human languages. Instrumentalists typically believe that it makes no sense to ask which of two or more recursive definitions

[15]   Ibid., p. 95.

of the sentences of a language is the grammar which users of that language in fact employ.[16]

The leading metaphysical idea of Chomsky's account of language is, then, in my view embodied in his proposal to treat language as an essentially subjective phenomenon.[17] I will try to show in the chapters which follow that Chomsky's subjectivism does indeed provide a framework within which his various and characteristic philosophical commitments can be integrated. Before proceeding to detailed investigations of these commitments, though, I may perhaps first mention some ways in which Chomsky's subjectivism has influenced linguistics as an empirical enterprise.

Linguists working in the Chomskian tradition draw a distinction between grammars which are 'psychologically realistic' and grammars which are 'observationally adequate'. On this account, a grammar is psychologically realistic if and only if it is in fact employed by the language user in producing and interpreting utterances. An observationally adequate grammar, on the other hand, is one which provides a recursive definition of the set of sentences which constitutes the language of the language user. Linguists influenced by Chomsky typically claim that the appropriate goal for linguistic research is the construction of grammars which are psychologically realistic, and not merely observationally adequate.[18] This goal follows, of course, directly from an interest in explaining linguistic productivity by postulating a mentally represented grammar, since it makes sense to explain the productive aspect of language in terms of a given grammar only if that grammar does in fact provide the psychological basis for productive language use.[19]

[16] For a recent defence of linguistic objectivism, see J. Katz, *Language and Other Abstract Objects*, Oxford, 1981. For an influential instrumentalist account of linguistics, see Z. Harris, 'Distributional Structure', reprinted in J. Fodor and J. Katz, eds., *The Structure of Language*, Englewood Cliffs, 1964.

[17] Katz arrived at a similar conclusion about the nature of Chomsky's linguistic revolution, but did so on the basis of a slightly different account of Chomsky's problem orientation. See Katz, op. cit., p. 24.

[18] For a discussion of these matters, see J. Fodor, T. Bever, and M. Garrett, *The Psychology of Language*, New York, 1974.

[19] See L. Hutchinson, 'Grammar as Theory', in D. Cohen, ed., *Explaining Linguistic Phenomena*, Washington, 1974, p. 45.

Of course, the goal of constructing psychologically realistic grammars places constraints on grammar construction which go beyond those implied in the goal of constructing grammars which are observationally adequate.[20] A recursive definition of a language can be observationally adequate without *ipso facto* being the grammar which language users employ in producing and interpreting utterances.[21] To determine whether a given grammar is in fact psychologically realistic, the linguist must consider evidence of kinds which would not be relevant to determining its observational adequacy. In fact, linguists have in recent years developed a number of psycholinguistic techniques for obtaining these kinds of evidence.[22] Chomsky's linguistic subjectivism has thus influenced the empirical practice of linguistics by fostering psycholinguistic investigations of grammars.[23]

It is well known that Chomsky rejected the 'corpus-based' methodology of his structuralist predecessors in favour of an 'intuitionistic' methodology. A corpus-based methodology is one which requires us to determine facts about linguistic structure solely with respect to distributional relations between linguistic entities in a corpus of attested utterances.[24] Chomsky's intuitionistic methodology, on the other hand, involves reliance on the beliefs (or intuitions) which language users have about the structural characteristics of the sentences

[20] For arguments that these additional constraints are excessive and indefensible, see Katz, *Language and Other Abstract Objects*, pp. 83–9.

[21] See P. Kiparsky, 'Linguistic Universals and Language Change', in E. Bach and R. Harms, eds., *Universals in Linguistic Theory*, New York, 1968, p. 121.

[22] See Fodor, Bever, and Garrett, *The Psychology of Language*, ch. 5 for an account of important psycholinguistic techniques.

[23] Chomsky himself has recently appeared to question the assumption that psycholinguistic investigations of grammars have a particularly important role to play in the evaluation of grammars. (See N. Chomsky, *Rules and Representations*, Oxford, 1980, ch. 5.) But Chomsky has neither repudiated linguistic subjectivism nor claimed that psycholinguistics has no legitimate role to play in the evaluation of grammars. He has merely insisted that psycholinguistic evidence has no privileged role in this context, and that it must be carefully interpreted.

[24] For an influential account of the corpus-based methodology of Chomsky's structuralist predecessors, see Z. Harris, *Methods in Structural Linguistics*, Chicago, 1951.

of their languages.[25] Chomsky's acceptance of an intuitionistic methodology seems to have been dictated by his rejection, on ontological grounds, of the still vaguely objectivistic proposal to regard a language as 'the totality of utterances that can be made in a speech-community' in favour of the patently subjectivistic claim that a language is embodied in 'the mental reality underlying actual [linguistic] behavior'.[26]

Linguistic subjectivism implies that the properties of sentences and languages are constituted by the (largely unconscious) beliefs of language users. In this case, it is natural to suppose that language users' explicit beliefs (or 'intuitions') about their language are an appropriate source of evidence about that language. On the other hand, linguistic objectivism implies that the properties of sentences and languages do not depend on the beliefs of language users, and thus can (and should) be investigated in the same way in which scientists investigate the properties of other objectively existent entities. And in this case, it is natural to suppose that the corpus of utterances current in some speech community is the appropriate object of linguistic inquiry. Chomsky's linguistic subjectivism thus appears to have influenced the empirical practice of linguistics by fostering the now widespread view that an appropriate methodology for linguistics is intuitionistic in character.

It is well known that Chomsky has rejected the possibility of employing mechanical discovery procedures in linguistics.[27] Chomsky's views on this matter also seem to have been dictated by his acceptance of a subjectivistic ontology for linguistics. Certainly, an objectivistic account of language seems to suggest that any given language has an objective reality which is independent of the subjective linguistic beliefs of its users. And in this case, we might expect it to be possible to employ a completely mechanical (i.e. fully objective) procedure for the

[25] For a brief account of his intuitionistic methodology, see N. Chomsky, *Aspects of the Theory of Syntax*, Cambridge, 1965, p. 20.

[26] L. Bloomfield, 'A Set of Postulates for the Science of Language', reprinted in M. Joos, ed., *Readings in Linguistics I*, Chicago, 1966, p. 26; and Chomsky, *Aspects*, p. 4.

[27] See N. Chomsky, *Syntactic Structures*, The Hague, 1957, ch. 6.

discovery of facts about that language. But the possibility of (successfully) employing such a mechanical discovery procedure seems, on the other hand, to be ruled out by a subjectivistic account of language. Linguistic subjectivism implies that the structure of a language is a function of its subjective structure. In this case, then, no method for the discovery of the structure of a language can be successful unless it permits investigation of, or incorporates substantive assumptions about, the subjective structure of that language. Linguistic subjectivism implies, in other words, that there is and can be no purely objective discovery procedure for linguistic structure.[28] Chomsky's linguistic subjectivism thus appears to have influenced the empirical practice of linguistics by undermining the once widely accepted claim that linguists ought to employ mechanical discovery procedures in their investigations of linguistic structure.

I claim, then, that the leading metaphysical idea inherent in Chomsky's account of language is embodied in the claim that linguistic phenomena are essentially subjective in nature. I have here briefly considered how this idea was suggested by Chomsky's consideration of the phenomenon of linguistic productivity. I have also briefly indicated how this idea has influenced developments in the empirical study of language. In the following four chapters, I will try to indicate how this idea, the metaphysical component of Chomsky's account of language, also serves to unify his characteristic philosophical commitments.

[28] My account of Chomsky's views here may appear to be inconsistent with his claim that a major goal of linguistic research is the construction of a theory of language acquisition. (See Chomsky, *Aspects*, p. 4.) If it is possible to construct such a theory it trivially follows that it is possible to construct a discovery procedure for grammars. For language-learners do, at least on Chomsky's account, discover a grammar for their language; and a theory of language acquisition therefore does constitute a discovery procedure. (See B. Derwing, *Transformational Grammar as a Theory of Language Acquisition*, Cambridge, 1973, p. 60.) This appearance of inconsistency can, however, be dissolved in the following way. When Chomsky rejected the possibility of constructing discovery procedures for linguistic structure, he was rejecting the possibility of constructing only those objectivistic procedures which incorporate no substantive assumptions about the range of possible subjective linguistic experience. But his own theory of language acquisition does incorporate very powerful assumptions of this kind. There is, then, no inconsistency in Chomsky's views.

1

CHOMSKY'S INDIVIDUALISM

1 *Introduction*

According to Chomsky, linguistics is 'a subfield of psychology' concerned with 'the mental reality underlying actual [linguistic] behavior'.[1] Chomsky's views on the nature of linguistics might usefully be contrasted with those of Schleicher, a nineteenth-century historical linguist, according to whom linguistics is the study of languages as 'natural organisms which, without being determinable by the will of man, grew and developed in accordance with fixed laws'.[2]

Chomsky's programmatic statement about the nature of linguistics reflects or instantiates the philosophical thesis known as *methodological individualism*, according to which all social phenomena, such as language, are to be explained, ultimately, in terms of the characteristics of individual human beings. On the other hand, Schleicher's account embodies the philosophical thesis known as *methodological collectivism*, according to which some characteristics of social phenomena, such as language, are *sui generis* with respect to the characteristics of individual human beings, and must therefore be explained in non-psychological terms.[3]

I may perhaps mention here that Chomsky's methodological individualism is just what one would expect in view of his

---

[1] N. Chomsky, *Reflections on Language*, London, 1976, p. 160; and *Aspects of the Theory of Syntax*, Cambridge, 1965, p. 4.

[2] F. Schleicher, *Darwinism Tested by the Science of Language*, trans. A. Bikkers, London, 1869, pp. 20–1.

[3] I will here treat linguistic objectivism, of the kind espoused by Katz in his book *Language and Other Abstract Objects* (Oxford, 1981), as a species of linguistic collectivism. This is appropriate, I think, because both objectivism and collectivism concur in regarding languages as entities at least some of the properties of which are *sui generis* with respect to the psychological properties of language users. According to objectivism, languages have *sui generis* properties because they are abstract (Platonic) objects. According to standard, non-objectivist, versions of collectivism, languages have *sui generis* properties because they are socially constituted entities.

characteristically subjectivistic account of language. Indeed, the individualistic methodological position which Chomsky embraces is more or less dictated by his acceptance of the metaphysical claim that linguistic phenomena are essentially subjective in nature. If the properties of a language 'must be those that are given to it by ... the organism that has invented it', then it is natural to suppose that linguistics is 'a subfield of psychology'. These claims, surely, simply record two aspects of the same underlying intuition about the nature of language. Chomsky's acceptance of them thus illustrates the unity of his system of ideas, and, ultimately, the dependence of that system on his characteristically subjectivistic account of language.

In recent years, most research in linguistics has embodied the individualistic methodological orientation in effect advocated by Chomsky.[4] This orientation has, however, recently been challenged. It has been suggested that collectivism rather than individualism provides the appropriate methodological orientation for linguistics. This suggestion threatens both individualism as a general thesis, and the currently individualistic character of Chomskian linguistics. This suggestion is also of interest because it has been embodied in arguments which are similar to those which have been employed in the philosophical debate about individualism.

I will here be concerned, then, to undermine the suggestion that collectivism rather than individualism provides the appropriate methodological basis for linguistics. More specifically, while I will not primarily be concerned to show that individualism provides the correct orientation for linguistics, I will be concerned to refute suggestions that there are a priori reasons for suggesting that individualism is inappropriate as a methodological orientation for linguistics.

---

[4] I do not mean to suggest here that pre-Chomskian linguistics was inevitably or wholly collectivistic in its methodological orientation. There is a sense in which Paul, Saussure, Bloomfield, and Sapir, among others, all adopted an individualistic point of view about linguistic phenomena. (This point is perhaps arguable in the case of Saussure. I defend it at Section 7 below.)

2   Individualism and Collectivism

Many recent discussions in the philosophy of the social sciences have been addressed to two divergent proposals about the appropriate methodology for empirical social scientific inquiry. Popper, Watkins, Agassi, and others have advocated a position which they call methodological individualism, while Mandelbaum, Gellner, Goldstein, and others have advocated a position which we may call methodological collectivism.[5]

Individualism and collectivism may be contrasted in the following way.[6]

Let us grant the irreducible ontological distinctiveness of human social institutions, processes, and events on the one hand, and human individuals on the other hand. Let us also grant that certain predicates, which we can call *C*-predicates, apply to social phenomena; that certain predicates, which we can call *I*-predicates, apply to individuals; and that at least some *C*-predicates cannot be defined in terms of *I*-predicates and vice versa.

Then, according to methodological individualism: (i) an adequate description of some social phenomenon may involve *C*-predicates; (ii) but any 'ultimate' explanation of this phenomenon will 'essentially' involve only *I*-predicates. That is, *C*-predicates will figure in such an explanation only in laws of the form

> L_I The state of affairs which obtains when various individuals can be characterized by the *I*-predicate I_i causes the state of affairs which obtains when a particular social entity, event, or process can be characterized by the *C*-predicate C_j.

Of course, laws invoked in explanations of social phenomena must contain *C*-predicates, as laws of the form L_I do, if

---

[5]   See the papers collected in J. O'Neill, ed., *Modes of Individualism and Collectivism*, London, 1973.

[6]   See J. Watkins, 'The Human Condition', in R. Cohen *et al.*, eds., *Essays in Memory of Imre Lakatos*, Dordrecht, 1976, p. 710; and A. Danto, 'Methodological Individualism and Methodological Socialism', reprinted in O'Neill, *Modes*, pp. 323–4.

descriptions of the phenomena they are invoked to explain irreducibly contain C-predicates, as they may according to (i) above. On the other hand, the requirement that C-predicates appear only in the consequent clauses and never in the antecedent clauses of such laws captures the basic ontological intuition behind the individualistic methodological injunction: only individual human beings are causal agents in the formation, development, and functioning of human social institutions.

By contrast, according to methodological collectivism, (i') an adequate description of the behaviour, beliefs and habits of individual human beings may involve I-predicates; (ii') but an 'ultimate' explanation of these phenomena may 'essentially' involve C-predicates as well as I-predicates. In particular, such an explanation may involve laws of the form

L_C The state of affairs which obtains when a social institution can be characterized by the C-predicate C_i
causes the state of affairs which obtains when certain
individuals can be characterized by the I-predicate I_j.

The possibility that at least one C-predicate may in this way appear in the antecedent clause of a law involved in the explanation of facts about individuals captures, in turn, the basic ontological intuition behind the collectivistic methodological position: at least some characteristics of individual human beings are causally dependent on the characteristics of their social institutions.

A word now on the qualification 'ultimate' in (ii) and (ii') above. At least on one interpretation, methodological individualism does not rule out the construction or deny the heuristic utility of laws of the form L_C or

L_C' The state of affairs which obtains when a social insti-
  • tution can be characterized by the C-predicate C_i
causes the state of affairs which obtains when a (possibly distinct) social institution can be characterized
by the C-predicate C_j.

Likewise, methodological collectivism does not rule out the

construction or deny the heuristic utility of laws of the form L_I or

L_I' The state of affairs which obtains when certain individuals can be characterized by the I-predicate I_i causes the state of affairs in which those individuals can be characterized by the I-predicate I_j.

What individualism does rule out is the claim that there are laws of the forms L_C or L_C' which cannot, in turn, be derived from laws of the forms L_I and L_I'. According to individualism, laws of the forms L_C and L_C' are in no sense 'ultimately' explanatory. Heuristically useful though they may be, they provide, in the end, only 'halfway' explanations, and are themselves in principle derivable from laws of the forms L_I and L_I'. According to individualism, it is only laws of these latter forms which can be said to provide 'rock bottom' or 'ultimate' explanations of social phenomena.[7] Likewise, what collectivism rules out is the claim that every law of the form L_I or L_I' is underivable from laws of the forms L_C and L_C'. According to collectivism, some laws of the forms L_I and L_I' are not 'ultimately' explanatory. Heuristically useful though such laws may be, at least some of them provide, in the end, only 'halfway' explanations, and are themselves in principle derivable from laws of the forms L_C and L_C'. According to collectivism, at least certain aspects of individual human behaviour have 'rock bottom' explanations only in terms of laws of these latter forms.

We may note in passing an asymmetry between individualism and collectivism. Whereas individualism requires that only laws of the forms L_I and L_I' are to be invoked in any 'ultimate' explanation of social or individual phenomena, collectivism implies only that not every law of these forms is to be construed as providing an 'ultimately' explanatory principle. In particular, collectivism is consistent with the possibility that at least some characteristics of individuals and social entities

[7] See J. Watkins, 'Historical Explanations in the Social Sciences', reprinted in O'Neill, *Modes*, p. 168.

are the effects of causes which are themselves independent of social phenomena. Individualism, on the other hand, rules out the possibility that there are any aspects of individual or social phenomena which are 'irreducibly' dependent on *sui generis* characteristics of social institutions.

It should be noted that this asymmetry makes collectivism somewhat harder to criticize than individualism. Whereas individualism is inconsistent with the claim that there is an 'ultimate' explanation of some human phenomenon which 'irreducibly' involves laws of the forms L_C or L_C', collectivism is not inconsistent with the claim that there is an 'ultimate' explanation of some human phenomenon which 'irreducibly' involves laws only of the forms L_I and L_I'. In fact, collectivism is only inconsistent with the claim that every 'ultimate' explanation of every human phenomenon involves laws only of the forms L_I and L_I'. Collectivism is separately consistent with each allegedly 'ultimate' individualistic explanation; it is inconsistent only with individualism itself.

Another way of characterizing this asymmetry is also available. We might say that advocates of collectivism have two 'degrees of freedom' in avoiding criticism, whereas advocates of individualism have only one. With respect to an allegedly 'ultimate' individualistic explanation of some phenomenon, collectivists can both deny that this is in fact an 'ultimate' explanation, and point out that this possibility is anyway not precluded by collectivism. With respect to an allegedly 'ultimate' collectivistic explanation, however, individualists can only deny that this is in fact an 'ultimate' explanation, since the possibility of its being so is precluded by individualism.[8]

---

[8] This asymmetry can also be explicated in terms of the distinction drawn by Watkins between 'all–some' and 'some–some' metaphysical statements. (See J. Watkins, 'Confirmable and Influential Metaphysics', *Mind* lxvii (1958), pp. 345-7.) Individualism can be cast in the form of the 'all–some' statement *MI*: For every human phenomenon, there is an 'ultimate' explanation which 'irreducibly' involves only laws of the forms L_I and L_I'. Likewise, collectivism can be cast in the form of the 'some–some' statement *MC*: For some human phenomena, there are 'ultimate' explanations which 'irreducibly' involve laws of the forms L_C and L_C'. The asymmetry then follows as a consequence of the fact that 'all–some' statements such as *MI* are inconsistent with the negations of their instantiations, whereas 'some–some' statements such as *MC* are not inconsistent with the negations of their instantiations.

The importance of this asymmetry will emerge in the course of this chapter, where I criticize arguments which are alleged to provide a priori grounds for abandoning the currently individualistic methodological orientation of linguistic research. Criticism of these arguments will sometimes involve the reduction of allegedly 'ultimate' collectivistic explanations of linguistic phenomena to individualistic explanations of these phenomena. While the possibility of carrying out such reductions suggests the viability of the currently individualistic methodological orientation of linguistics, it does not, in view of this asymmetry, undermine collectivism and thus establish individualism as a methodological thesis of general validity and applicability.[9]

Before considering the bearing of linguistics on the debate about these positions, it is appropriate to mention one final proviso on the interpretation of individualism and collectivism. Individualism and collectivism can, and for the sake of clarity should, be distinguished from a variety of related theses.[10] In particular, neither individualism nor collectivism is an ontological thesis, though each, as we have seen, is responsive to certain ontological intuitions. Individualism does not imply the non-existence of things, such as social institutions, which are neither individual human beings nor physical objects. Likewise, collectivism does not imply that individual human beings have no ontological status which is independent of their status as participants in social institutions. Keeping this proviso in mind will be helpful in what follows.

---

[9] Of course, it might be suggested that collectivism is not an entirely empty metaphysical thesis and thus must be supposed to hold in certain specified domains; that it must, then, surely hold in the domain of linguistic phenomena, which are paradigmatically social phenomena; and that MC can therefore be taken to entail the thesis MC^*: For every linguistic phenomenon, there is an 'ultimate' explanation which 'irreducibly' involves laws of the forms L_C and $L_C{}^l$. In this case, of course, any reduction of collectivistic explanations in linguistics would have critical bearing on the status of collectivism as a general methodological thesis. If MC does entail MC^*, then undermining the latter thesis undermines the former, more general, thesis.

[10] See Danto, 'Methodological Individualism and Methodological Socialism', pp. 320–1.

3   *Linguistic Individualism*

Within the central tradition of research in Chomskian linguistics, individualism has provided the dominant methodological orientation. This orientation is revealed in Chomsky's claim that linguistics is 'a subfield of psychology' and in his remark that language 'has no existence apart from its mental representation' by its users.[11] Recently, Chomsky's remarks on linguistic methodology have been even more explicitly individualistic in character. He has said, for instance, that though we expect to find the grammar of a language 'physically represented in . . . the adult brain, . . . the language [itself] is epiphenomenal'.[12] Indeed, Chomsky appears explicitly to reject a collectivistic account of language when he claims that 'it does not follow that there exists a "shared language", a kind of "superlanguage" in terms of which each individual's understanding of his own language must be explained'.[13] It seems clear from these statements that the characteristics of a language are what they are, according to Chomsky, because of certain characteristics of its individual users. And this, of course, is exactly what the advocate of individualism would expect: the users of a language are the only causal agents in its formation, development, and functioning.

Further examples of this methodological orientation could easily be proliferated, but we may, I think, assume here that Chomskian linguists are strongly committed to an individualistic methodology. This commitment has, however, recently been challenged by a number of linguists and philosophers.

Sanders has suggested that there are facts about language which admit of no adequate explanation in terms of the psychology of language users. He concludes that linguistic theories must involve

claims about what is culturally real [and] though knowledge . . . about cultural objects obviously affects, influences and guides the behavior of

---

[11] Chomsky, *Reflections*, p. 160; and *Language and Mind*, New York, 1972, p. 95.
[12] N. Chomsky, *Rules and Representations*, Oxford, 1980, pp. 82–3.
[13] Ibid., p. 118.

individual human beings, the existence of such knowledge does not explain or fully determine either the cultural objects themselves or the behavior of the individuals who possess this knowledge.[14]

According to Sanders, then, language is a human social institution which has certain characteristics which cannot be explained in terms of facts about the actions, beliefs, and habits of individual participants in that institution. And this claim is, of course, inconsistent with methodological individualism and thus threatens to undermine linguistic individualism.

Watkins has recently constructed a thought experiment about the invention of language which he thinks reveals the need to posit a 'pre-attunement' of the cognitive capacities of the inventor and his or her imitators. Since Watkins sees no way of accounting individualistically for this 'pre-attunement', he proposes instead to explain it in terms of a collectivistic theory of natural selection.[15] According to Watkins, then, language is a human social institution an explanation of the origins of which cannot be given solely in terms of the characteristics of its individual inventors and users. And this claim, of course, is inconsistent with methodological individualism and thus threatens to undermine linguistic individualism.

Katz has recently argued that the constraints imposed on grammar construction by the dominant individualistic methodology of linguistics 'so drastically limit the abstractness of grammars that the best theories of natural languages are ruled out'.[16] Katz claims that the objectivistic view that 'grammars are theories of abstract objects' provides a better methodological orientation for linguistics.[17] According to Katz, then, language is a human social institution the characteristics of which cannot adequately be accounted for in individualistic terms. And this claim is, of course, inconsistent with methodological individualism and thus threatens the linguistic individualism which Chomsky espouses.

---

[14] G. Sanders, 'Issues of Explanation in Linguistics', in D. Cohen, ed., *Explaining Linguistic Phenomena*, Washington, 1974 pp. 12–13.
[15] See Watkins, 'The Human Condition'.
[16] Katz, *Language and Other Abstract Objects*, p. 25.   [17] Ibid., p. 3.

The arguments of Sanders, Watkins, and Katz motivate an examination of the relation between individualism and linguistics. Watkins's argument is, perhaps, especially salient in this regard, since it marks a drastic change of heart by one of the earliest and staunchest advocates of methodological individualism. In Sections 4 to 6 below, I will explicate and criticize these arguments, and defend the claim which they challenge: that individualism provides the appropriate methodological orientation for linguistics. In Sections 7 and 8, I will consider related arguments which can be extracted from the earlier work of Saussure and from the contemporary research of sociolinguists.

4 *Methodological Objections*

Sanders presents three arguments in support of the claim that collectivism rather than individualism provides the appropriate methodological basis for linguistics:

(*a*) Sanders seems to have been led to his advocacy of collectivism by the observation that an individualistic methodological orientation for linguistics threatens the autonomy of linguistics as a discipline, since it leaves linguistics with no 'natural domain' of enquiry. If the study of language is really just the study of individuals' (tacit and explicit) beliefs about language, as an individualistic methodology seems to suggest, then linguistics is, as Chomsky has claimed, really just 'a subfield of psychology'. According to Sanders, if theories of languages

are merely abbreviations for certain portions of the actual knowledge or behavior of their speakers, then it would be quite easy to show that the traditional domain of linguistics is not a natural domain, and that all grammars ... must be appropriately reducible to theories of human psychology or physiology.[18]

It is not clear that this observation can be (or is even meant to be) taken seriously as an argument against linguistic individualism. We may still ask, however, what kind of motivation it might provide for advocating a collectivistic rather than an

----

[18] Sanders, 'Issues', p. 11.

individualistic methodological orientation for linguistics. Three considerations seem to be relevant here.

First, this observation seems to embody a rather extreme form of disciplinary parochialism, and we may want to dismiss it for this reason alone.

Second, it is, surely, an open empirical question whether linguistics is a natural domain of enquiry in any strong sense which might be related, for instance, to those ontological questions which form the background to the debate between individualists and collectivists. In any event, the fact that linguistics has existed for some time as a distinct academic discipline provides no conclusive reason for supposing that its domain of enquiry is a natural one in this strong sense. If Sanders assumes that linguistics ought to constitute a natural domain of enquiry in this strong sense, then he may well pre-empt issues associated with the debate between individualists and collectivists. Invoking this assumption may thus render question-begging the argument supporting Sanders's collectivistic conclusion.

Third, the autonomy of chemistry, for instance, as a natural domain of enquiry, in some weaker, non-pre-emptive sense, is not, presumably, threatened by the fact that its laws may be, and in some cases actually are, derivable from those of physics. Why then should the autonomy of linguistics, in this weaker sense, be threatened by the possibility that linguistic facts may be explicable in psychological terms?

On these grounds, then, I think we can safely dismiss the 'domain problem' as a plausible motivation for abandoning an individualistic methodological orientation in linguistics.

(*b*) Linguists of a Chomskian persuasion have, by and large, accepted the heuristic utility of Chomsky's famous distinction between linguistic competence and linguistic performance. Although there is a certain amount of controversy about how this distinction ought to be drawn, it is customarily drawn in the following way.[19] Language users' competence is embodied

[19] For the standard account of the competence–performance distinction, see N. Chomsky, *Aspects of the Theory of Syntax*, Cambridge, 1965, pp. 3–4. For objections to this account, see B. Derwing, *Transformational Grammar as a Theory of Language Acquisition*, Cambridge, 1973, ch. 8.

in their tacit knowledge about their language. This tacit knowledge provides the basis for linguistic performance, or behaviour. For a variety of essentially non-linguistic reasons, users' performance may not accurately reflect their competence. Users' competence nevertheless (partially) determines their actual performance.

Sanders's second reason for rejecting linguistic individualism, then, is embodied in his claim that an individualistic methodological orientation undermines precisely this familiar and useful distinction, while a collectivistic orientation in fact justifies it. According to Sanders,

the fact that linguistic theories are about cultural objects and events rather than psychological ones underlies the familiar distinction recognized by linguists [between competence and performance, a distinction the significance of which] has apparently only been questioned by those essentially individualistic philosophers who assume that linguistic theories are at least partly about human behavior rather than wholly about human language.[20]

Sanders's claim here rests, I think, on a dubious assumption. He appears to assume that an individualistic theory of a language is, in effect, a theory about the overt linguistic behaviour (i.e. performance) of users of that language. But this assumption is incorrect. The linguistic individualist is perfectly free to suppose, and generally will suppose, that a theory of a language is, in effect, a theory about those psychological characteristics of language users which underlie their overt linguistic behaviour. Individualism is not to be confused with behaviourism. But only some such confusion could motivate Sanders' assumption that 'individualistic philosophers . . . assume that linguistic theories are at least partly about human behavior'. Of course, if individualists can distinguish between overt linguistic behaviour and its psychological basis, then they can recognize, and indeed will be inclined to recognize, the existence of some distinction quite similar to

<hr />

[20] Sanders, 'Issues', p. 13.

that usually drawn by linguists between competence and performance.[21]

I think we can conclude, then, that the appropriateness of an individualistic methodological orientation for linguistics cannot be undermined by appealing to the salience of the competence/performance distinction.

(*c*) I have already mentioned Sanders's main argument against linguistic individualism. According to Sanders, there are facts about languages which are not currently explicable in individualistic terms and which it seems implausible to suppose ever will be so explicable. From this claim, Sanders concludes that 'there are in fact irreducible cultural objects and laws . . . [and] the burden of proof thus rests with advocates of methodological individualism'.[22]

In order to determine the force of this argument, it will be useful first to mention Watkins's important distinction between 'detailed explanations' and 'anonymous explanations'.[23] A detailed individualistic explanation of some linguistic fact would involve reference to the actual behaviour and beliefs of specified individual language users. An anonymous individualistic explanation of this fact would, on the other hand, involve reference to the idealized behaviour and beliefs of typical, unspecified language users.

Perhaps it is a detailed explanation of certain kinds of linguistic facts which Sanders supposes it is now impossible to give and implausible to believe ever could be given. If so, I entirely agree, but am at a loss to see how this supposition threatens linguistic individualism. The impossibility at issue is, surely, a practical one. It results from the practical inaccessibility of various relevant data. But linguistic individualism would be

---

[21] Of course, linguists such as Bever have proposed drawing the competence-performance distinction differently from Chomsky. (See T. Bever, 'The Psychology of Language and Structuralist Investigations of Nativism', in G. Harman, ed., *On Noam Chomsky*, Garden City, 1974.) But this has typically been for reasons which are irrelevant to the debate between individualists and collectivists.

[22] Sanders, 'Issues', p. 12.

[23] See J. Watkins, 'Ideal Types and Historical Explanation', reprinted in O'Neill, *Modes*, pp. 155–65.

undermined here only if the impossibility at issue were a matter of principle and not just of practice. Since Sanders provides no reason for believing that this impossibility is one of principle, we can conclude, I think, that linguistic individualism is not threatened by the fact that linguists are unable to provide detailed individualistic explanations of certain kinds of linguistic facts.

Perhaps we should conclude, then, that Sanders is instead claiming that it is impossible to give even anonymous individualistic explanations of such facts. If this is what he claims, then linguistic individualism might indeed be threatened by his argument. Individualists are committed to the availability of anonymous individualistic explanations of linguistic facts. Sanders, however, provides no reasons for supposing that these kinds of explanations are unavailable, and furthermore neglects to mention the fact that such anonymous individualistic explanations have been widely employed in recent years, particularly in historical linguistics.[24] Perhaps Sanders finds such explanations inadequate. If so, some argument to this effect is called for.

Sanders, in short, either thinks that the acknowledged unavailability of detailed individualistic explanations of linguistic facts tells against linguistic individualism, in which case he is wrong on a point of fact about the individualist's commitments. Or he thinks that the alleged unavailability of anonymous individualistic explanations of such facts tells against linguistic individualism, in which case he appears, in the absence of supporting arguments, to be wrong on a point of fact about linguistics.

I think we can conclude, then, that none of Sanders's arguments against linguistic individualism can be accepted. I turn now to Watkins's thought experiment, and consider its relevance to the issue under discussion.

---

[24] See F. D'Agostino, 'Ontology and Explanation in Historical Linguistics', *Philosophy of the Social Sciences* xv (1985).

5 *Individualism and the Origin of Language*

Watkins's thought experiment was not intended to undermine linguistic individualism, as Sanders's arguments were. Nevertheless, as Watkins himself recognizes, this experiment does have implications for linguistic individualism, and so must be considered here.[25]

Watkins's thought experiment can be reconstructed in the following way.[26]

We are asked to consider two of our remote, pre-linguistic ancestors, Alpha and Beta, and their development of a rudimentary language. Watkins discusses several stages in this development, but since the conclusions he draws from his consideration of each such stage are similar, we can limit our exposition of his experiment to one such stage—the stage, for instance, at which Alpha and Beta begin to use names to refer to things.

On the (Hobbesian) view which Watkins is considering, a name begins as a mark—that is, as an object, sound, or inscription which an individual uses to remind himself or herself of some other object(s). But a mark is not yet a name, since it has significance only for its inventor/user, whereas a name has shared, public significance.

Suppose, then, that Alpha has invented some marks. The problem which Watkins addresses is that of explaining how Alpha can get Beta to use these marks in the same way as he does, thus turning them into names. Watkins correctly points out that any of the teaching methods, such as ostension, which Alpha might employ will be effective only if Beta is already aware of their significance. According to Watkins, for ostension to be an effective teaching method, Beta 'must already have some inkling about the significance of pointing; and she must have learnt to make private marks for herself; . . . Beta must be just about as inventive, and in the same sorts of ways, as Alpha; otherwise, names will never get established in their cave'.[27]

[25] See Watkins, 'The Human Condition', p. 714 n. 2.
[26] Ibid., pp. 696–7.
[27] Ibid., p. 697.

From this, Watkins concludes that Alpha and Beta must have 'collaborated spontaneously . . . as if by a kind of pre-established harmony'.[28] Furthermore, Watkins seems to feel that it is precisely the need to posit a pre-established harmony between Alpha and Beta which militates against explaining their collaboration individualistically. He seems to think that there can be no individualistic explanation of the required attunement of the cognitive capacities of Alpha and Beta. Watkins appears to suggest that this 'pre-attunement' of (innately based) individual linguistic capacities must be explained in terms of the theory of 'group selection'—that is, in terms of a theory of natural selection which takes a group or population of organisms, rather than the individual organism, as the unit on which selective pressures operate, and which proposes that these pressures favour the survival of individual organisms which have characteristics which are advantageous to the group as a whole, whatever their (possibly negative) consequences for the individuals who possess them.[29]

If Watkins is right about these matters, then language is a human social institution the phylogenetic development of which cannot be explained individualistically. And this, of course, threatens both individualism in general and the currently individualistic methodological orientation of linguistic research.[30] To defend linguistic individualism, I must then now try to undermine Watkins's argument.

The first thing one might say about that argument is that Watkins's use of teleological language—specifically, his reference to 'pre-attunement'—though no doubt intended metaphorically, seems to have prevented him from seeing that this attunement of capacities can, despite his denial of this, be seen as just a 'happy coincidence'.[31] In particular, what Watkins's use of

[28]   See Watkins, 'The Human Condition', p. 701.   [29]   Ibid., pp. 707 and 712.

[30]   Watkins does not seem to have realized to what an extent Chomskian linguistics is based on an individualistic methodological orientation. He approvingly quotes Chomsky's individualistic maxim that 'language is "reinvented" each time it is learned' in the context of an otherwise anti-individualistic discussion of language. Ibid., p. 715 n. 20.

[31]   Ibid., p. 712.

teleological language may have prevented him from noticing is the existence of those precursors of Alpha and Beta whose cognitive capacities were not suitably matched and who thus between themselves never managed to establish any language-like communicative system. This consideration does not show, of course, that the attunement of the linguistic capacities of Alpha and Beta can be explained individualistically. What it does show, though, is that what needs to be explained need not be described collectivistically. On this account, what needs to be explained is a conjunction of facts about individuals (that Alpha had some cognitive capacity at some time and that Beta had it then too), and not a fact about the group constituted by those individuals. And, I would guess, it is precisely the salience of this point which reference to pre-attunement tends to disguise.

These considerations make it clearer, I think, what Watkins has to establish in order to support his anti-individualistic claim about explanations of the origin of language. Watkins must establish that we cannot explain the series of 'happy coincidences' (of attunements of cognitive capacities) which were necessary for the development of language without appealing to the causal efficacy of certain 'irreducibly' social factors such as group selective pressures on individuals.

It is not clear that Watkins actually argued (or intended to argue) to this effect. Nevertheless, I think there is an argument for this thesis implicit in Watkins's discussion of his thought experiment. This argument has something like the following form.[32]

(i) Evolution has selected for a linguistic capacity the immediate selective consequences of which for lone individual possessors of it may be negative. (As will emerge below, this is, I think, an unwarranted assumption in this case.)

(ii) It is hard to see how this could have happened given the individualistic assumption that selective pressures operate on individuals and operate negatively on individuals who have characteristics with negative (individual) selective consequences.

[32] Ibid., pp. 706–7.

(iii) We can, however, explain the development of a linguistic capacity by pointing out that shared possession of such a capacity by a group of individuals would have positive (immediate) selective consequences for that group since an ability to communicate increases the chances of surviving attacks by predators.

(iv) 'Group-selective' pressures must be invoked, then, in explaining the development of such a linguistic capacity—in explaining the series of 'happy coincidences' which constituted this development.

This argument is, I think, particularly vulnerable on one point. That is, premiss (i) seems patently incorrect. A capacity for making marks, for instance, even though unshared by others, can hardly be supposed to have negative selective consequences, as, for instance, an altruistic moral sense might have. (It was the problem of explaining the development of altruism which, in part, motivated the theory of group selection to which Watkins appeals.) At worst, then, individualistic selective pressures ought to be neutral with respect to the inheritance of the language capacity. Furthermore, it may even be plausible to suppose that this capacity has positive selective consequences even for its lone possessors. Even the ability to give objects private marks may be a useful one from the point of view of individual survival. In any event, once premiss (i) is rejected, in neither case does an individualistic explanation of the sharing of linguistic capacities seem to be inadequate. If Alpha and Beta share a capacity to use marks, then this may be because both inherited this capacity from one of their precursors, who may have shared it with none of her or his fellows but who would not for this reason have been so disadvantaged biologically as to be unable to survive long enough to reproduce and thus to pass this capacity along, eventually, to Alpha and Beta. On this account, then, the fact that Alpha and Beta share this capacity *is* just a 'happy coincidence', but not an individualistically inexplicable one.

Watkins's thought experiment thus does not have the anti-individualistic implications he seems to think it has. This experiment thus does not undermine either methodological individualism as a general thesis or the currently individualistic methodological orientation of linguistics. I turn now to Katz's objectivistic arguments against linguistic individualism.

6 Objectivist Objections

According to Katz, 'theories in linguistics are not psychological theories', as linguistic individualists such as Chomsky claim. This is so, in particular, Katz says, because 'the grammatical component in the speaker-hearer's information processing mechanism can be a false theory of the grammatical structure of the language'.[33] In this case, of course, linguistic individualism is threatened, since it identifies the theory of a language with the language user's theory of that language. If the language user's theory of language is a false theory, then this identification is clearly unwarranted. Katz presents three major arguments in support of his anti-individualistic claim that 'linguistic theories are not about psychological phenomena':[34]

(*a*) According to Katz, the claim that 'linguistic theories are not about psychological phenomena [as the individualist alleges] but straightforwardly about sentences and language [as the objectivist or collectivist claims] rests on the general epistemological distinction between knowledge that we have of something and the thing(s) that we have knowledge of'. Katz claims that linguistic individualists ignore this distinction and so are driven to the 'astounding claim that "English", "French", etc. and "natural language" are not concepts of linguistic science'. According to Katz, individualists can avoid being driven to this 'astounding claim' only if they can 'provide an explanation of how talk of natural languages can be conceived of as logical construction out of [individualistically respectable] talk about their speakers'.[35]

Katz's argument here appears to derive its plausibility from the assumption that concepts such as 'English' and 'French'

---

[33] Katz, *Language and Other Abstract Objects*, pp. 51 and 87.
[34] Ibid., p. 77.
[35] Ibid., pp. 77, 80, and 81.

are in fact legitimate and necessary concepts of linguistic science. While this assumption may itself seem plausible, it cannot in fact be sustained. Two considerations are relevant here.

In a distinct but related context, Chomsky argued that the notion of a language (such as English) is not a legitimate concept of linguistic science because it can be given no coherent definition. In Chomsky's view, the existence of linguistic variation and its social embodiment in dialects presents a crucial problem for those, like Katz, who hold that notions such as 'English' are legitimate concepts of linguistic science. Chomsky says in this regard: 'How broadly should the "superlanguage" German extend? To Dutch? If not, why not, since it presumably will cover dialects that differ from one another more or less in the way some of them differ from Dutch.' According to Chomsky, it is for this reason doubtful 'that one can give any clear or useful meaning to the "everyday sense" of the term "language"' on which Katz's argument appears to depend.[36] The notion of a language, then, is not a legitimate concept of linguistic science, and the fact that linguistic individualists may be able to provide no account of this notion thus fails to tell against their methodological commitments.[37]

Furthermore, the notion of a language (such as English), even if legitimate, is not a necessary concept for any adequately explanatory theory in linguistics. Of course, it may appear that we need to invoke a shared language in order to explain, for

---

[36] Chomsky, *Rules and Representations*, p. 118. By the way, it is not entirely clear that the notion of a language cannot be defined in individualistically acceptable terms. Bickerton, for instance, has suggested that it may be possible to construct 'polylectal' grammars which would characterize the variant idiolects current in some speech community. (See D. Bickerton, 'The Structure of Polylectal Grammars', in R. Shuy, ed., *Sociolinguistics: Current Trends and Prospects*, Washington, 1973.) But this possibility only strengthens the conclusion of my argument here. If it were possible to construct such polylectal grammars, then individualistic linguists would certainly not be driven to the 'astounding claim' that 'English' is not a concept of linguistic science.

[37] This same argument appears, and was indeed intended by Chomsky, to undermine Dummett's contention that language is irreducibly social in character. See M. Dummett, 'What is a Theory of Meaning?', in S. Guttenplan, ed., *Mind and Language*, Oxford, 1975, pp. 134–5.

instance, how individuals are able to communicate with one another. This is certainly the way in which we would normally and informally explain mutual intelligibility. Why are Alf and Beth able to communicate with one another? They are able to do so because they both speak (i.e. have knowledge of) the shared language English. But such an informal explanation, while intuitively satisfying, is certainly not necessary. Another explanation of mutual intelligibility is available, and this explanation does not involve reference to the (possibly illegitimate) notion of a shared language. Such an explanation might have the following form.

Alf and Beth are able to communicate with one another because each has a capacity to effect a mapping between phonetically represented utterances and semantically represented meanings (or, perhaps, beliefs). And these capacities are similar enough for Alf and Beth each to tend to map the other's phonetically represented utterances to semantically represented meanings (or beliefs) which are similar (or identical) to the meanings (or beliefs) which these utterances were intended by their user to report. And these capacities are similar in this way because both Alf and Beth acquired them on the basis of evidence about phonetic–semantic mappings which, given strong innate constraints on language acquisition, induced the construction of theories about these mappings which are sufficiently similar to ensure mutual intelligibility. There seems to be no reason, then, to suppose that the concept of a language is an explanatorily necessary concept for linguistics. I have just shown that this concept can be dispensed with even in accounting for mutual intelligibility. Katz's first anti-individualistic argument thus fails.

(b) According to Katz, the individualist 'construes [grammars] as representing cognitive structures . . . [which] have to reflect the characteristics of the . . . medium in which the speaker's knowledge is realized'. Katz claims that it is for this reason that individualistically 'interpreted theories in linguistics are too severely restricted . . . to be optimal grammars'.[38] Katz presents two arguments for this claim.

[38] Katz, *Language and Other Abstract Objects*, p. 83.

First, Katz considers 'the set [*S*] which contains all the simplest grammars that predict and explain every grammatical fact about each sentence of English'. According to Katz, it is possible that 'no grammar in the set [*S*] satisfies the psychological constraints imposed by [individualism, since] none is realizable in the information processing system underlying human linguistic ability', while 'some grammar *G** . . . is best as an empirical theory of the relevant aspects of this information processing system'.[39] There are two cases to be considered here.

The grammar *G** explains and predicts the same grammatical facts as do grammars in the set *S*. In this case, according to Katz, the 'psychological constraints that [individualists] impose on grammars are excessive in asking us to pass over the best scientific theory in favor of lesser ones'.[40] Katz's point here is that the grammar *G** is inferior as a theory of English to grammars in the set *S* because it is, by hypothesis, not one of 'simplest grammars that predict and explain every grammatical fact about each sentence of English', and is, therefore, methodologically inferior to these grammars. Two considerations are relevant here.

Katz's argument appears to depend on an assumption which in this context is and must be controversial. Katz appears here to assume that there are grammatical facts (to be predicted and explained) which are independent of facts about language users. If this assumption is correct, it of course follows that the 'psychological constraints that [individualists] impose on grammars are excessive'. If there are 'objective' grammatical facts, then grammars in the set *S* clearly provide better explanations of these facts than does the grammar *G**. But to assume that there are objective grammatical facts in this sense is, of course, to prejudge precisely the question which is at issue in the debate between individualists and (objectivistic) collectivists. Collectivists claim that such facts exist, while individualists deny that this is so. This argument must be rejected, then,

[39] Katz, *Language and Other Abstract Objects*, p. 86.
[40] Ibid., p. 86.

because it depends on an assumption which, in effect, begs precisely the question at issue.

It is, in any event, not clear that grammars in the set S are explanatorily equivalent to the grammar G^*. Even if there are objective linguistic facts, the individualistically acceptable grammar G^* appears to be explanatorily superior to grammars in the set S. This is so because linguists might even in this case still have a legitimate interest in accounting for the explicit intuitive knowledge of these objective facts which language-users exhibit. And in this explanatory context, attribution to the user of the grammar G^* can, while attribution to the user of a grammar in the set S cannot, legitimately be invoked. The grammar G^* does provide a basis for explaining the language-user's explicit intuitive knowledge of these facts. Grammars in the set S, on the other hand, provide no adequate basis for explaining the language-user's knowledge of these facts since grammars in the set S are, by hypothesis, not 'realizable in the information processing system' underlying the language-user's ability to manifest knowledge of these facts. Linguistic objectivists or collectivists will thus be obliged, just as individualists are, to invoke the grammar G^* in order to explain language-users' intuitive knowledge of facts about their language. And in this case, it is, at best, not clear that the individualistic account is methodologically inferior to the objectivistic account. Katz's argument here must be rejected, then, even if there are objective facts about languages. It simply fails to establish that individualistically acceptable grammars are methodologically inferior to grammars which are psychologically unconstrained.

The second case to be considered is that in which the grammar G^* does not predict and explain the same grammatical facts as do grammars in the set S. According to Katz, this is a possibility since G^* may make 'false, though in principle underivable, predictions about the grammatical structure of sentences'. In this case, Katz claims that 'in forcing them to prefer G^*, the [individualists'] philosophical commitment forces them to accept a false theory needlessly'.[41]

[41] Ibid., p. 88.

It is, of course, possible that the grammar G^* and grammars in the set S might diverge in their predictions about various grammatical facts. What Katz needs to establish, though, is that the predictions of G^* are incorrect just where they diverge from the predictions of grammars in the set S. How could this be established? Katz himself accepts Chomsky's intuitionistic methodology, even if he does not accept Chomsky's subjectivistic individualism.[42] But in this case, Katz must suppose that we can determine the truth of claims about grammatical facts by consulting our linguistic intuitions. In particular, Katz must suppose that we can use linguistic intuitions as a basis for adjudicating the divergent claims about certain grammatical facts which issue from G^* and from grammars in the set S. But, according to Katz, those predictions of G^* which diverge from predictions of grammars in the set S are 'in principle underivable'. And this means that these predictions cannot be derived by language-users as intuitions which they have about their language. But in this case, we have no intuitive warrant for saying that the divergent predictions of G^* are false, and, therefore, no warrant for claiming, as Katz does, that individualists' 'philosophical commitment forces them to accept a false theory needlessly'. For all that linguistic intuition tells us, the divergent predictions of G^* might well be true and those of grammars in the set S false. This argument must be rejected then. It simply fails to establish any basis for Katz's anti-individualistic conclusion.

Second, Katz asks us to suppose that

we are visited by intelligent aliens from outer space, who can communicate with us in English just as well as we do with one another ... [though] examination shows that these creatures have minds or brains so radically different that the grammatical systems realizable in theirs as knowledge of a natural language are nothing like the systems realizable in our minds or brains.

According to Katz, 'since they take possible grammars to be those that ... are realizable within the human mind or brain,

---

[42] Katz, *Language and Other Abstract Objects*, p. 64.

[individualists] would have to [claim] that the aliens do not speak English'—a claim which Katz considers 'counter-intuitive'.[43]

It is clearly correct to say, as Katz does, that the claim that the aliens in his example do not speak English is a 'counter-intuitive' claim. But this admittedly counter-intuitive claim bears on the acceptability of linguistic individualism only if individualists are forced by their methodological commitments to accept it. Certainly, individualists would be forced to accept this claim if their methodological commitments required them to explicate the notion 'speaks the same language as' in terms of the notion 'has the same mentally represented grammar as'. But I see no reason to suppose that linguistic individualism does require such an explicatory strategy. Two considerations are relevant here.

As I have already pointed out, linguistic individualists have principled reasons for supposing that the notion of a shared language is neither coherent nor explanatorily significant. In this case, what needs to be explained in Katz's hypothetical example is not the fact that the aliens 'speak English', but, rather, the fact that they are able to communicate with certain human beings.

This reformulation of the problem posed by Katz's example suggests, then, that it can be assimilated to a case already considered—that of Alf and Beth. Thus, we can say of the alien Mork and the human being Mindy, just as we could say of Alf and Beth, that they are able to communicate because each has a capacity to effect a mapping between phonetically represented utterances and semantically represented meanings (or beliefs). And these capacities are similar enough for each to tend to map the other's phonetically represented utterances to semantically represented meanings (or beliefs) which are similar (or identical) to the meanings (or beliefs) these utterances were intended by their user to report. Of course, in this case we cannot, as we could in the case of Alf and Beth, also explain the similarity of

[43]   Ibid., pp. 89–90.

these capacities. Katz does not tell us, and it is hard to imagine in detail, how the aliens acquired the ability to communicate with certain human beings. But we need no more invoke the notion of a shared or objective language to explain their acquisition of this ability than we needed to invoke this notion in order to explain how Alf and Beth acquired sufficiently similar linguistic abilities. This argument must be rejected, then. It simply fails to establish any basis for Katz's anti-individualistic conclusion.

(c) According to Katz, individualism 'offers us nothing stronger than a nativistic account of how human beings might be genetically programmed to think that some class of propositions [are] true no matter what, but offers us no account of what it is for propositions to be true no matter what'. Katz claims that individualism thus 'falls short of what is required to explain the necessary truths expressed by the analytic sentences of natural languages'.[44] In support of this claim, Katz adapts a number of arguments of Frege and Husserl.

The most telling of Katz's arguments is an adaptation of Frege's argument for the uniqueness of the laws of logic. According to Katz, 'beings whose semantic laws flatly contradict ours are ecumenically pictured [by linguistic individualists] as having laws that hold for them just as we have laws that hold for us'. Katz claims that such ecumenical tolerance is, however, misplaced, since 'if their laws flatly contradict ours, then their laws claim that at least one analytic proposition is false'. And this, according to Katz, 'is enough to establish . . . that we have run up against . . . a novel variety of falsehood'.[45]

Clearly, it would make sense to claim that any alien semantic law which contradicts a human semantic law embodies 'a novel variety of falsehood' only if there are analytic propositions in Katz's sense; only, that is, if there is at least one proposition the truth-value of which is, as Katz says, 'not relative at all but absolute (and hence . . . the same for any rational creature no matter how radically different its cognitive processes from

---

[44] Katz, *Language and Other Abstract Objects*, pp. 94–5.
[45] Ibid., p. 173.

ours)'.[46] But Katz provides no (new) reasons to suppose that there are propositions of this kind. His third argument will thus fail to carry much weight with those who have been persuaded by Quine and others that there are no analytic propositions in Katz's sense.[47] It fails, then, to establish any non-controversial basis for accepting his anti-individualistic conclusion.

Katz's arguments against linguistic individualism fail to undermine that methodological thesis. Each appears to depend on assumptions about the individualist's commitments and resources that cannot in fact be sustained.

The recent arguments of Watkins, Sanders and Katz motivated my defence of linguistic individualism. But such a defence must also involve consideration of a number of other arguments which are alleged to undermine this thesis. Some of these arguments are to be found in Saussure's theory of language and, in an abstract form, in the philosophical debate about methodological individualism. I will consider them now.

7 *Saussure's Arguments*

Saussure is no doubt quite rightly regarded as the father of modern linguistics. When he gave his now famous lectures on linguistics (in Geneva from 1906 to 1911), questions about the appropriate (ontological and) methodological orientation of linguistics were seen to be of great significance. Although Saussure explicitly rejected the ontological collectivism of those nineteenth-century historical linguists influenced by Hegel, his own methodological views cannot readily be categorized either as obviously individualistic or as obviously collectivistic.[48]

---

[46] Ibid., p. 6.

[47] See W. V. Quine, 'Two Dogmas of Empiricism', in *From a Logical Point of View*, Cambridge, 1953.

[48] Bopp and Schleicher were prominent collectivistic linguists of this period. Bopp claimed that 'languages are to be considered organic natural bodies, which are formed according to fixed laws [and] develop as possessing an inner principle of life'. (See O. Jespersen, *Language*, London, 1922, p. 65.) And Schleicher claimed that 'languages are natural organisms which, without being determinable by the will of man, grew and developed in accordance with fixed laws'. (Schleicher, *Darwinism Tested*, pp. 20–1.) For his rejection of such ontologically collectivistic views, see F. de Saussure, *Course in General Linguistics*, trans. W. Baskin, London, 1959, p. 5.

While I believe that his methodological orientation was fundamentally an individualistic one, he seems at many places to give arguments against such an orientation. Three of these arguments are especially significant:

(*a*) A powerful theme running through Saussure's lectures is embodied in his claim that language 'is the social side of speech, outside the individual, who can never create nor modify it by himself'; or again, that 'the individual does not have the power to change [his language] in any way once it has become established in the linguistic community'; or yet again, that 'no individual, even if he willed it, could modify in any way [the structure of his language]; and what is more, the community itself cannot control so much as a word; it is bound to the existing language'.[49]

These claims appear to threaten linguistic individualism in quite a radical way. They appear, in particular, to be inconsistent with a thesis which is at the very heart of the individualistic position: that individuals are the only causal agents in the formation, development, and functioning of social institutions such as language. If individuals are, as Saussure alleges, powerless to alter the structures of their languages—which nevertheless have been altered in the course of their histories—then individuals cannot have been (and *a fortiori* cannot have been the only) causal agents in the development of language.

It is interesting to note that Saussure's argument here is similar to one which Mandelbaum has presented in the course of recent philosophical discussions of individualism. Mandelbaum has claimed, in particular, that 'societal facts . . . exercise external constraints over individuals', from which it presumably follows that individuals do not and cannot freely create and alter the institutional frameworks which they inhabit.[50]

My problem here is to meet the challenge to linguistic individualism posed by both versions of this argument. There are a number of possibilities in this regard:

[49] Saussure, *Course*, pp. 14, 69, and 71.
[50] M. Mandelbaum, 'Societal Facts', reprinted in O'Neill, *Modes*, p. 234.

(*i*) Those who employ this argument apparently hope to undermine linguistic individualism by citing the fact that individual language-users experience 'resistance' when they attempt to alter the structures of their languages, and believe, on the basis of this experience, that they are powerless to alter these structures. But individualism is not threatened by the fact that language-users believe that they are powerless to alter their languages, so long as this belief has no basis in objective fact. The individualist is not, in general, committed to the claim that individuals' beliefs about social institutions are true, but only to the claim that such beliefs (and the actions which are based on them) are causally constitutive of these social institutions. The fact that language-users believe that they are, in the face of 'resistance', powerless to alter their languages thus provides no reason for the individualist to suppose that language-users are powerless in this way. If Saussure and Mandelbaum claim that individuals' feelings of constraint and impotence tell against individualism, then their argument cannot be sustained, and it does not, after all, threaten linguistic individualism.

(*ii*) If, on the other hand and as seems more likely, Saussure and Mandelbaum claim that individuals not only believe, but rightly believe, in the existence and efficacy of institutional 'resistance' then their argument would threaten individualism. Even in this case, of course, the individualist could still follow Watkins in holding that 'the social environment by which any particular individual is confronted and frustrated and sometimes manipulated and occasionally destroyed is, if we ignore its physical ingredients, made up of other people, their habits, inertia, loyalties, rivalries, and so on'.[51] The individualist could suggest, in other words, that the collectivist is correct in claiming that institutional frameworks resist individual inter-ventions, but is wrong in supposing that these frameworks are themselves irreducibly social entities. On an individualistic account, individual interventions in institutional frameworks are resisted by the other individuals whose behaviour, beliefs, and

---

[51] Watkins, 'Historical Explanations', p. 176 n. 8.

habits causally constitute these frameworks. And this possibility is, of course, consistent with individualism. Its advocates do not claim, and are not obliged to claim, that particular individuals have the unconstrained capacity unilaterally to alter their institutional framework. They are merely obliged to claim that whatever alterations are effected in institutional life are, in the end, causal consequences of individual interventions in it.

This reply may not seem to be a terribly forceful one. It may seem that I have here defended individualism in a question-begging way. I have, after all, merely here suggested that individualism is not really threatened by the claim that institutions 'resist' individuals since such institutions are anyway just causal consequences of individuals' behaviour, beliefs, and habits. But collectivists would, of course, dispute just this suggestion, pointing out that social institutions are not, on their view, just the causal consequences of such factors. Collectivists might reasonably say that I have here defended individualism in a way which presupposes the truth of individualism, and that my argument is therefore viciously circular.

This charge is actually quite well founded. The counter-argument which I have developed merely provides a kind of 'consistency proof' for individualism with respect to certain fundamentally uncontroversial facts about social life. It merely shows that individualism has the conceptual resources with which to deal with such facts. It does not, however, show that the individualist's treatment of these facts is the correct one, and thus fails to provide any 'inductive support' for individualism. Nevertheless, I think we can strengthen the impact of this part of our discussion.

(*iii*) I mentioned earlier that Saussure's methodological views are not easily categorized. While his apparently collectivistic claim that 'the individual does not have the power to change' the language has motivated my discussion to this point, consideration of remarks of his apparently inconsistent with this claim may help both to clarify our understanding of his position, and to develop an individualistic account of language change which is responsive to the problem of linguistic 'resistance'.

Preliminarily, we might observe that Saussure drew a sharp, if somewhat elusive, distinction between language (*langue*) and speaking (*parole*). Language, according to Saussure, is the system of conventions which is shared by the members of a linguistic community; 'it is the social side of speech'; or 'it is the whole set of linguistic habits which allow an individual to understand and be understood by' others.[52] Speaking, on the other hand, is, according to Saussure, embodied in the individual's use of these conventions in order to communicate with others.[53] Furthermore, although conceptually distinct, language and speaking manifest a kind of double-sided empirical interdependence. According to Saussure, language 'is both a social product of the faculty of speech and a collection of necessary conventions that have been adopted by a social body to permit individuals to exercise that faculty'; or 'language is necessary if speaking is to be intelligible and produce all its effects; but speaking is necessary for the establishment of language'.[54] Explicating the claim that language and speaking might be both conceptually distinct and empirically interdependent will perhaps help us to dissolve the apparent inconsistency between Saussure's collectivistic and individualistic tendencies. It may also help us to construct an individualistic model of language change which is responsive to the problem of linguistic 'resistance'.

Since a language is a system of shared linguistic conventions, it is apparently nothing more than a truism that any one individual does not have the ability unilaterally to alter this shared system simply by adopting some set of linguistic habits which differ from those characteristic of other members of the speech community. And this fact accounts for the 'resistance' which is experienced by individual linguistic innovators. On the other hand, the actions of individuals do causally constitute language change when it occurs. Since language is the social product of speaking, it is, according to Saussure, 'in speaking that the germ

[52] Saussure, *Course*, pp. 14 and 77.
[53] Ibid., p. 19. See also J. Culler, *Saussure*, London, 1976, pp. 29–30.
[54] Saussure, *Course*, pp. 9 and 18.

of all change is to be found'.[55] Language change occurs, on this account, when a group of language-users change their individual habits of speaking in some co-ordinated way—perhaps by imitating the changed speaking habits of individual innovators in their midst.

Saussure, then, after all proposes to give an explanation of language change which is both individualistic in character and provides an individualistic solution for the problem of linguistic 'resistance'. He appears in this respect, then, to be only superficially a collectivist. The authority of his insightful discussion of language cannot, then, here be invoked against linguistic individualism.

(*iv*) We can, perhaps, further strengthen the impact of our discussion by considering two attempts to provide, in outline at least, an individualistic explanation of language change.

The first such attempt was Saussure's, and it was clearly intended to provide an anonymous individualistic explanation of a change, in the sixteenth century, in the conjugation of the German copula. According to Saussure, the replacement of *was* by *war* occurred because 'some speakers, influenced by *waren*, created *war* through analogy; this was a fact of speaking; this new form, repeated many times and accepted by the community, became a fact of language'.[56]

The second such attempt was Sapir's. Saussure's influence on Sapir will be obvious here. This attempt has, moreover, the additional virtue of addressing a question the significance of which Saussure himself did not yet clearly see. Under what conditions are individually initiated changes accepted by the linguistic community? Sapir's problem was that of explaining the evolution of *teeth* and *geese* as plural forms of the words *tooth* and *goose* respectively. Sapir claims that

failing the precedent set by such already existing types of vocalic alternation as SING-SANG-SUNG, it is highly doubtful if the detailed conditions that brought about the evolution of TEETH and GEESE from TOOTH and GOOSE would have been potent enough to allow the native

---

[55] Saussure, *Course*, p. 98.   [56] Ibid.

linguistic feeling to win through to an acceptance of these new types of plural formation as psychologically possible.[57]

In short, Sapir proposes, in a characteristically individualistic way, to explain the imitation of linguistic innovations in terms of their perceived 'psychological possibility'.

What is evident, I think, is that both these attempts to provide schematic explanations of language change were individualistic in character, and were at the same time responsive to the problem of linguistic 'resistance'. Each of these schematic explanations has, in essence, the following abstract form. Individuals in a linguistic community may develop habits of speaking which differ from those current in the community as a whole. If these habits are perceived by other members of that community to be 'psychologically possible', then they will be imitated by other speakers and thus gradually come to be shared by the members of that community. Linguistic 'resistance' is experienced when members of a linguistic community do not find the innovative linguistic behaviour of one of their fellows 'psychologically possible'.

Our discussion so far does not, of course, establish that such individualistic explanations of language change are, in fact, superior to collectivistic alternatives.[58] Nevertheless, our discussion does appear to clarify some issues which are relevant to the problem under consideration. Specifically, it appears to show that the problem of linguistic 'resistance' poses no principled difficulty for an individualistic account of language change. Individualistic accounts of language change in the face of 'resistance' not only can be, but have been, given. These considerations dispose, I think, of Saussure's first argument against linguistic individualism.

(b) A second argument against linguistic individualism has the following form. According to Saussure, 'no society, in fact, knows or has ever known language other than as a product inherited from preceding generations'.[59] In this case, linguistic

[57] E. Sapir, *Language*, London, 1963, pp. 60-1.
[58] See D'Agostino, 'Ontology and Explanation'.
[59] Saussure, *Course*, p. 70.

individualism reverses the order of causal dependence between the social institution of language and the individuals who participate in that institution. The individualistic claim that language is a product of the behaviour, beliefs, and habits of individuals is undermined by the fact that those habits, in particular, themselves depend on a historically pre-existent language. As Saussure says, language cannot 'be a function of the speaker [but is instead] passively assimilated by the individual'.[60]

This argument, like that discussed at (*a*) 'above, also has affinities with a more abstract argument which has been employed by recent philosophical critics of individualism. Gellner, for instance, criticizes individualism for ignoring the fact that 'for any individual, the mores, institutions, tacit presuppositions of his society are an independent and external fact'.[61] And Goldstein echoes this criticism when he notes that 'for the most part, people are born into their [social] relationships, and it seems entirely a reversal of actual fact to say that such relations "are the product of people's attitudes to each other ..."'. According to Goldstein, it seems more reasonable to say that 'for the most part the proper attitudes towards one's [fellows] are cultivated during the enculturation process ... [and] that the kinds of dispositions to be found in people of any given type are socially induced dispositions'.[62]

Goldstein's remarks, in particular, make it clear how such considerations threaten individualism. If an individual's beliefs or dispositions are 'socially induced', then it does not suffice, to warrant individualism, to establish that social institutions are the products of individuals' beliefs and dispositions. On Goldstein's account, these beliefs and dispositions are themselves causal products of the institutional characteristics which the individualist invokes them to explain. My problem here, then, is to undermine the anti-individualistic implications of

---

[60]   Saussure, *Course*, p. 14.

[61]   E. Gellner, 'Explanations in History', reprinted in O'Neill, *Modes*, p. 258.

[62]   L. Goldstein, 'Two Theses of Methodological Individualism', reprinted in O'Neill, *Modes*, p. 284.

these considerations. Once again, there seem to be a number of possibilities:

(i) We might concede the collectivistic claim that individuals' beliefs and dispositions are causally conditioned by pre-existent social frameworks. But we might, in spite of this concession, deny what the collectivist then claims: that this concession undermines individualism. And we might support our rejection of this claim by an argument of the following form.

The invalidity of individualism does not follow from the (conceded) causal efficacy of social frameworks so long as advocates of individualism can provide individualistic explanations of the formation, development, and functioning of those frameworks—so long, that is, as they can show that that which is causally efficacious in the formation of beliefs and dispositions is itself the product of the behaviour, beliefs, and habits of individuals. In other words, individualists can acknowledge that there are true causal laws which exhibit the dependence of individual characteristics on institutional characteristics without *ipso facto* conceding the invalidity of individualism. And they can do this in virtue of their distinction between 'half-way' and 'rock-bottom' explanations. Individualists can concede that collectivistic laws can be formulated, but can avoid the anti-individualistic implications of the argument under consideration by claiming that these laws can, in turn, be derived from individualistically acceptable laws.

The ultimate success of this strategy depends, of course, on actually providing 'rock-bottom' individualistic explanations of those collectivistic laws which, the individualist claims, merely offer 'half-way' explanations of, for instance, the enculturation of individuals into a linguistic community. Since providing such explanations is ultimately an empirical enterprise, and thus outside the scope of my discussion, I cannot claim here to have provided 'inductive support' for individualism. What I can claim to have shown, though, is that we need not concede the invalidity of individualism when we concede that individuals' dispositions and beliefs are 'socially induced'. Individualism does, after all, have the conceptual resources with which to deal with this fact.

(ii) But we can, I think, offer a stronger and more positive reply to this kind of collectivistic criticism of individualism. In particular, we can defend individualism by arguing against the collectivistic claim that individuals' beliefs and dispositions are 'socially induced'. An argument to this effect has the following form.

The claim that an individual's beliefs are 'socially induced' seems to suggest (and Saussure, at least, certainly took it to suggest) that the individual passively assimilates those beliefs during the enculturation process. But this suggestion is implausible, especially in the case of language acquisition. It seems to require that language-learners be instructed in the linguistic beliefs which they will eventually come to hold. But this requirement is, with unimportant exceptions, never satisfied in the case of language acquisition. Though language-learners may eventually acquire a variety of (partly tacit) beliefs about their language, they will, in nearly every case, never have been explicitly instructed in such beliefs. They will, rather, simply have been exposed to linguistic behaviour which was guided by certain beliefs, and, on the basis of such behavioural evidence, will have constructed (possibly unconscious) hypotheses about the beliefs which guided that behaviour.[63] But in this case, it is surely incorrect to speak of language-learners 'passively assimilating' beliefs about their language. It is, rather, they who actively construct such beliefs as will eventually guide their behaviour. And they do so on the basis of evidence about behaviour in which such beliefs are merely implicit. The only sense, then, in which language-learners' beliefs are 'socially induced' is, roughly, the same sense in which beliefs about the natural world are 'naturally induced'—that is, the sense which follows in both cases from the fact that we check those beliefs (which we ourselves construct) against

[63]   See D. Slobin, *Psycholinguistics*, London, 1974, p. 55.

empirically relevant evidence. But here, surely, the collectivist's argument collapses. For the evidence which is empirically relevant for the language-learner is, after all, provided by the behaviour of other individual language-users.

I claim, then, that the following account of language learning is a plausible one. On the basis of the observed linguistic behaviour of individuals in their environment, language-learners construct a set of beliefs such that the behaviour which they subsequently guide is communicatively successful. Clearly, this account of language learning is entirely free of any dependence on collectivistic notions such as the 'social induction' or 'passive assimilation' of beliefs.[64]

It would appear, then, that individualism can be defended against the collectivistic charge that it is inconsistent with facts about the 'social induction' of individuals' beliefs and dispositions. We can defend individualism from this charge by showing, as I have just tried to, that this 'fact' is, after all, not a fact at all. In short, Saussure's second argument against linguistic individualism cannot be sustained.

(*c*) A third argument against linguistic individualism is, in effect, a logically stronger version of the argument we have just considered and rejected. According to this argument, social institutions and their characteristics are logically, and not merely historically, prior to the characteristics of individuals. Saussure alluded to this argument when he claimed that 'language is necessary if speaking is to be intelligible and produce all its effects'.[65]

A similar claim about the logical priority of social characteristics to individual characteristics has also been made in the course of recent philosophical discussions of methodological individualism. Gellner, for instance, has claimed that while the

---

[64] The situation is, I think, no better from a collectivistic point of view if we replace references to 'social instruction in beliefs' with references to 'social shaping of dispositions'. Evidence about language learning seems to indicate that very little such 'shaping' of the learner's dispositions occurs or is effective. See Slobin, *Psycholinguistics*, p. 58.

[65] Saussure, *Course*, p. 60.

individualistic social scientist 'may in some cases account for the social facts in terms of the interaction of individual decisions with prior "social facts", any attempt to eliminate these altogether will only lead to a regress'.[66] Indeed, Gellner's remarks promise to be most helpful in illuminating the alleged strength of the collectivistic position here. They appear to suggest that the individualist is faced with the following situation:

(i) The claim that institutional characteristics are logically prior to individual characteristics is uncongenial to the individualistic position. We might try to reconcile individualism with this uncongenial claim by providing an individualistic explanation of the (phylogenetic) development of social institutions such as language.

(ii) This attempt will fail, however, since any explanation of the development, for instance, of some system of linguistic conventions C will necessarily involve reference to other (possibly non-linguistic) conventions C'.

(iii) This will be the case since only those individuals sharing conventions C' could achieve the kind of spontaneous cooperation necessary for the adoption of conventions C as shared linguistic conventions.

(iv) Since the argument of (iii) applies as well to individualistic attempts to explain the development of the conventions C', an infinite regress threatens. This regress can be avoided only by conceding that there are conventions which are *sui generis*— conventions for the development and social acceptance of which there is no individualistic explanation. And this concession does, of course, undermine linguistic individualism and, by implication, individualism as a general methodological thesis.

This argument appears to threaten individualism in quite a radical way. I must, then, now try to undermine it in order to safeguard the claims of linguistic individualism.

Let me begin by suggesting that premiss (iii) above is false. If this premiss is false, no infinite regress of explanations

---

[66] Gellner, 'Explanations in History', p. 259.

threatens, and it is thus unnecessary for the individualist to concede the existence of *sui generis* social conventions. An argument supporting this suggestion might have the following form.

Premiss (iii) appears to depend on the assumption that the individualist is committed to some sort of 'contractualist' account of the development of language. From such an account, it would follow that a 'contract' between individuals to adopt linguistic conventions *C* could be 'negotiated' only between individuals who had already adopted those conventions *C'* in terms of which such a negotiation could itself meaningfully be undertaken. But this assumption about the individualist's commitments is false. We can, I think, easily show that this is so by considering again our analysis of Watkins's thought experiment. What emerged from that analysis was the claim that individuals do not, on the individualistic account, need to negotiate an agreement to adopt certain linguistic conventions. On that account individuals are able jointly to adopt certain linguistic conventions because they are, as a matter of contingent psychological fact, able to use certain private 'linguistic' conventions, and to recognize as similar the similar private 'linguistic' conventions which other individuals have independently adopted. On this account, then, it is not that individuals conspire to adopt certain linguistic conventions, in a way which might require other, pre-existent conventions. It is, rather, merely that each of a group of individuals is equipped with such cognitive capacities as enable him or her to use certain private conventions in ways which are socially meaningful.

On this individualistic account, then, the possibility that a group of individuals might develop certain linguistic conventions does not depend on their negotiating an agreement to do so, but, rather, on a happy coincidental attunement of their cognitive capacities. Since this attunement of capacities is a fact of nature, rather than itself the result of some prior conventional agreement, no infinite regress of conventions threatens, and the individualist is not, after all, forced to concede the existence of *sui generis* social conventions.

Saussure's third argument does not, then, threaten linguistic individualism.[67]

This counter-argument is not, perhaps, conclusive. Collectivists might reply, for instance, that their argument against individualism does not depend on the assumption that its advocates are committed to a 'contractualist' account of the development of social institutions, and is, therefore, not undermined by our contention that this assumption is false. More specifically, collectivists might claim that our reconstruction of their argument imposes on them a view which they do not hold—namely, premiss (ii): that the development of linguistic conventions *C* requires other, pre-existent conventions *C'*. Collectivists might say that their position is not that this development depends on pre-existent social conventions. It is, rather—new premiss (ii')—that it depends on pre-existent social facts, which, in turn—new premiss (iii')—themselves depend on other pre-existent social facts.[68] Given this revised reconstruction of the collectivists' argument, it might appear that an infinite regress of explanations again threatens individualism, and now in a way which cannot be avoided by pointing out, what the collectivist here claims never to have disputed, that individualism is not committed to a 'contractualist' account of the development of social institutions such as language.

But this move by collectivists can, I think, also be blocked. In our discussion of Watkins's thought experiment, we have

---

[67] It may be noted that our counter-argument appears to apply with equal force to collectivistic claims about explanations of the ontogenetic development of language. The acquisition of a capacity to employ linguistic conventions appears to require an (innately based) ability to construct for oneself hypotheses about the conventions which guide the behaviour of others. The construction of such hypotheses does not depend on the existence of antecedent conventions. It is, rather, governed by those psychological laws which describe the innately based ability and attribute it to the language-learner. Language-learners, in other words, do not conspire with mature members of their community to adopt the linguistic conventions of that community—in a way which might require pre-existent conventions. Rather, they simply find themselves able to adopt such conventions. Here too, then, the individualistic account appears to be free of those 'contractualist' assumptions which the collectivist claims to find in it.

[68] The collectivist's response here depends, of course, on the assumption that there are social facts which are not themselves constituted by social conventions. I see no reason for supposing that this assumption is unwarranted.

already examined an argument of the form now under consideration. Watkins too appeared to claim that pre-existent and irreducible (but non-conventional) social facts must be invoked in explaining the (phylogenetic) development of language. Since we have already seen how this claim can be undermined in the case of Watkins's argument, we can, I think, safely dismiss this new reconstruction of Saussure's third argument. This argument simply fails to threaten linguistic individualism.

In this section, I have examined three Saussurean arguments against linguistic individualism. In each case, I claim to have undermined the argument in question, and thus to have ensured that it provides no a priori reasons for supposing that individualism is not an appropriate methodology for linguistics. In the next section, I will consider the relevance of sociolinguistics to the currently individualistic methodological orientation of Chomskian linguistics.

8 *The Relevance of Sociolinguistics*

The work of the sociolinguist Labov may perhaps be taken to embody an empirically motivated repudiation of the currently individualistic methodological orientation of Chomskian linguistics. Various programmatic statements by Labov may seem suggestive in this regard. Labov, for instance, claims that 'it now seems clear that one cannot make any advance towards understanding the mechanisms of linguistic change without serious study of the social factors which mediate linguistic evolution'.[69] Furthermore, Labov's work has sometimes been interpreted by his critics as embodying a collectivistic methodological orientation. Bickerton, for instance, has argued that the kinds of grammars Labov constructs 'must be based on the behavior of groups [and may therefore] be misleading with regard to the contents of individual rule systems'.[70]

The impression that Labov's methodological orientation is collectivistic rather than individualistic is further reinforced by

[69] W. Labov, *Sociolinguistic Patterns*, Philadelphia, 1972, p. 252.
[70] Bickerton, 'Polylectal Grammars', p. 19.

his own discussion of these two points of view. He explicitly contrasts an 'individualistic approach [which] is reflected in most current theories of language change' with a tradition which emphasized 'the importance of social facts in linguistic change', and appears to commit himself unequivocally to the apparently collectivistic tradition.[71]

Of course, Labov's apparently collectivistic methodological orientation poses a threat to linguistic individualism only if his theory of language change is superior to that provided by his individualistic rivals, and only if that theory embodies collectivistic rather than individualistic assumptions about the basis of language change. I will not here consider whether the first of these conditions in fact obtains, though I am inclined to think that it does.[72] I will, however, try to show that Labov's account of language change, though different in significant ways from more obviously individualistic accounts, nevertheless embodies an individualistic, and not a collectivistic, methodological orientation.

Labov defines language 'as an instrument used by members of the community to communicate with one another'. From this definition, he takes it to follow that 'the origin of a linguistic change is not the act of some one individual whose tongue slips, or who slips into an odd [linguistic] habit of his own'. Given his definition of language, it follows, according to Labov, that 'language has changed only when a group of speakers use a different pattern to communicate with one another'—only, that is, when a variation in language use has been 'propagated' through the linguistic community. According to Labov, variations in language use can be assumed to be 'introduced by one individual', but the real problem involved in explaining language change arises when we try to account for the '"propagation" or acceptance by others' of individually introduced variations.[73] Labov proposes that we account for the propagation of linguistic variants by assuming that 'any group of

---

[71] Labov, *Sociolinguistic Patterns*, pp. 260 and 263.
[72] See D'Agostino, 'Ontology and Explanation'.
[73] Labov, *Sociolinguistic Patterns*, p. 277.

speakers which regards itself as a close social unit will tend to express its group solidarity by favoring tl `se linguistic innovations which set it apart from other speakers which are not part of the group'.[74] According to Labov, then, the propagation of individually introduced linguistic variants is co-ordinated because individuals who are members of a group each react in a similar way to this variant. Propagation of a variant occurs when acceptance of that variant would express the cohesiveness of a group.

Clearly, Labov's model of language change differs from the individualistic models of Saussure and Sapir, for instance. The question which remains is whether this difference is as significant as it may appear. Is Labov's model of language change a collectivistic alternative to the obviously individualistic models of Saussure and Sapir? I do not think that it is. Two considerations have special relevance here.

First, Labov himself appears to believe that social groups can be defined in an individualistically acceptable way. He claims that 'the social status of an individual is determined by the subjective reactions of other members of society'.[75] In this case, however, it appears that a group is, on Labov's account, simply a collection of individuals to each of whom other individuals react in a particular way. The fact that Labov's explanation of language change makes reference to groups of individuals thus cannot be taken as an indication that that explanation is collectivistic in character.

Second, references to groups figure in Labov's explanation of language change only, as it were, in indirect discourse. Labov does not claim that groups have properties which cause their members to accept or reject particular linguistic variants. He claims, rather, that individual members of groups believe that certain linguistic variants would have social significance if they were adopted. But individualists can certainly acknowledge that the beliefs that individuals have about the social significance of their actions can be causally efficacious in determining their

[74] Ibid., p. 314.
[75] Ibid., p. 285.

behaviour. Beliefs about social significance are, after all, things which individuals have.

From these two observations, it appears to follow that the conditions under which an individually introduced variant is accepted by a group are those which obtain when individual members of that group (itself individualistically defined) believe that this variation, if adopted, would serve to distinguish members of that group from members of other groups in the wider linguistic community.

On analysis, then, Labov's account of language change does not seem to involve any irreducibly collectivistic assumptions, and thus does not provide a genuinely collectivistic alternative to more obviously individualistic accounts. Whatever its explanatory superiority to them, then, it does not threaten the currently individualistic methodological orientation of Chomskian linguistics.[76]

There is, however, another way in which Labov's work might be construed as posing a threat to linguistic individualism. Labov has been interpreted by Bickerton, among others, as claiming to show that there is a social level of linguistic description which is *sui generis* with respect to any individual level of description. Specifically, he is alleged to claim to show that there are social regularities of language use where, at the level of the individual, only random variation exists.[77] Bickerton's characterization of Labov's work is also interesting because it has the effect of connecting it with a criticism of individualism which is familiar in the philosophical context. For Gellner has claimed that the 'argument in favour of [irreducible] social facts is historically associated with the presence of statistical

---

[76] This conclusion seems to apply with equal force to another apparently collectivistic approach to the study of language—that embodied in Hymes's 'ethnography of speaking'. While Hymes seems to refer in a collectivistic way to the 'adaptation of language to social contexts', his fundamentally individualistic orientation is indicated by his proposal to view 'the interaction of language with social life . . . as a matter of human action, based on a knowledge . . . that enables persons to use language'. See D. Hymes, 'Models of the Interaction of Language and Social Life', in J. Gumperz and D. Hymes, eds., *Directions in Sociolinguistics*, New York, 1972, pp. 43 and 53.

[77] See Bickerton, 'Polylectal Grammars', p. 19.

regularities where none can be found at the molecular, individual level'.[78]

Labov's findings might threaten linguistic individualism, then, if Bickerton has correctly interpreted them. The existence of *sui generis* regularities at the social level might imply the existence of ultimate laws of a form not countenanced by individualism as ultimate. I say 'might' here because Watkins has argued that 'the existence of those actuarial regularities . . . which we can control . . . does not, as has often been alleged, support' the collectivist position.[79]

We must, then, now consider the *sui generis* statistical regularities which Labov is alleged to have uncovered. There are two points to be made here. First, Labov himself denies that these regularities are resoluble at the individual level only into random variation. According to Labov, these regularities 'are universal and binding on each individual' and are observable at the individual level as well as at the social level.[80] Second, Labov in any event notes that these regularities can be controlled by manipulating the conditions under which individual behaviour giving rise to them occurs.[81] But in this case, Watkins's proviso would appear to apply. Social regularities which can be controlled by manipulating the conditions under which individual behaviour occurs are surely not causally *sui generis*. For these reasons, then, it seems that Labov's discovery of these social regularities in language use cannot be taken to threaten the currently individualistic methodological orientation of Chomskian linguistics.

Before concluding this section, I must first mention two problems which remain for Labov's account of language change.

The first problem is a technical one concerning Labov's account of the relation between individually introduced variants and their acceptance by groups. Labov claims that a variant will be accepted by a group if its acceptance would serve to

---

[78] Gellner, 'Explanations in History', p. 252.

[79] Watkins, 'Historical Explanations', p. 170.

[80] W. Labov, 'Where Do Grammars Stop?', in Shuy, *Sociolinguistics*, p. 80.

[81] See W. Labov, 'Methodology', in W. Dingwall, ed., *A Survey of Linguistic Science*, College Park, 1971, p. 465.

distinguish members of that group from members of other groups. The problem here is that of explaining why every individual variation from community norms is not accepted by some group, since every such variation is potentially distinctive.

The second problem is an interpretative one. Why does Labov appear to identify his approach as a non-individualistic one if it is, as I claim to have shown, really an individualistic one after all? To answer this question, it may be helpful to recall Watkins's distinction between individualism *per se* and 'psychologism', a species of individualism according to which 'all large-scale social characteristics are . . . a reflection of individual characteristics'.[82] Since Labov appears to be unaware of this distinction, and since most standard individualistic accounts of language change are specifically psychologistic in nature, it may have been natural for Labov to identify his approach as a non-individualistic one in contrast to the psychologistic approaches which he opposes.

In this section, I have examined two ways in which Labov's theory of language change might bear on the validity of linguistic individualism. I think I can claim to have shown that in neither of these ways does this theory undermine the currently individualistic methodological orientation of Chomskian linguistics. Having already disposed of anti-individualistic arguments of Sanders, Watkins, Katz and Saussure, I think I can conclude, more generally, that Chomsky's individualistic methodological orientation is not currently at risk. In Section 9 below, I will consider some implications of this orientation.

9   *Implications of Linguistic Individualism*

In previous sections of this chapter, I have distinguished individualism and collectivism, indicated the currently individualistic methodological basis of Chomsky's account of language, and defended the viability of this methodology. In this section, I conclude my discussion of linguistic individualism by considering some of its implications.

I have already mentioned Chomsky's claim that 'language

---

[82] Watkins, 'Historical Explanations', p. 173.

has no existence apart from its mental representation'. I have also already mentioned Watkins's distinction between individualism and psychologism. I might now mention Gellner's discussion of 'social monadism', the view that 'every social event must have its habitat in the individual psyche'.[83] With these considerations in mind, we can now ask whether and to what extent Chomsky is committed to a psychologistic or monadistic account of language. I believe that Chomsky is, in fact, thoroughly so committed. From his conception of language, it would seem to follow more or less directly that language is a social institution which is a 'reflection of individual characteristics', and one which has 'its habitat in the individual psyches' of its users.

That Chomsky's account of language is psychologistic or monadistic in nature is important to the extent to which one finds these doctrines implausible. And Gellner, for one, does do so. He says:

If individualism is to degenerate into what could be called social monadism, the desperate incorporation of complex and difficult relations into the related terms or individuals, then it must be admitted to be true 'in a sense'. 'Algy met the bear, the bear was bulgy, the bulge was Algy': the individual may consume what Durkheim and others have called social facts, but he will bulge most uncomfortably, and Algy will still be there. I suspect that actual investigators will often, though perhaps not always, prefer to have Algy outside the bear.[84]

Gellner's remarks suggest that Chomsky's acceptance of a psychologistic account of language is philosophically disreputable. But I do not think that the Chomskian linguist ought to be too much bothered by Gellner's scruples here. For one thing, the move by linguists towards a psychologistic position was not a 'desperate' attempt to assimilate social characteristics to individual ones. This move was, rather, quite a natural one to make in the context of the empirical problems with which Chomsky has characteristically been concerned. There are, for

[83] Gellner, 'Explanations in History', p. 262.
[84] Ibid.

instance, interesting and difficult problems involved in explaining how language-users decode the acoustically encoded messages of their interlocutors. In the context of this problem, it seems quite natural to suppose that language-users have 'consumed' the 'social facts' which determine the relationship between sound and meaning in their language.[85] Indeed, it is only by accepting some such supposition that we can explain the phenomenon of mutual intelligibility.

It would appear, then, that psychologism or monadism is a natural, rather than a 'desperate' explanatory strategy for linguistics. This is, of course, consistent with Gellner's claim that social monadism is in general implausible, since he does admit that social scientists will 'perhaps not always' prefer collectivistic accounts of social phenomena to monadistic ones. But the naturalness of such an orientation in the linguistic context may, in fact, suggest that this orientation is also appropriate in other contexts of social explanation. If the problem of explaining mutual intelligibility makes monadism a natural research strategy for linguistics, then the existence of similar problems in other social domains surely suggests that a monadistic strategy might also be appropriate in those domains.[86] As Chomsky himself has suggested, the monadistic methodological orientation of linguistics may be exemplary for other social sciences.[87] This, then, is one important implication of Chomsky's individualistic methodological orientation.

A second important implication of Chomsky's linguistic individualism derives from the insight which it provides into the revolutionary character of Chomsky's account of language. That Chomsky's work has had a revolutionary impact on linguistics has become virtually a truism. What has not become

---

[85] See Chomsky, *Language and Mind*, pp. 168–9; and J. Fodor, T. Bever, and M. Garrett, *The Psychology of Language*, New York, 1974, ch. 1.

[86] Garfinkel, for instance, has suggested that the appropriate strategy for explaining individuals' general ability to make sense of their social environment involves the supposition that they have 'consumed' those 'social facts' which constitute that environment. See H. Garfinkel, 'Remarks on Ethnomethodology', reprinted in Gumperz and Hymes, *Directions in Sociolinguistics*.

[87] See Chomsky, *Reflections*, ch. 1.

the subject of widespread consensus is in just which respects Chomsky's account of language in fact constituted a revolutionary break with the accounts offered by his predecessors. Bach characterizes the Chomskian revolution as a revolution of method, Lyons as a revolution of rigour, and Hymes claims that it resulted from Chomsky's demonstration of the formal inadequacy of previous modes of linguistic explanation.[88]

There is, I think, at least a grain of truth in each of these characterizations. But my own view is that Chomsky's most revolutionary contribution to linguistics was embodied in his advocacy of a thoroughly individualistic point of view.

We have already seen that Saussure was torn between individualism and collectivism. And although Bloomfield and Sapir, the other 'founding fathers' of modern linguistics, could perhaps be said to have anticipated Chomsky in their fundamentally individualistic methodological orientation, neither of them seems to have been as fully aware as Chomsky was of the implications of this orientation. Specifically, neither of them seems to have noticed, as Chomsky did, that such an orientation presupposes and implies a thoroughly subjectivistic account of language. When Chomsky claims that linguistics is 'a subfield of psychology', he goes much further, I think, than either Bloomfield or Sapir were prepared to go. Sapir believed, for instance, that 'we can profitably discuss ... speech ... as an institutional or cultural entity, leaving the organic or psychological mechanism back of it as something to be taken for granted'.[89] And Bloomfield claimed that 'we can pursue the study of language without any reference to any one psychological doctrine'.[90] I do not claim, of course, that Bloomfield and Sapir were collectivists. I do claim, though, that Chomsky saw more clearly than either of them just what was entailed by the individualistic orientation which he inherited from them.

---

[88] See E. Bach, 'Structural Linguistics and the Philosophy of Science', *Diogenes* xxxi (1965), p. 123; J. Lyons, *Noam Chomsky*, London, 1970, p. 43; and D. Hymes, 'Review of *Noam Chomsky*', reprinted in Harman, *On Noam Chomsky*, p. 325.

[89] Sapir, *Language*, p. 11.

[90] Bloomfield, *Language*, p. vii.

In fact, Chomsky's understanding of the implications of this commitment exceeded that even of his teacher Harris, who could only entertain the idea of interpreting linguistic theories as psychological theories, but opted in the end to treat language in objectivistic or instrumentalist terms.[91] In retrospect, then, Chomsky seems to have had an almost uniquely clear understanding of the implications of an individualistic methodological orientation for linguistics.

This concludes my discussion of Chomsky's individualism. In Chapter Two, I will consider a related Chomskian claim—the claim that language-users know the grammars of their languages.

---

[91] See Harris, *Methods*, pp. 16–20.

2

CHOMSKY'S MENTALISM AND RATIONALISM

1 Introduction

According to Chomsky, 'certain well-founded conclusions about the nature of language . . . are relevant to the problem of how knowledge is acquired and how the character of human knowledge is determined by certain general properties of the mind'. Chomsky elsewhere claims that these conclusions support 'what might fairly be called a rationalist conception of the acquisition of knowledge', as opposed, in particular, to an empiricist one. More specifically, he suggests that 'contemporary research [in linguistics] supports a theory of psychologically a priori principles that bears a striking resemblance to the classical doctrine of innate ideas'.[1] Katz, among others, joins Chomsky in making such claims, declaring that 'enough is now known in the theory of language to afford a substantial basis for deciding between the empiricist and rationalist hypotheses', and concluding that such a decision favours a rationalist account of human learning.[2] We can call the claim that research in linguistics supports a rationalist account of learning *linguistic rationalism*.

Commentators on linguistic rationalism, both hostile and friendly, have agreed on its philosophical interest and importance and a lively debate has developed in connection with various problems associated with this doctrine. Cooper has argued, for instance, that Chomsky's neo-rationalism is dissimilar enough from the rationalism of Descartes and Leibniz so that 'there is little of philosophical contention in Chomsky's

---

[1] N. Chomsky, 'Linguistics and Philosophy', in S. Hook, ed., *Language and Philosophy*, New York, 1969, p. 59; and 'Recent Contributions to the Theory of Innate Ideas', *Synthese* xvii (1967), pp. 9 and 2.

[2] J. Katz, *The Philosophy of Language*, New York, 1966, p. 245.

doctrine'.[3] Danto, on the other hand, sees a 'considerable parity between Locke's thought and Chomsky's' and claims that 'what Chomsky has chosen to think of as innate ideas [do not] correspond in any measure to what Locke rejected'.[4] More concretely, Goodman, Putnam, and Stern have questioned the force of Chomsky's arguments for a rationalist account of language learning, while Cohen, Harman and Quine have claimed that Chomsky's criticisms of empiricist accounts of learning undermine only weak and unimaginative versions of empiricism.[5] And Derwing has challenged the claims about language in terms of which Chomsky has constructed his arguments about the relative merits of empiricist and rationalist accounts of language learning.[6]

Despite the importance and interest of these criticisms, much of the debate about linguistic rationalism has been concerned with Chomsky's distinct, but allegedly related, claim that language-users know the grammar of their language. Chomsky says, for instance, that 'every speaker of a language has mastered and internalized a generative grammar that expresses his knowledge of his language'.[7] And Katz also refers to language-users' 'internalized knowledge of the grammar' of their language.[8] We can call the claim that language-users know the grammar of their language *linguistic mentalism*.

Before discussing the alleged relation between linguistic rationalism and linguistic mentalism, I may perhaps indicate how Chomsky's advocacy of linguistic mentalism is consistent

[3] D. Cooper, 'Innateness: Old and New', *Philosophical Review* lxxxi (1972), p. 466.

[4] A. Danto, 'Semantical Vehicles, Understanding, and Innate Ideas', in Hook, *Language and Philosophy*, p. 130.

[5] See N. Goodman, 'The Emperor's New Ideas'; W. V. Quine, 'Linguistics and Philosophy'; and K. Stern, 'Neorationalism and Empiricism'—all in Hook, *Language and Philosophy*; H. Putnam, 'The "Innateness Hypothesis" and Explanatory Models in Linguistics', *Synthese* xvii (1967); G. Harman, 'Reply to Arbini', *Synthese* xix (1969); and L. J. Cohen, 'Some Applications of Inductive Logic to the Theory of Language', *American Philosophical Quarterly* vii (1970).

[6] See B. Derwing, *Transformational Grammar as a Theory of Language Acquisition*, Cambridge, 1973, esp. ch. 4.

[7] N. Chomsky, *Aspects of the Theory of Syntax*, Cambridge, 1965, p. 8.

[8] J. Katz, *The Underlying Reality of Language and Its Philosophical Import*, New York, 1971, p. 131.

with his advocacy of linguistic subjectivism, and thus illustrates the unity of his system of ideas. In general, there is a close relation between the subjectivistic and mentalistic points of view. According to subjectivism, a grammar of a language describes the psychological basis of linguistic competence. According to linguistic mentalism, individuals' knowledge of a grammar provides the (psychological) basis for their linguistic competence. Linguistic mentalism is, then, just that version of linguistic subjectivism according to which a grammar provides the psychological basis for linguistic competence because it is known by the language-user whose competence it describes. Linguistic mentalism, in other words, is just a species of linguistic subjectivism. Chomsky's advocacy of these two theses thus illustrates the unity of his system of ideas and the central organizing role which subjectivism has in that system. (It will be the burden of much of the argument of this chapter, however, to show that a commitment to linguistic subjectivism does not require a commitment to linguistic mentalism.)

That the debate about linguistic rationalism has crucially involved questions about the merits of linguistic mentalism is due to a widespread belief, shared by both supporters and opponents of linguistic rationalism, that linguistic rationalism presupposes linguistic mentalism. Cooper, for instance, opposes linguistic rationalism and suggests that it 'stems, primarily, from a certain [mentalistic] view about what it is to know a language' and can therefore be discredited 'to the extent that the relevant view of knowing a language is discredited'.[9] On the other hand, Graves *et al.* support linguistic rationalism, but in effect agree with Cooper that it is necessary to establish linguistic mentalism as a bridge between the scientific claims of linguistics and the philosophical claims inherent in linguistic rationalism.[10] We can call the claim that linguistic mentalism is needed to provide a bridge between linguistic rationalism and facts about language the *bridge thesis*.

[9] D. Cooper, *Knowledge of Language*, London, 1975, pp. 5–6.
[10] See C. Graves *et al.*, 'Tacit Knowledge', *Journal of Philosophy* lxx (1973), p. 318.

The bridge thesis derives its plausibility from an argument of the following kind. (*a*) It seems reasonable, perhaps even necessary, to explain various facts about language learning by assuming that certain innate mental structures or faculties mediate the language acquisition process. (*b*) The traditional philosophical debate between empiricists and rationalists was, however, not concerned with questions about the existence of innate mental structures or faculties. This debate was concerned with questions about the existence of innate ideas and innate knowledge. In particular, both empiricists and rationalists agreed on the existence of innate structures or faculties, but empiricists denied, while rationalists asserted, the existence of innate knowledge and innate ideas. (*c*) In order to support linguistic rationalism, it is thus necessary to argue that the innate mental structures or faculties postulated by linguists constitute knowledge innately possessed by language-learners. (*d*) But the argument called for in (*c*) could be provided only if language-learners acquire propositional knowledge about their language. This is so because it is necessary to postulate innate knowledge in order to explain the acquisition of propositional knowledge about language, whereas it is unnecessary to postulate innate knowledge in order to explain the acquisition merely of linguistic skills, dispositions, or habits. (*e*) In order to warrant attribution to language-learners of innate ideas or innate knowledge, it is thus necessary to warrant attribution to language-users of knowledge of the grammar of their language. In order to warrant linguistic rationalism, it is, in other words, necessary to warrant linguistic mentalism.

The soundness of this argument for the bridge thesis has been widely assumed in the literature about linguistic rationalism. Graves *et al.* actually provide an argument for the bridge thesis which resembles the one just outlined, while Edgley, Wells, Danto, and Cooper all seem to accept the bridge thesis on roughly this basis.[11]

---

[11] See C. Graves *et al.*, 'Tacit Knowledge', *Journal of Philosophy* lxx (1973), p. 318. See also R. Edgley, 'Innate Ideas', in G. Vesey, ed., *Knowledge and Necessity*, London, 1970; D. Cooper, *Knowledge of Language*; and R. Wells, 'Innate Knowledge', and A. Danto, 'Semantical Vehicles'–both in Hook, *Language and Philosophy*.

My position here is this. On the one hand, I agree with the opponents of linguistic rationalism that linguistic mentalism is unwarranted. On the other hand, I claim that a case can be made for linguistic rationalism. Since the bridge thesis implies that it is necessary to employ what might be called a *mentalistic strategy* for supporting linguistic rationalism, it is clear that the two claims I endorse are consistent only if the bridge thesis is false. I will, then, argue here that the bridge thesis is false. I will, in particular, develop and deploy two non-mentalistic strategies for supporting linguistic rationalism.

2   *Mentalism and the Object of Linguistic Inquiry*

According to linguistic mentalism, language-users know the grammar of their language. I will here initially be concerned to consider what a grammar is taken by linguists to be and what kind of knowledge of a grammar linguistic mentalists attribute to language-users.

Kant revolutionized philosophical psychology by asking how our experience of the causal connection of events is possible, given that no such connection is manifested in sensation; and by answering that it is the human mind which imposes a causal connection between events which are in sensation merely temporally successive.[12] Likewise, Chomsky revolutionized linguistics by asking how our perception of the structure of sentences is possible, given that this structure may be nowhere overtly marked in the acoustic signal which impinges on us; and by answering that the language-user imposes perceptual structure on events which are in sensation linguistically unstructured.[13] The force of this common approach is to emphasize that the individual is an active interpreter, rather than a merely passive recipient, of sensations.

We can say that the language-user's ability to impose perceptual structure on linguistically unstructured acoustic sensations is an aspect of her or his linguistic *competence*.

---

[12] See I. Kant, *Prolegomena to Any Future Metaphysics*, trans. P. Lucas, Manchester, 1953, pp. 56–7.

[13] See N. Chomsky, *Language and Mind*, New York, 1972, pp. 133–4.

According to Chomsky, the fundamental goal of linguistic research is the development of theories of linguistic competence.[14]

If the goal of linguistic research is the construction of theories of linguistic competence, we can now properly ask what form a theory of competence ought to take. Moravcsik has given an insightful answer to this question. He claims that an explanatory theory of linguistic competence ought to specify (a) what individuals with this competence are able to do, (b) what psychological processes underlie manifestations of this competence, and (c) what structural characteristics language-users must have if the psychological processes underlying manifestations of their competence are to occur.[15]

As Moravcsik points out, the specification called for in (a) delineates the competence for which an explanatory theory is sought. Though constructing such a specification may involve difficult methodological and formal problems, it is clear that such a specification could not by itself constitute an explanatory theory of the competence in question.[16] Such a specification would, at best, constitute a description of that competence. An explanation of that competence would in addition specify the characteristics of individuals with that competence which enable them to manifest it in the ways described by that specification. Paradigmatically, then, an explanatory theory of linguistic competence is a theory of the psychological structures and processes which provide the basis for manifestations of that competence.

[14] See Chomsky, *Aspects*, p. 4. Chomsky of course denies that the language-user's competence can be identified with the ability to impose linguistic structure on unstructured sensations. He insists instead, in a way which pre-empts debate about linguistic mentalism, that the user's competence is embodied in knowledge of the grammar of the language. I see nothing wrong in using the term 'competence' in the way I do, but it should be noted that my usage differs from Chomsky's in this respect.

[15] See J. Moravcsik, 'Competence, Creativity and Innateness', *Philosophical Forum* i (1969), pp. 407-9.

[16] Among the methodological problems involved in constructing a description of linguistic competence is that of distinguishing behaviour which manifests the competence more or less directly from behaviour which is from this point of view contaminated by extra-linguistic influences. In Chomsky's terminology, this is the problem of distinguishing between linguistic competence and linguistic performance. See *Aspects*, pp. 10-15.

Viewed abstractly, a grammar is a mathematical function which induces a mapping between linguistic stimuli (acoustic sensations) and their corresponding percepts (structural descriptions of sentences).[17] It does this by defining certain levels of representation intermediate between representations of its input and output, and by defining certain operations on these representations. In Moravcsik's terms, then, a grammar is a descriptive delineation of the language-user's competence—of his or her ability to effect such a mapping.

Given a grammar which does adequately describe the language-user's competence, we can reasonably ask how and on what basis that competence is to be explained. One plausible strategy for answering this question involves the invocation of what we might call *normal realist assumptions*, according to which the concepts which figure in a descriptively adequate scientific theory can be taken to describe real, though perhaps presently unobservable, entities and events underlying the observable entities and events described by that theory.[18] In terms of such realist assumptions, a plausible explanatory theory of language-user's competence would thus be one which attributes to them a capacity to manipulate the representations and to perform the operations specified by the grammar of their language.[19] It is clear, moreover, that such a theory would satisfy Moravcsik's desiderata for theories of linguistic competence. Such a theory would identify the processes underlying manifestations of linguistic competence with the operations on linguistic representations defined by the grammar which describes that competence. And it would imply that these processes occur because language-users incorporate a mental mechanism the operations of which are defined by the rules of that grammar. Furthermore, at least some of the empirical consequences of supposing that grammars and theories of linguistic competence are related in this way have experimentally been confirmed.

---

[17] See Chomsky, *Language and Mind*, p. 125.
[18] See E. Nagel, *The Structure of Science*, New York, 1961, ch. 6.
[19] See N. Chomsky and J. Katz, 'What the Linguist is Talking About', *Journal of Philosophy* lxxi (1974), pp. 362–3.

It has been shown, for instance, that some of the intermediate representations of linguistic entities defined by descriptively adequate grammars are involved in the mental processing of linguistic stimuli.[20]

Given that such a realist strategy is both a priori appropriate and has received empirical support, we can thus see how a grammar of a language might provide the basis for explaining the language-user's competence. A realist theory of linguistic competence would attribute to language-users a mental mechanism the operations of which are defined by the grammar of their language.

The standard mentalistic strategy for supporting linguistic rationalism involves a preliminary argument, according to which the grammar which we realistically attribute to the language-user is in fact known by the language-user to whom we attribute it. To establish this mentalistic claim, those who accept the standard strategy argue that the mentalistic assumption that language-users know the grammar of their language has excess explanatory power with respect to the merely realist assumption that this grammar describes the psychological basis of linguistic competence.

I will later consider an argument of this kind and conclude that it is not sound; that linguistic mentalism cannot be supported; and that a non-mentalistic strategy for supporting linguistic rationalism must be developed. First, though, it is necessary to clarify the mentalistic claim that language-users know the grammar of their language.

Many philosophers concerned with linguistic mentalism have accepted Ryle's claim that knowledge is a matter either of knowing how to do something or of knowing that something is the case.[21] On this account, a person who has knowledge of

---

[20] See J. Fodor, T. Bever, and M. Garrett, *The Psychology of Language*, New York, 1974, ch. 5.

[21] See G. Ryle, *The Concept of Mind*, Harmondsworth, 1973, p. 29. Harman and Schwartz have urged the importance of this distinction to discussions of linguistic mentalism. See G. Harman, 'Psychological Aspects of the Theory of Syntax', *Journal of Philosophy* lxiv (1967); and R. Schwartz, 'On Knowing a Grammar', in Hook, *Language and Philosophy*.

some proposition *p* has typically reflected that *p*, been aware of *p*, will assert *p* on suitable occasions, and is capable of understanding formulations of *p*.[22] According to linguistic mentalism, typical language-users know the grammar of their language. But they have obviously never been aware of that grammar and may be unable to formulate or even to understand formulations of the knowledge they are alleged to have. For this reason, it would seem that the knowledge of grammar postulated by linguistic mentalism is not knowledge-that, or, at least, not any ordinary kind of knowledge-that. On the other hand, to say that a grammar merely describes the language-user's ability or know-how is not in this context to say enough. For the mentalistic defender of linguistic rationalism, the latter claim would not involve attributing to the language-user anything the acquisition of which would involve innate knowledge.

Chomsky has refused to accept the claim that the dichotomy between knowing-how and knowing-that is exhaustive of the various kinds of knowledge a person might be said to have. He suggests that we might, in addition, have tacit knowledge—propositional knowledge which we are unaware of having and cannot report having which nevertheless guides our behaviour.[23] It is this kind of tacit knowledge of grammars which linguistic mentalism attributes to language users.

Although such tacit knowledge differs in obvious ways from typical cases of knowledge-that, it is clear that mentalistic defenders of linguistic rationalism must claim that it is a kind, though not the ordinary kind, of knowledge-that. This is so because the existence of innate knowledge-how was not at issue in the debate between empiricists and rationalists, at least according to the epistemic interpretation of that debate to which linguistic mentalism is meant to be responsive.[24]

The requirement that the tacit knowledge of grammar attributed to language-users be a kind of knowledge-that

[22] See S. Stich, 'What Every Speaker Knows', *Philosophical Review* lxxx (1971), pp. 485–6.
[23] See Chomsky, 'Linguistics and Philosophy', p. 87.
[24] See Cooper, *Knowledge of Language*, p. 27.

provides a desideratum, then, which any adequate argument for linguistic mentalism must satisfy. One strategy for satisfying this desideratum involves arguing that the knowledge of grammar attributed to language-users must be a kind of knowledge-that because the attribution of this knowledge to users plays the same role in explaining their behaviour as do attributions of ordinary kinds of knowledge-that in explaining other kinds of behaviour.

An argument for linguistic mentalism, then, must satisfy two conditions. (*a*) It must show that attributing tacit knowledge of a grammar to language-users has excess explanatory power over attributing to them a mental structure the operations of which are described by that grammar. (*b*) It must show that this tacit knowledge is a kind of knowledge-that. In Section 4, I will consider an argument which is alleged to satisfy these two conditions. Before doing so, however, I will first consider some standard, and I think mistaken, criticisms of linguistic mentalism.

3　*Standard Criticisms of Linguistic Mentalism*

I will here consider three arguments against linguistic mentalism and attempt to show that each of them fails. Although these arguments are more or less widespread in the literature about linguistic mentalism, I will focus my discussion by considering the versions of them presented by David Cooper in his book *Knowledge of Language*.

(*a*) In Chapter 3 of his book, Cooper claims that one of the reasons why we might say that language-users know the grammar of their language is that they can be said to follow the rules of this grammar. Cooper aims to undermine linguistic mentalism by undermining the claim that language-users follow the rules of a grammar in any sense relevant to the validity of linguistic mentalism. He begins his discussion by considering the relation between rule-following and linguistic mentalism.

Cooper points out that in order to be relevant to linguistic mentalism, rule-following must involve more than merely rule-conforming behaviour. While the behaviour of a child correctly performing certain arithmetical calculations conforms to the Peano axioms, we would not, of course, normally be inclined to infer from this fact the claim that the child was following these (axiomatic) rules, or that she or he knew them.[25] Behaviour which conforms to rules, then, does not provide adequate evidence to support the claim that individuals whose behaviour does so conform follow or know the rules in question.

Cooper next considers what he calls a paradigmatic case of rule-following, which he calls rule-following$_1$. Rule-following$_1$ involves what Cooper calls consultative acts. Those who are rule-following$_1$ typically consult certain rules and arrange their behaviour to conform to those rules. Cooper points out that there is no sense, at least no obvious one, in which native speakers of a language follow the rules of its grammar in this paradigmatic way. He then notes that if rule-following$_1$ were the only kind of rule-following, then language-users could not reasonably be said to follow the rules of a grammar and thus could not reasonably be said to know that grammar. In other words, if rule-following$_1$ were the only kind of rule-following, linguistic mentalism could not be supported.[26]

Cooper next considers the possibility of extending the idea of rule-following to include what he calls rule-following behaviour, and suggests that linguistic mentalism might (though it need not) be supported if language users in fact exhibit this behaviour. We exhibit rule-following behaviour, according to Cooper, if (i) our behaviour regularly conforms to some rule R; (ii) our R-conforming behaviour is extended to situations new to our experience; and (iii) we criticize deviations from R-conforming behaviour. Cooper then extends the notion of rule-following to include the activities of someone who exhibits rule-following behaviour but who is not rule-following$_1$. Such a person is, rather, rule-following$_2$.[27]

Cooper now claims that an argument from analogy justifies this extension of the sense of rule-following to include

[25] See Cooper, *Knowledge of Language*, p. 39.
[26] Ibid., pp. 43–4.
[27] Ibid., p. 44.

rule-following$_2$ as well as rule-following$_1$. He notes in this regard that there are two kinds of analogical argument which might justify such an extension.[28]

The first kind of analogical argument might be called an analogical inference. According to this argument, both rule-followers$_1$ and rule-followers$_2$ exhibit rule-following behaviour, and it is thus reasonable to infer that the latter are similar to the former in other ways as well, and, in particular, to infer that the latter, like the former, perform consultative acts. On this account, the only difference between them is that rule-followers$_1$ perform these consultative acts consciously (at least in principle), while rule-followers$_2$ perform them unconsciously. An analogical inference of this kind suggests what might be called a mentalistic view of rule-following$_2$.[29]

The second kind of analogical argument might be called an analogical extension. According to this argument, both rule-followers$_1$ and rule-followers$_2$ exhibit rule-following behaviour, and it is thus reasonable to say that both are rule-following. On this view, no further similarities between the two are assumed to exist. In particular, it is not assumed that rule-followers$_2$ perform consultative acts. This argument suggests what might be called a behaviouristic view of rule-following$_2$.[30]

Cooper next points out that only the mentalistic view of rule-following$_2$ supports linguistic mentalism. For only on this view do rule-followers$_2$ (unconsciously) consult the rules of their grammar, and only on this view, then, could they be said to know those rules.[31]

Cooper's fundamental strategy in attempting to undermine linguistic mentalism involves an argument against the mentalistic account of rule-following$_2$. I will now outline this argument. After I have done so, I will indicate why I think that it fails.

Cooper's argument against the mentalistic view of rule-following$_2$ has the following form.[32] (i) The fact that individuals

[28] See Cooper, *Knowledge of Language*, pp. 46–7.
[29] Ibid., pp. 48–9.
[30] Ibid., p. 49.
[31] Ibid., pp. 49–50.
[32] Ibid., pp. 53–7.

exhibit rule-following behaviour is the only evidence to support the claim that they are rule-following$_2$. (ii) But rule-following behaviour conforms to every behaviourally equivalent rule R_1, R_2, R_3, etc. (Rules are behaviourally equivalent if conformity to them leads to the same overt behaviour. Clearly, there are (possibly infinitely) many behaviourally equivalent rules to which any particular kind of rule-following behaviour conforms.) (iii) But since rule-following behaviour is, by (i), the only evidence as to which rule rule-followers$_2$ are following, and since, by (ii), this behaviour conforms to every behaviourally equivalent rule, we have no way, then, of determining which of these behaviourally equivalent rules rule-followers$_2$ are actually following. (iv) But we can determine which of a number of behaviourally equivalent rules rule-followers$_1$ are following. We can make this determination, for instance, by asking rule-followers$_1$ which of a number of behaviourally equivalent rules they are following. (v) Rule-following$_1$ and rule-following$_2$ are thus fundamentally dissimilar. (vi) Since rule-following$_1$ and rule-following$_2$ are fundamentally similar according to the mentalistic view of rule-following$_2$, this view is thus discredited. (vii) Linguistic mentalism is thus itself discredited, since only the mentalistic view of rule-following$_2$ supports it.

This is Cooper's argument. It fails because of the falsity of the claim—(iii) above—that rule-following behaviour is the only evidence as to which rule the language user is following. Cooper seems to think that this claim follows unproblematically from the (perhaps correct) claim—(i) above—that rule-following behaviour provides the only evidence that the language user is rule-following. But I do not see that this is so. There are two points to be made here.

First, the fact that exhibiting rule-following behaviour may be criterial for saying that individuals are rule-following does not imply that rule-following behaviour is the only kind of evidence as to which rule they are following. In particular, this is, on Cooper's own account, clearly not the case in instances of rule-following$_1$, where other kinds of evidence typically are available, and must be invoked, as in the case of rule-following$_2$, to determine which of a number of behaviourally equivalent rules rule-followers$_1$ are in fact following. In suggesting that such evidence is unavailable in cases of rule-following$_2$, Cooper thus appears to beg precisely the question at issue: how similar are rule-following$_1$ and rule-following$_2$?

Second, it seems that evidence bearing on the problem of behavioural equivalence is available in the case of rule-following$_2$. In particular, much of the psycholinguistic research of recent years has been directed to obtaining evidence as to which of a variety of behaviourally equivalent grammars the language-user is actually employing.[33] Of course, this evidence is not as direct as that obtained when we ask rule-followers$_1$ which rule they are following, nor is it particularly easy to obtain or to interpret.[34] But these difficulties are not insurmountable. They do not preclude the possibility of determining which of a number of behaviourally equivalent sets of rules the language-user is following$_2$.

For these reasons, then, I have to conclude that Cooper has not here established that rule-following$_1$ and rule-following$_2$ are fundamentally dissimilar; that he has not discredited the mentalistic view of rule-following$_2$; and that he has not, therefore, undermined the support which that view may provide for linguistic mentalism.

(*b*) In Chapter 5 of his book, Cooper discusses linguistic intuitions and the support which their availability allegedly lends to linguistic mentalism. According to most linguists, language users have intuitions about properties of and relations between the sentences of their language, on the basis of which

[33] For an argument that constituency-based transformational grammars and dependency-based transformational grammars are not explanatorily equivalent despite their behavioural equivalence, see W. Levelt, *Formal Grammars in Linguistics and Psycholinguistics*, The Hague, 1974, iii, pp. 32–63. This argument can be taken to suggest that language users consult the dependency-based grammars, which are explanatorily superior according to Levelt, even though their behaviour conforms to the rules of both kinds of grammars.

[34] For a discussion of some of the difficulties involved in obtaining and interpreting psycholinguistic evidence, see J. Wirth, 'Logical Considerations in the Testing of Linguistic Hypotheses', in D. Cohen and J. Wirth, eds., *Testing Linguistic Hypotheses*, Washington, 1975.

they are able to make intuitive judgements about those sentences. Native speakers of English might, for example, agree that (1) below is odd in a way in which (2), (3), and (4) are not, and that (2) and (3) are related in a way in which neither is to (4).

(1) *If the is were could*
(2) *The boy likes the girl*
(3) *The girl is liked by the boy*
(4) *Temperatures today were high*

Furthermore, on the standard view, a grammar is, among other things, a theory intended to account for such intuitive judgements by showing, for instance, what it is about (1) which makes it odd, and what it is about (2) and (3) which makes them somehow related.[35]

In this chapter, Cooper considers an argument which is alleged to show that the availability of linguistic intuitions supports linguistic mentalism. His strategy here is to undermine this argument and thus to undermine the claim that it does support linguistic mentalism. Cooper reconstructs this argument in the following way:[36]

(i) When language-users judge (2) and (3) to be somehow related, they are in effect judging that they have some particular property in common. (ii) In judging that these sentences have some particular common property, language-users are exhibiting their acquaintance with the properties of these sentences. (iii) A grammar of English is, among other things, a theory about the properties of sentences such as (2) and (3), and so will indicate which particular properties (2) and (3) share. (iv) When language-users judge (2) and (3) to be somehow related, they are in effect exhibiting their acquaintance with (or knowledge of) the grammar which specifies the ways in which these sentences are related. (v) Linguistic mentalism is supported, then, by the availability of linguistic intuitions.

---

[35] Not all linguists agree that grammars ought to be responsive to such intuitive judgements. See, for instance, G. Sampson, *The Form of Language*, London, 1975. For some objections to Sampson's position on this matter, see, however, F. D'Agostino, 'Rethinking Transformational Linguistics', *British Journal for the Philosophy of Science* xxvii (1976).

[36] See Cooper, *Knowledge of Language*, p. 94.

Cooper presents two objections to this argument. I will first outline these objections before saying why I think that they are not decisive.

First, Cooper objects to the claim that the fact that language-users judge (2) and (3) to have something in common shows that language-users judge (2) and (3) to have some particular, specified property in common. In effect, Cooper claims that this redescription has no excess explanatory force. Once we have conceded that users judge (2) and (3) to have something in common, we have said all that there is to say about such judgements.[37]

Second, Cooper challenges the idea that a grammar of English ought to explicate the similarity of (2) and (3) by representing these sentences in some way which displays the particular properties which they have in common. According to Cooper, to think that this similarity can or ought to be explicated in this way is to commit a mimetic fallacy. Cooper claims, in particular, that it makes no more sense to suppose that we can or ought to explicate the similarity of (2) and (3) in this representational way than it does to suppose that we can or ought to explicate the similarity of objects of a particular kind by representing them in some way which displays their common properties.[38]

Cooper's first objection is indecisive in a way which clearly reveals the unacceptability of his methodological commitments. To claim that we have said all that there is to say about users' intuitive judgements once we have conceded that users believe that (2) and (3) have something in common is to claim, in effect, that these judgements are in need of no real explanation. On Cooper's account, users do simply make such judgements and there is nothing about their ability to do this which requires explanation. On this view, we need not ask why or on what basis users make such judgements; they simply do.

But Cooper's position here is surely indefensible method-ologically; he simply asks us to abdicate the responsibility for

---

[37] See Cooper, *Knowledge of Language*, p. 95.
[38] Ibid., p. 97.

explaining phenomena by insisting, in many cases in defiance of common sense, that there is nothing problematic about these phenomena. And it is by no means obvious that there is nothing problematic about intuitive linguistic judgements. A problem arises, for instance, when we consider the ways in which such judgements are systematically related. Cooper's approach must inevitably fail to come to grips with this problem since, for Cooper, the notion of relatedness is an unanalyzed primitive term. This approach must for this reason fail to capture differences between various kinds of relatedness. Sentences (2) and (3) above, for instance, are not related to each other in the same way in which (3) and (5) below are, though both of these pairs of sentences are judged by users of English to have something in common.

   (5)   *The car was parked by the curb*

It would seem, then, that Cooper's first criticism of this argument must stand or fall with the propriety of his methodological views. Since we must reject these views, we must also, then, reject this criticism.

   Cooper's second objection also seems to be misplaced. It is, in particular, unconvincing to claim, as he does, that there is no way of explicating the similarity of objects of a particular kind in a representational way which displays their common properties. Objects of a certain kind might share many properties which are criterial for that kind. A representation of these objects in the form of a statement to this effect would surely display their common properties. But in this case, I do not see that it is illegitimate or fallacious to explicate intuitively accessible notions of similarity in terms of representational schemata of the kind which linguists use to account for linguistic intuitions.

   Since neither of Cooper's objections to this argument is convincing, I believe that we can conclude, then, that his attempt to undermine this argument fails. Linguistic mentalism is not threatened by Cooper's objections to this argument.

   (*c*) In Chapter 6 of his book, Cooper discusses the productivity of language and the support for linguistic mentalism which this is alleged to provide. When linguists claim that language use is productive, they refer, as we have already seen, to the fact that language-users are able to produce and to understand sentences which they have not before produced or encountered.[39] Most linguists suppose that the existence of this ability supports linguistic mentalism. Cooper seeks in this chapter to undermine an argument to this effect.

This argument is reconstructed by Cooper in the following way.[40] (i) Language-users are able to deal appropriately with sentences of their language which they have not previously encountered. (ii) Language-users are able to do this because such novel sentences are similar in various ways to those which they have previously encountered. (iii) But such novel sentences are, in an important sense, similar to familiar sentences only in highly abstract, non-observable ways. (iv) We cannot, then, explain how language-users deal appropriately with novel sentences by supposing that they observe similarities between these sentences and sentences with which they are familiar, and interpret the former by way of analogy with the latter. This is so because, by (iii), there may be no observable similarities between these sentences. (v) But since the grammar of a language specifies the abstract ways in which both familiar and novel sentences are similar, we could explain linguistic creativity by assuming that language-users know the grammar of their language and use this knowledge to deal in an appropriate way with novel sentences. (vi) The existence of linguistic productivity thus supports linguistic mentalism.

Cooper tries to undermine this argument by challenging the claim—(ii) above—that language users are able to deal appropriately with novel sentences because these sentences are similar in various ways to familiar ones. Cooper believes that this claim is not only wrong, but entirely misguided. He denies that it is the similarity of novel and familiar sentences which enables language-users to deal appropriately with the novel sentences. He claims instead that it is the fact that language-users deal with

---

[39] See Chomsky, *Language and Mind*, p. 100.
[40] See Cooper, *Knowledge of Language*, pp. 102–3.

a novel sentence in one way rather than another which makes that sentence similar to familiar sentences.[41] Cooper seems to be arguing, in effect, that there is no problem of productivity to be solved because there is nothing problematic about linguistic productivity. According to Cooper, language use simply is productive in the sense at issue, and it is the behaviour of language-users, not itself in need of explanation, which makes it so.

For reasons like those cited at (*b*) above, I find this claim fatuous. Furthermore, Cooper's account of this problem simply begs what must be an important question, even from his rather perverse point of view. When we are told that it is the fact that language users deal with a particular sentence S_1 in the same way in which they deal with another sentence S_2 (but not in the same way in which they deal with a third sentence S_3) which makes S_1 and S_2 (but not S_1 and S_3) similar, then we are surely entitled to ask what it is about S_1 (or for that matter about language-users who encounter S_1) which inclines them to deal with it in one way rather than another. As soon as we raise this kind of question, we are led to claim—as in (ii) above—that users deal with a novel sentence in one way rather than another because that sentence is similar to some familiar sentences (but not to others). Cooper's strategy here seems, then, to be self-defeating. We must, I think, conclude that this objection fails to undermine linguistic mentalism.

This concludes my discussion of three of the standard arguments against linguistic mentalism. Each of them, I think, fails to undermine that thesis. My conclusion to this effect should not, however, be taken to suggest that the arguments for linguistic mentalism which Cooper has criticized are themselves sound. Indeed, I will try to show in Section 5 that linguistic mentalism cannot, in fact, be sustained.

4   *The Standard Argument for Linguistic Mentalism*

The most sophisticated argument for linguistic mentalism is that provided by Graves *et al.* In particular, this argument

---

[41] Ibid., pp. 121–2.

avoids certain objections to, and thus supersedes earlier arguments of a similar kind due to Fodor, Moravcsik, and Arbini.[42] Because all of these arguments have the same general form, we can consider the argument of Graves *et al.* the *standard argument* for linguistic mentalism.

As I have already pointed out, this argument is intended to establish the explanatory superiority of the mentalistic assumption that language-users have tacit knowledge of a grammar to the realist assumption that language users incorporate a mental mechanism the operations of which are described by that grammar. In fact, one of the reasons why this argument is such an important one is that it avoids the pitfalls of arguments, such as some of those which Cooper criticized, which attempt to provide warrant for linguistic mentalism by justifying an extension of the ordinary application of the notion 'knowledge-that'. The defects of arguments of this latter kind are, of course, precisely those of all 'essentialist' arguments, which attempt to warrant basically empirical claims in terms of considerations about the 'essential' meanings of the concepts involved in the formulation of those claims. That such 'essentialist' arguments are inappropriate in the empirical context was clearly seen and forcefully stated by Popper, who urged that the important thing about any empirical claim is its relations to the problem it is intended to solve—a consideration in which questions of excess explanatory power, for instance, can, while those of 'essential' meaning cannot, justifiably figure.[43] I claim, then, that the standard argument for linguistic mentalism has the merit of avoiding inappropriate questions about 'essential' meaning and focusing instead on questions about explanatory power.

The question remains, of course, whether Graves *et al.* have in fact justified the claim that linguistic mentalism does have

---

[42] See Graves *et al.*, 'Tacit Knowledge'. See also J. Fodor, 'The Appeal to Tacit Knowledge in Psychological Explanation', *Journal of Philosophy* lxv (1968); R. Arbini, 'Comments on Linguistic Competence and Language Acquisition', *Synthese* xix (1969); and Moravcsik, 'Competence, Creativity and Innateness'.

[43] See K. Popper, 'Autobiography of Karl Popper', in P. Schilpp, ed., *The Philosophy of Karl Popper*, LaSalle, 1974, pp. 12–23.

excess explanatory power with respect to linguistic realism. This is the question I now propose to address.

The standard argument for linguistic mentalism has the following abstract structure:

(i) More or less straightforward empirical considerations support the realist claim that language-users incorporate a neurally embodied mental mechanism *M* the operations of which underlie manifestations of their linguistic competence.

(ii) There are nevertheless things which language-users are able to do which cannot be explained solely on this realist basis.

(iii) These abilities can be explained, however, on the assumption that language-users have tacit knowledge of the grammar of their language.

(iv) Attribution to language-users of such knowledge thus has excess explanatory power with respect to the claim that they incorporate a mental mechanism *M*.

(v) We are thus warranted in supposing that language-users have tacit knowledge of the grammar of their language.

An argument of this general kind has the following specific form:

(*a*) There are situations in which it is appropriate and legitimate to explain an individual's explicitly manifested knowledge of some set of propositions by assuming that this individual knows a theory which entails each of the propositions which she or he knows. (Notice that the plausibility of this assumption increases with *n*, the number of distinct but related propositions known by the individual and entailed by the theory. If *n* is very large, only the attribution of knowledge of a theory is likely to provide a unified account of what appears to constitute a unified domain of propositional knowledge.)

The validity of this conjectural explanation of the individual's knowledge can, of course, easily be tested. We can test this explanation, for instance, by determining whether the theory in question does entail each of the propositions the individual knows and by determining whether the individual does know the theory in question. And we can make this latter determination, in ordinary cases of the kind here under consideration, simply by asking the individual to expound the theory in question. Furthermore, while an explanation of this kind may involve the conjecture that the individual knows a theory which he or she has not perhaps yet explicitly manifested knowledge of, such an explanation clearly does not involve attributing to the individual any problematic kind of knowledge. We attribute to him or her propositional knowledge of the ordinary kind. We attribute knowledge of a kind which, we expect, he or she has been aware of having, can report having, can understand formulations of, etc.[44]

(*b*) Language-users are capable of making a potentially infinite number of assertions about their language. In a whole range of cases, for instance, language-users will, when queried, typically assert that a given string of words either is or is not an acceptable sentence of their language. These assertions are explicit manifestations of language-users' propositional knowledge about their language. Observation statements reporting these assertions should, then, take the form O: the language-user knows proposition p.[45]

(*c*) If O is taken as an *explanandum* for which some theory is to be offered as *explanans*, then it is a logical requirement on that theory that it contain epistemic predicates, since O itself does.[46]

(*d*) A theory T which attributes to language-users the mental mechanism M does not contain epistemic predicates, and so fails to satisfy the logical requirement set out in (*c*) above.[47]

(*e*) On the other hand, a theory T^*, which attributes to language-users knowledge of the grammar of their language does contain epistemic predicates and so does not fail to satisfy the logical requirement at issue. In particular, an explanation of O in terms of the theory T^* has the following, logically unexceptionable form. According to T^*, language-users know the grammar of their language. This grammar entails the proposition

[44] See Graves *et al.*, 'Tacit Knowledge', pp. 321 and 324.
[45] Ibid., pp. 324 and 328.
[46] Ibid., p. 326.
[47] Ibid.

p. Language-users know whatever is entailed by the grammar of their language. Language-users therefore know *p*. The theory *T**, in other words, entails the observation statement *O*.[48]

(*f*) The theory *T** thus has excess explanatory power with respect to the theory *T*. It is thus necessary to attribute to language-users knowledge of the grammar of their language in order to explain their ability to make assertions about that language.

This argument for linguistic mentalism thus appears to satisfy the first of the two desiderata for such arguments. It seems to establish the excess explanatory power of linguistic mentalism.[49] Of course, since language-users are not aware of the grammar and cannot expound it when asked to do so, the knowledge of it attributed to them by the theory *T** must be tacit knowledge rather than any ordinary kind of propositional knowledge.[50]

(*g*) Nevertheless, the tacit knowledge attributed to language-users by the theory *T** is similar to ordinary kinds of propositional knowledge. This is so because the attribution of tacit knowledge to language-users plays the same role in explaining their explicitly manifested propositional knowledge as does the attribution of ordinary kinds of propositional knowledge in explaining other kinds of manifestations of explicit propositional knowledge.[51]

This argument for linguistic mentalism thus appears also to satisfy the second of the two desiderata for such arguments. It seems to establish that the knowledge of grammar attributed to language-users is a kind of, though not quite the ordinary kind of, propositional knowledge.

This, then, is the standard argument for linguistic mentalism. In Section 5 I will present a number of considerations which show, I think, that this argument does not in fact provide an adequate warrant for linguistic mentalism.

[48] Ibid.
[49] Ibid., p. 321.
[50] Ibid., p. 325.
[51] Ibid.

5   *Criticisms of the Standard Argument*

I claim that the standard argument for linguistic mentalism
fails, and that a mentalistic strategy for supporting linguistic
rationalism must, therefore, also fail. In particular, I claim that
the standard argument fails because it does not in fact establish
that a theory which attributes to language-users knowledge of
a grammar has excess explanatory power with respect to a
theory which attributes to users a mental mechanism the
operations of which are described by that grammar. I claim,
in other words, that the theory T can explain everything which
can be explained by the theory T^*.

In arguing to this effect, I will, in particular, try to establish
three points. (*a*) It is questionable that language-users have
knowledge of the propositions which they assert about their
language on any basis which is relevant to the validity of
linguistic mentalism. (*b*) It is not the case, in any event, that
such propositional knowledge, if such there be, could not be
explained by a realist theory which merely attributes to
language-users a mental mechanism M. (*c*) The force of the
standard argument is anyway vitiated by a confusion between
requirements for justifying knowledge claims and requirements
on explanations of manifestations of knowledge.

(*a*) I claim that the standard argument for linguistic mentalism
fails because it is questionable whether the *explananda* for
which the mentalistic theory T^* is invoked as *explanans* are
statements of the form O: the language-user *knows p*. Of
course, if the *explananda* in this case do not contain epistemic
predicates, then their *explanans* need not contain such predicates
either, and the attribution to language-users of knowledge of a
grammar would thus no longer be warranted by its alleged excess
explanatory power. In fact, Graves *et al.* themselves recognize
that this is the case. They point out that the attribution to
language-users of knowledge of a grammar has excess explanatory
power only on the assumption that their assertions about their
language are manifestations of their propositional knowledge.[52]

---

[52]   See Graves *et al.*, 'Tacit Knowledge', p. 327.

The question, then, is whether language-users' assertions about their language are manifestations of their propositional knowledge. The main thing to note here is that these assertions do not come labelled, as it were, as manifestations of knowledge. We are, then, warranted in considering them as such only given what amounts to an observational theory which specifies the conditions under which it is appropriate to describe an assertion as a manifestation of propositional knowledge. Graves *et al.* do not seem to realize this, since they provide no reason for describing language-users' assertions about their language as manifestations of their propositional knowledge. Perhaps they feel that it is obvious that they are such.

I will argue here that it is not obvious that language-users' assertions are manifestations of their propositional knowledge. I will, in particular, suggest that there is at least one observational theory, to which one might reasonably suppose Graves *et al.* to subscribe, in terms of which it is at best problematic whether such assertions are to count as manifestations of language-users' propositional knowledge. (At (*b*) below I will consider an observational theory according to which language-users' assertions are manifestations of their propositional knowledge. But I will also there show that an explanation of language-users' knowledge involving this observational theory does not incorporate any mentalistic assumptions.)

The observational theory in question is due to Ayer and has recently been widely canvassed as an explication of the concept of knowledge.[53] According to this theory, there are three conditions which must be satisfied if assertion of the proposition *p* is to be given the description *O*: the individual knows *p*. These are (i) the individual asserts *p*, (ii) the individual has some warrant for asserting *p*, and (iii) *p* is true.

Ignoring (iii) and granting that (i) is satisfied in the case of the language-user, we can now ask whether condition (ii) is also satisfied in this case. I claim that Graves *et al.* can answer 'Yes' here only on pain either of begging the question of the

[53]   See A. J. Ayer, *The Problem of Knowledge*, London, 1956.

validity of linguistic mentalism or of undermining linguistic mentalism.

If we claim that language-users' warrant for asserting *p* is their propositional knowledge of the grammar of their language, then our claim presupposes the truth of a claim (i.e. linguistic mentalism) the truth of which it was invoked to guarantee. An argument involving this claim is thus circular, and cannot be held to provide support for linguistic mentalism.

If, on the other hand, we claim that language-users' warrant for asserting *p* is their knowledge of some proposition *q* (which is not a description of the grammar of their language), then we undermine the standard argument for linguistic mentalism. If language-users' knowledge of *q* warrants their assertion of *p*, then we could explain their knowledge of *p* by assuming that they know *q*. In this case, the assumption that language-users also know the grammar of their language would be explanatorily otiose, and the standard argument for linguistic mentalism would thus be undermined.

There is, then, at least one observational theory, in terms of which language-users cannot be held to have propositional knowledge about their language on any grounds which are relevant to the truth of linguistic mentalism.

Frankly, I do not consider this particular criticism of the standard argument a very powerful one. For one thing, Ayer's explication of the concept of knowledge is itself by no means obviously satisfactory. There are well-known internal problems with this explication, and it involves both essentialist and justificationist assumptions which are controversial.[54] Nevertheless, this criticism may still have some force, if only because it seems likely that Graves *et al.* do find Ayer's account of knowledge congenial.[55]

---

[54] See E. Gettier, 'Is Justified True Belief Knowledge?', *Analysis* xxiii (1963).
[55] See Graves *et al.*, 'Tacit Knowledge', p. 320, where they appear to endorse this account of knowledge for all but 'directly evident beliefs', which, they claim, do not require justification to count as instances of knowledge. Since they present no arguments for this claim, or for their claim that intuitive linguistic judgements are directly evident beliefs, it is not possible to evaluate the force of the present argument as a criticism of their position.

In any event, whatever the force of this criticism of the standard argument, it does at least have the merit of making clear something which seems to have escaped the notice of Graves *et al.*—the 'theoretical' (i.e. non-observational) character of the description O: the language-user knows p. In fact, this point immediately suggests a second criticism of the standard argument for linguistic mentalism.

(*b*) I claim that there is an explanation of language-users' knowledge about their language, if such they have, which does not attribute to them knowledge of the grammar of their language. I claim, in other words, that language-users' knowledge about their language can be explained merely by attributing to them a mental mechanism M the operations of which are described by the grammar of that language. I claim, in short, that a mentalistic theory of linguistic competence has no excess explanatory power with respect to a realist theory.

My claim to this effect depends on the plausibility of a particular observational theory T_O, according to which it is appropriate to describe language-users' assertions about their language as manifestations of their knowledge of that language. This theory can be formulated in the following way.[56] When an individual asserts a proposition p, this event can rightly be described by the observation statement O: the individual knows the proposition p, just when p reports a belief of the individual which has been arrived at by a reliable method.

It should be clear that the theory T_O, in conjunction with the theory T (which attributes to language-users the mental mechanism M), does warrant using statements of the form O to describe language-users' assertions about their language. In attributing the mechanism M to language-users T does attribute to them a reliable mechanism for arriving at beliefs about their language.[57] In this way, it resembles those theories of

---

[56] I heard Richard Grandy advocate this account in a lecture at the Massachusetts Institute of Technology on 1 October 1976.

[57] On my account, M is the mechanism which provides the basis for language-users' ability to produce and interpret the sentences of their language. It is arguable whether users' ability to make meta-linguistic judgements about these sentences is in any way related to the ability simply to understand them. Levelt has suggested

perception which explain a person's ability to form beliefs about the properties of objects by attributing to them certain sensory-neural mechanisms. In this case, then, the conditions specified by the theory T_O are satisfied, and language-users can be said to manifest their knowledge of their language when they make assertions about it.

Furthermore, it should be clear that the theory which consists of the conjunction of T and T_O does entail observation statements of the form O, without attributing to language-users any knowledge of the grammar of their language. We can easily see that this is so. The theory T attributes to language-users a mental mechanism M the operations of which are such as to lead, in the appropriate circumstances, to users' assertion of the proposition p. The theory T thus entails (and therefore explains) the uninterpreted observation statement o: the language user asserts p. But since T attributes to language-users a mental mechanism which provides a reliable basis for making such assertions, the conditions specified by the observational theory T_O are satisfied, and, given o, T_O entails that language-users know the proposition p. That is, the conjunction of T and T_O — neither of which attributes knowledge of a grammar to the language-user—entails the interpreted observation statement O: the language-user knows p. Attribution to language-users of knowledge of the grammar of their language thus has no excess explanatory power over the attribution to them of a mental mechanism described by that grammar. Since this latter attribution is anyway independently warranted, and in any case not here at issue, we must then conclude that the standard

that the relation between these two abilities is unknown, while Moravcsik has argued that 'the fact that a speaker has intuitions about what is and what is not a grammatical sequence is one of the causal factors responsible for his ability to generate the right sequences of language'. (See Levelt, *Formal Grammars* iii, p. 10; and Moravcsik, 'Competence, Creativity and Innateness', p. 414.) I have no interesting opinion on this matter. What I do claim is that any interesting theory of the full range of behaviour involved in linguistic competence will have to account for both of these abilities, whatever their relation to one another. But attribution to language-users of a mental mechanism described by such a theory will enable us to explain users' intuitions about their language, and will enable us to do so without attributing to them any knowledge of grammar.

argument for linguistic mentalism is inadequate, and that linguistic mentalism cannot be recommended on the grounds that it is explanatorily superior to linguistic realism.

(*c*) I claim, finally, that the standard argument for linguistic mentalism fails because it embodies a confusion between requirements on justifying claims to knowledge and requirements on explanations of manifestations of knowledge. This confusion undermines an assumption implicit in the standard argument for linguistic mentalism.

> *A* Any explanation of a manifestation by the language user of knowledge of some proposition *p* must involve the attribution to the user of knowledge of some other proposition or system of propositions.

I claim that this assumption is implicit in the standard argument since some such assumption is necessary to warrant the inference from the logically correct claim that *explanans* must contain epistemic predicates if *explanandum* does to the unjustifiable claim that no *explanans* can be adequate unless it attributes to language-users knowledge of some system of propositions which entails the propositions which they explicitly assert. No justification for this assumption is provided by Graves *et al.* in their account of the standard argument. Nevertheless, if we try to construct an argument to justify this assumption, we will see that it is undermined by the confusion which I have mentioned.

An argument in support of assumption *A* might have the following form. (i) It is reasonable to require that

> *R* Any claim to know some proposition *p* (which is not itself immediately knowable) must be justified in terms of a claim to know some other proposition *q*, where knowing *q* would warrant knowing *p*.

(ii) There are cases in which it is plausible to explain a manifestation of knowledge of *p* by attributing to the person who manifests that knowledge knowledge of the same proposition *q* which would also serve as a justificatory warrant for his claim to know p. (iii) On the basis of (ii), we make the plausible conjecture

> C Whenever knowing some proposition q would be relevant to justifying a claim to know some proposition p, then attribution of knowledge of q may also be relevant to explaining manifestations of knowledge of p.

(iv) And finally, the locus of the confusion: the inference from the conjecture C to the assumption A.

The inference from C to A is, of course, fallacious. The fact that a particular strategy may always be relevant to explaining manifestations of knowledge does not entail a requirement always to employ such a strategy in such contexts. The assumption A is thus unsupported. Since the standard argument for linguistic mentalism depends on this unsupported assumption, it is itself undermined, and is thus incapable of providing warrant for linguistic mentalism. (The argument I have here outlined and criticized may also fail to support assumption A because it relies, at R, on a requirement which cannot be sustained if we accept the account of knowledge which was presented at (b) above.)

I claim, in conclusion, that the standard argument for linguistic mentalism fails to support that thesis, and that it fails largely because it does not establish the excess explanatory power of linguistic mentalism with respect to a realist account of linguistic competence. Since linguistic mentalism is unsupported, I furthermore claim that any mentalistic strategy for supporting linguistic rationalism must also fail. Since I nevertheless believe that linguistic rationalism can be supported, I will shortly present two non-mentalistic strategies for doing so. I must, however, first consider what kind of theory of linguistic competence remains once we have rejected the standard mentalistic account.

Linguistic mentalism was intended to provide a basis for explaining linguistic competence. It is clear that it would, if sustainable, have been satisfactory in this regard. Having rejected this thesis as unsupported, I am, then, now obliged to provide an alternative account of linguistic competence. This is particularly important in view of the widespread belief that the only alternative to a mentalistic account of linguistic competence is a behaviouristic one.[58]

A behaviouristic account of linguistic competence identifies language-users' competence with their dispositions to behave in certain ways in certain kinds of circumstances. A behaviouristic theory of competence is, then, just a convenient axiomatic representation of this set of dispositions. Such a theory is recommended by Cooper, Stich, Quine, and others.[59] But a behaviouristic account of competence is descriptive without being explanatory. Such an account (intentionally) does not indicate what it is about linguistically competent individuals which enables them to behave in the ways described by the axiomatic representation of their behavioural capacities which it provides. My rejection of a mentalistic account of linguistic competence requires the formulation, then, of an account of linguistic competence which is both non-mentalistic and explanatory.

As an alternative to both mentalistic and behaviouristic accounts of linguistic competence, I propose a realist account, according to which language-users' linguistic competence is described by a grammar of their language and is based on their incorporation of a mental mechanism the operations of which are described by that grammar.

It is clear that this realist account of linguistic competence meets the following three requirements. (i) This account is fully

---

[58] This belief is manifested in a *non sequitur* which infects much of the discussion of linguistic mentalism. Supporters of this thesis frequently suggest that it is entailed by the anti-behaviouristic requirement that a theory of competence postulate mental states and processes underlying manifestations of competence. For instances of this *non sequitur*, see Katz, *The Underlying Reality*, pp. 130-1; Moravcsik, 'Competence, Creativity and Innateness', pp. 416-7; and D. Slobin, *Psycholinguistics*, London, 1974, pp. 6-7.

[59] See Cooper, *Knowledge of Language*, ch. 5.; S. Stich, 'What Every Grammar Does', *Philosophia* iii (1973), p. 92; and W. V. Quine, 'Methodological Reflections on Current Linguistic Theory', reprinted in G. Harman, ed., *On Noam Chomsky*, Garden City, 1974, pp. 106-7.

explanatory, since it attributes to language-users certain psychological structures and processes, on the basis of which manifestations of their competence are conjectured to occur. (ii)
This account is thus superior to a behaviouristic account since it
is, while a behaviouristic account is not, fully explanatory in
this sense. (iii) This account is not, however, equivalent to
Chomsky's preferred mentalistic account. While both the realist
and the mentalistic accounts interpret grammars as psychological
theories (and in this way differ from a behaviouristic account),
the realist account merely attributes to language-users a mental
mechanism, while the mentalistic account postulates, in
addition, that a description of this mechanism is an object of
knowledge for those users to whom it is attributed.

My proposal, then, is to regard a grammar as a description of
the (possibly neurally embodied) mental mechanism the
operations of which provide the basis for manifestations by
language-users of their linguistic competence. That this realist
account of linguistic competence is a psychological theory
shows that we can reject Chomsky's mentalism without undermining his much more significant subjectivistic account of
language. We do not destroy the essential unity of Chomsky's
system of ideas, then, when we reject his mentalistic account of
linguistic competence.

This completes my discussion and criticism of linguistic
mentalism. I will now outline two non-mentalistic strategies for
supporting linguistic rationalism.

6 *Linguistic Rationalism*

In Section 5, I in effect rejected the standard mentalistic
strategy for supporting linguistic rationalism. That strategy is
based on acceptance of an epistemic interpretation of the
empiricist–rationalist debate, according to which that debate
was concerned with questions about the existence of innate
ideas and innate knowledge, but not with questions about the
existence of innate mental structures or faculties. I claim to
have shown that this strategy for supporting linguistic rationalism
must fail because linguistic mentalists have failed to establish

that descriptions of the mental mechanisms empirically postulated by linguists are in fact objects of knowledge for the language-users to whom these mechanisms are attributed.

I will here consider two alternatives to the standard mentalistic strategy for supporting linguistic rationalism. I claim that neither of these strategies fails in the way the standard strategy does.

The first of these strategies, like the standard strategy, is based on acceptance of the epistemic interpretation of the empiricist–rationalist debate. But where the standard strategy involves the assumption that the mental mechanisms empirically postulated by linguists are objects of knowledge, this strategy adopts something like the opposite assumption. This strategy involves assuming that ideas are, or can be taken to be, mental structures of a certain kind. This strategy in other words involves the assumption that references to ideas can be replaced by references to particular kinds of mental structures, and that this replacement does not involve the loss of significant, explanatorily relevant, content. On this assumption, empirically warranted postulations of innate mental mechanisms become relevant to the debate about the existence of innate ideas. Since such a strategy involves the claim that ideas can be simulated by mental structures of a certain kind, we can call it a *simulative* strategy for supporting linguistic rationalism.

The second non-mentalistic strategy for supporting linguistic rationalism differs from both the standard strategy and the simulative strategy. While both of these strategies involve acceptance of the epistemic interpretation of the empiricist–rationalist debate, this strategy presupposes the plausibility of a facultative interpretation of that debate. This strategy, in other words, involves the assumption that the empiricist and rationalist positions can be distinguished in terms of the claims they involved about the kinds of innate mental faculties by which learning is mediated. On this assumption, research in linguistics is relevant to determining whether the innate mental faculties which mediate language acquisition are a kind countenanced by rationalists, but not by empiricists. Since this strategy depends on a facultative interpretation of the empiricist–rationalist debate, we can call it a *facultative* strategy for supporting linguistic rationalism.

It is obvious that both of these non-mentalistic strategies involve non-trivial interpretative assumptions about the empiricist–rationalist debate. In order to provide a basis for evaluating the plausibility of these assumptions, I will shortly offer general characterizations of the empiricist and rationalist positions. Before doing so, though, I must first consider the account of the relation between philosophical and empirical claims which both of these non-mentalistic strategies presuppose.

As I pointed out when discussing the bridge thesis, the standard mentalistic strategy for supporting linguistic rationalism is attractive largely with respect to a particular, positivistic account of the relation between philosophical and scientific theories, according to which philosophical claims are more or less completely immune to the impact of empirical criticism.[60] It is primarily in virtue of this account that it makes sense to suppose that a bridge is needed to close the gap between Chomsky's empirical theory of language and philosophical claims about the acquisition of knowledge.

Since I have rejected linguistic mentalism and must therefore abandon any mentalistic strategy for supporting linguistic rationalism, I am obliged to defend an assumption to which I am thus driven—that a bridge is not needed to close the (allegedly logical) gap between empirical and philosophical claims. My position here will necessarily be that empirical theories can bear directly on philosophical claims. There are at least two points to be made in defence of this claim.

In this particular case, I agree with Chomsky when he claims that 'it is a mistake to read Descartes, the minor Cartesians, Hume and others as if they accepted some modern distinction between "scientific" and "philosophical" concerns', and concludes that these philosophers advanced many detailed empirical

---

[60] Harman actually makes precisely this point in his criticism of linguistic rationalism. See his 'Psychological Aspects', p. 84.

claims about the learning process.[61] Chomsky is clearly right here. One need only inspect Descartes's *Optics* or his *Treatise of Man*, or Berkeley's *Essay Towards a New Theory of Vision* to be convinced of this. It follows from this point that the empirical nature of Chomsky's linguistic theory does not in itself suffice to establish that that theory has no bearing on the debate between empiricists and rationalists. On this view, that debate was, to an extent greater than that credited by positivistic philosophers, itself centrally concerned with matters of fact, and was thus a debate to which Chomsky's empirical theories might be relevant.

More generally, I agree with Watkins that even paradigmatically philosophical claims can and do have logical relations with paradigmatically empirical ones. Consider, for instance, the statement

> F Energy in any form can be transformed, directly and without loss, into energy of any other form.

The statement F is a philosophical statement *par excellence* since, for syntactic reasons, it is neither falsifiable nor conclusively verifiable. (The statement F is, apparently, an implication of Faraday's holistic field theory.) Nevertheless, although F cannot clash with any finite conjunction of singular empirical statements, it is not, for that reason, immune to empirical criticism. In particular, F can clash with certain empirical theories. In fact, F is inconsistent with Newtonian theory, according to which gravitational energy cannot be transformed directly into electrical energy. It is in virtue of this relation that philosophical statements such as F can influence the development of scientific theories (and vice versa). For instance, a scientist who accepted F could not consistently accept Newtonian theory and might thus be led to attempt to develop an alternative theory of gravitation consistent with F.[62]

---

[61] N. Chomsky, *Reflections on Language*, London, 1976, pp. 224–5.
[62] See J. Watkins, 'Confirmable and Influential Metaphysics', *Mind* lxvii (1958), pp. 353 and 355.

But in this case, it may be that a modern empirical account of language acquisition is inconsistent in this sense with a traditional philosophical account of learning, and could thus bear on its acceptability. This is not to say, of course, that any such inconsistency would decisively undermine the traditional philosophical account. This is so because the empirical theory with which such a philosophical account may be inconsistent may itself be false. Nevertheless, to say that some current empirical theory of language acquisition is inconsistent with some traditional philosophical account of learning is to say that we currently have (fallible) grounds for supposing that the philosophical account is incorrect.[63]

For these reasons, then, I think that I am entitled to conclude that my rejection of the bridge thesis does not foreclose the possibility of finding a means of supporting linguistic rationalism. In fact, I will shortly outline two strategies intended to do just this. Before doing so, however, I must first characterize the empiricist and rationalist accounts of learning.

Ignoring certain differences which are unimportant from our point of view, the empiricist position can be characterized in the following terms.

First, empiricists claim that the senses (including the inner sense of reflection on the mind's own activities) supply the mind with all of the materials out of which it constructs knowledge about the world. Locke held that the mind is *tabula rasa* (i.e. devoid of ideas) at birth, and that the senses supply it with all of the simple ideas which are the atomic components of our complex ideas about the world. Hume claimed that all of our ideas are either copied directly from sensory impressions or are compounded solely from ideas which were themselves so

[63] In suggesting that philosophical theories can be logically inconsistent with empirical theories, I am not, of course, suggesting that the former are 'refutable' in the technical sense. A theory is refutable in this sense only if it is inconsistent with syntactically singular statements of certain kinds. And empirical theories are not, of course, syntactically singular statements. See K. Popper, *The Logic of Scientific Discovery*, London, 1959, p. 41.

copied. And Mill held that all general terms are compounds of attributes which denote sensations.[64]

Second, empiricists claim that human beings have certain innate mental faculties which provide the basis for the manipulation of the data supplied by the senses. In particular, these are the faculties by means of which we are able to perceive the identity, similarity, co-existence or succession of the ideas made available in sensation. Locke referred to our faculties or natural powers for perceiving ideas to be the same or different, similar, and co-existent. Hume mentioned the principles which govern the imaginative faculty's operations, and numbered among these the associative relations of resemblance and contiguity. And Mill claimed that perceptions of resemblance and of the succession of sensations are irreducible effects of the nature of our mental faculties.[65]

Third, empiricists claim that there are no relations between ideas or sensations prior to experience in perception of their connection; that one idea or sensation has no power to suggest any other idea prior to experience of their relation. Locke held that no simple idea has any necessary relation to or inconsistency with any other. Berkeley insisted that there are no associative relations between ideas prior to experience. Hume claimed that we can discover a priori no relations between ideas, and that we have no a priori grounds for anticipating one such relation rather than any other. And Mill noted that the various properties of real kinds of things do not imply one another.[66]

Fourth, empiricists claim, on the other hand, that ideas or sensations become associated entirely as a result of experience of their constant conjunction in sensation. Locke claimed that

[64] See J. Locke, *An Essay Concerning Human Understanding*, ed. A. C. Fraser, New York, 1959, i, pp. 122-3 and 145; D. Hume, *A Treatise of Human Nature*, ed. L. A. Selby-Bigge, Oxford, 1888, pp. 1-3; and J. S. Mill, *A System of Logic*, London, 1947, p. 75.

[65] See Locke, *An Essay* i, pp. 169-71; Hume, *A Treatise*, pp. 10-11; and Mill, *A System*, p. 44.

[66] See Locke, *An Essay* i, p. 200; G. Berkeley, *An Essay Towards a New Theory of Vision*, in *Philosophical Works*, ed. M. R. Ayers, London, 1975, p. 9; Hume, *A Treatise*, pp. 8-13; and Mill, *A System*, p. 91.

our complex ideas of substances are constructed by combining those simple ideas which have been observed constantly to co-exist. Berkeley held that one idea comes to suggest another by constantly accompanying it and varying as it does. And Hume claimed that ideas become related in virtue of their constant conjunction in experience.[67]

Rationalists, on the other hand, can be characterized in the following terms.

First, rationalists claim that some or all of our ideas are innate in us, at least in the sense that we are born with a propensity for forming them, for which sensory experience merely provides the occasion, but not the cause. Descartes claimed that certain ideas are innate in this sense. Leibniz held that the senses provide only the occasion for eliciting ideas which are innate in us, and, more strongly, that we learn nothing from experience of which we have not already had an idea prior to experience. And Whewell claimed that we have a natural (i.e. innate) faculty for forming ideas and that these ideas pre-exist the sensations which provide the occasion for our experience of them.[68]

Second, rationalists claim that we have innate dispositions, prior to experience, to relate some ideas to others in certain ways. Descartes claimed that we infer certain ideas from others, not by virtue of learning to do so, but by a kind of natural (i.e. innate) calculation. Leibniz held that certain innate principles lead us to relate some ideas to others prior to any experience of their connection, and despite their logical independence. He also claimed that the mind is active in forming such relations prior to experience. And Whewell held

---

[67] See Locke, *An Essay* i, pp. 390–4; Berkeley, *New Theory*, p. 11; and D. Hume, *An Enquiry Concerning Human Understanding*, ed. L. A. Selby-Bigge and P. H. Nidditch, Oxford, 1975, p. 27.

[68] See R. Descartes, *Notes Directed Against a Certain Programme*, in *The Philosophical Works of Descartes*, ed. E. Haldane and G. Ross, Cambridge, 1911, i, pp. 442–3; and *Meditations on First Philosophy*, in Haldane and Ross, *Works* i, p. 160; G. Leibniz, *New Essays Concerning Human Understanding*, trans. A. Langley, New York, 1896, pp. 77–8; and *Discourse of Metaphysics*, in *Leibniz Selections*, ed. P. P. Wiener, New York, 1951, pp. 327–9; and W. Whewell, *The Philosophy of the Inductive Sciences*, London, 1967, i, pp. 44–5 and ii, p. 23.

that the mind combines sensations according to laws of its own nature.[69]

These two positions clearly suggest different accounts of learning.

Consider the empiricist account of how we learn that two kinds of events are 'causally' related. A set of events causes a set of complex ideas to arise in our minds. Each of these complex ideas is, in turn, some combination of those simple ideas which, given experience, we have a natural faculty for forming. We have a natural faculty for perceiving these complex ideas as partially ordered in time. We have a natural faculty for perceiving similarities between some of these complex ideas and for classifying those complex ideas which are similar as instances of the same general idea. We thus come to perceive the partially ordered sequence of complex ideas as a partially ordered sequence of instances of general ideas. We have a natural faculty for perceiving relations of constant conjunction between pairs of instances of general ideas. We thus come to perceive the causal relation of certain kinds of events when we realize that (i) some of our complex ideas are instances of a particular general idea; (ii) some of our complex ideas are instances of another general idea; (iii) events instancing the former of these general ideas have in our experience regularly been followed by events instancing the latter of these general ideas. On the basis of this perceived constant conjunction of instances of general ideas, we form the disposition to expect events instancing a particular general idea to be followed by events instancing another general idea. This disposition in effect constitutes our perception of the causal relatedness of these kinds of events.

Consider, on the other hand, a rationalist account of how such learning occurs. An event provides the occasion for a set of innate simple ideas to arise in our minds. Another event provides the occasion for another set of innate simple ideas so to arise. In virtue of innate predispositions, we take these complex ideas to be instances of certain innate general ideas. In

---

[69] See R. Descartes, *Optics*, trans. P. Olscamp, Indianapolis, 1965, p. 106; Leibniz, *New Essays*, pp. 77–8; and Whewell, *Inductive Sciences* i, p. 29.

virtue of an innate predisposition to associate instances of certain kinds of general ideas, we perceive a causal relation between the events giving rise to these two complex ideas. (On this account, we are, in other words, innately endowed with an expectation that certain kinds of events will be causally related to one another. No experience is necessary to form this expectation.) We will thus expect other pairs of events instancing these general ideas to be causally related in this same way. We will, in other words, expect events instancing these general ideas to be constantly conjoined in experience. If we encounter cases in which instances of these general ideas are not conjoined in experience, then we will modify the innate predisposition which provides the basis for this expectation. We will, in particular, make this disposition more specific by taking account of the ways in which non-conforming instances of the innately-related ideas differ from conforming instances. We will in this way eventually form a well-confirmed disposition to expect certain kinds of events to be causally related to one another.

The salient distinguishing features of these accounts of learning are easily characterized. (i) Rationalists claim that innate ideas exist; empiricists deny that this is so. (ii) Both empiricists and rationalists attribute to human beings certain innate faculties. (iii) Among these for rationalists, but not for empiricists, is a faculty for relating certain ideas to others prior to any experience of their conjunction in sensation.

These two positions are clearly distinct and there is therefore an issue between them as schematic accounts of human learning. I will now consider a proposal for interpreting these accounts in a way which makes empirical evidence about how learning actually does occur relevant to deciding between them.

7　*Simulation of Innate Ideas*

I will now consider a strategy for supporting linguistic rationalism which depends essentially on an insight due to Root.[70] Since

---

[70] See M. Root, 'How to Simulate an Innate Idea', *Philosophical Forum* iii (1971). See also N. Rescher, 'A New Look at the Problem of Innate Ideas', *British Journal for the Philosophy of Science* xvii (1966).

this strategy depends on the plausibility of Root's claim that empiricist and rationalist accounts of learning can adequately be simulated by certain devices E and R respectively, I will first describe these devices and consider their adequacy as simulations. I will then try to show how an argument supporting linguistic rationalism might be constructed on the basis of Root's proposal. I reserve to Section 9 below consideration of the extent to which such an argument actually does support linguistic rationalism.

Before describing the devices E and R, it will be helpful to describe a device D, which is alleged to provide a model of what is learned. The device D, that is, is alleged to be a model of the end-product of the learning process, as mediated by either E or R. It is important first to consider D because this device has features which are alleged to simulate the role which ideas play in mediating perception on both empiricist and rationalist accounts of perception.[71] Consideration of these features will thus enable us to ensure that we construct E and R in such a way that R does, while E does not, have features which could be said to simulate the role in learning of innate ideas.

Modifying Root's account slightly, we construct D so that it simulates the process by which experience of a particular event gives rise to the expectation that another event will be causally related to that event. We describe D in the following way.[72] Input to D has the form of complex representations of events. D stores a set of abstract representations and a set of relations on pairs of these abstract representations. D stores a 'comparator program', which compares an input complex representation with each of the stored abstract representations and computes the best match. D stores a 'relator program' which finds some relation among those stored for which the output of the comparator program is suitable input and uses this relation to compute the corresponding output in the form of an abstract representation.

---

[71] See Root, 'How to Simulate', p. 15.
[72] Ibid.

Given this description of *D*, it is clear that the following conditions obtain. (i) The complex representations in *D* correspond to (in the sense of being functionally equivalent to) the complex particular ideas which are, on the standard philosophical accounts, caused or occasioned to arise in the mind by certain sensory input. (ii) The abstract representations stored in *D* correspond to the general ideas under which particular complex ideas are, on the standard accounts, ranked as instances. (iii) The relations stored in *D* correspond to the expectations which, on the standard accounts, mediate our perception of causal relations. (iv) The 'relator program' maps one abstract representation onto another abstract representation just when, on the standard accounts, a complex idea produces the expectation that another complex idea will causally be related to it. It thus seems reasonable to claim that the device *D* simulates the process by which such expectations are mediated on the standard philosophical accounts of perception.

Given our interest in constructing suitable devices *E* and *R*, this description of the device *D* is important because it points to the kinds of features which *R* must incorporate if it is to have features which could be said to correspond to the innate ideas and expectations which rationalists claim provide a basis for learning. In particular, our description of *D* shows that *R* will have to contain abstract representations and relations defined on them, just as *D* does, since these representations and relations correspond to the ideas and expectations which, on the rationalist account, mediate the acquisition of knowledge.

With this in mind, we can now describe the device *E* in the following way. (I again modify Root's account slightly.)[73] The device *E* initially stores no complex or abstract representations. Input to *E* takes the form of complex representations, plus information about which such representations are representations of the same events. The device *E* does initially store an 'abstractor program', which takes as input sets of complex representations of instances of the same event and produces as

[73] See Root, 'How to Simulate', pp. 19–20.

output the subrepresentation of these representations which is common to all of them. The device E also initially stores an 'associator program', which takes as input pairs of abstract representations and produces as output a relation on those pairs of abstract representations the instances of which are constantly conjoined in input to E.

On the other hand, we can describe the device R in the following way.[74] The device R initially stores abstract representations and relations defined on those representations. Input to R takes the form of complex representations, plus information about which such representations are representations of the same events. The device R also initially stores an 'instantiator program', which takes as input a complex representation and determines which of the abstract representations stored by R this complex representation instances. The device R also initially stores a 'learning program', which takes as input a set of pairs of complex representations in the range of some relation stored in R, and produces as output a relation defined on that pair of subrepresentations of these input pairs, which is characteristic of just those pairs of input representations in this set which are conjoined in input to R.

Having described the devices E and R, I now consider whether they adequately simulate the learning process as described by empiricists and rationalists respectively. I claim that the differences between the standard rationalist and empiricist accounts of learning are all faithfully mirrored in differences in the features attributed to R and E.

(i) Just as empiricists deny, while rationalists assert the existence of innate ideas, so too does R initially store abstract representations, while E does not. Since these abstract representations are functionally equivalent to ideas (as we saw in our discussion of D), the fact that they are stored initially in R (but not in E) shows that these representations simulate the role in learning which rationalists (but not empiricists) assign to innate ideas.

[74] Ibid., pp. 21–2.

(ii) Just as empiricists deny, while rationalists assert, the existence of pre-experiential dispositions to relate certain ideas to others, so too does R, but not E, store relations between abstract representations. Since these relations are functionally equivalent to associative relations between ideas (as we saw in our discussion of D), the fact that they are stored initially in R (but not in E) shows that these relations simulate the role in learning which rationalists (but not empiricists) assign to innate associative dispositions.

(iii) Just as empiricists attribute to the learner certain innate mental faculties of generalization and association, so too does E initially store abstractor and associator programs, which are, clearly, functionally equivalent to these faculties.

By reason of these correspondences, I conclude that the devices E and R do adequately simulate the learning process as described by empiricists and rationalists respectively. But if this is the case, then we are warranted in claiming that the debate between empiricists and rationalists can be 'translated', without loss of significant content, into a debate about the relative merits of the devices E and R as simulations of the learning process as it is observed actually to occur. In particular, we can accept the epistemic interpretation of the empiricist–rationalist controversy, but can also claim that questions about the existence of innate ideas can be replaced by questions about the simulation of the learning process by devices which do or do not initially store certain kinds of representations and relations.

But it now finally becomes clear how research in linguistics could be relevant to the debate between empiricists and rationalists. It becomes clear how we could formulate a simulative strategy for supporting linguistic rationalism. In outline, such a strategy would involve the claim that the language acquisition process is better simulated by an R-like device than by an E-like device; and, in view of the correspondence between these devices and standard philosophical accounts of learning, that the rationalist account is therefore preferable, on empirical grounds, to the empiricist account. In particular, a crucial test between R and E (and thus between rationalism and empiricism) might be obtained by considering whether language learning appears to involve pre-experiential dispositions to form certain associative relations, as rationalism suggests. I address just this question in Section 9 below.

The success of such a strategy clearly depends, then, on establishing the empirical superiority of R to E as a simulation of the language learning process. But whatever such considerations reveal, it is clear that this strategy for supporting linguistic rationalism is not philosophically misguided, though it might fail because the evidence about language learning is better accounted for when this process is simulated by an E-like device. This strategy for supporting linguistic rationalism does not depend, as the mentalistic strategy did, on any philosophically controversial claim. It depends only on the plausible suggestion that we can translate philosophical accounts of learning into scientifically testable claims about simulations of the learning process.

In the next section, I will consider in outline a second non-mentalistic strategy for supporting linguistic rationalism.

8 *Innate Faculties*

Both the mentalistic and simulative strategies for supporting linguistic rationalism involve acceptance of the epistemic interpretation of the empiricist-rationalist debate. The strategy now to be considered depends, however, on the claim that that debate can adequately be represented as a debate about the kinds of innate mental faculties which it is necessary to attribute to the learner. On the assumption that these positions can be distinguished in this way, this strategy then involves an argument that empirical research in linguistics suggests the existence of innate mental faculties mediating the language acquisition process which are of a kind countenanced by rationalists, but not by empiricists.

The non-empirical burden of this strategy is clearly carried by the interpretative claim that empiricism and rationalism can be distinguished in the way suggested. Some commentators on the debate about linguistic rationalism appear to reject this claim.[75] I think, however, that their position rests on a straight-forward confusion. I believe that those who reject this in-terpretative claim do so because they invalidly infer the claim that empiricists and rationalists cannot be distinguished in terms of the kinds of innate mental faculties which they were willing to countenance from the undisputed fact that both empiricists and rationalists did countenance certain kinds of innate mental faculties. In any event, I will now attempt to defend this interpretative claim, deferring to Section 9 below discussion of empirical evidence about language learning which might bear on the success of a facultative strategy for supporting linguistic rationalism.

I claim that empiricism and rationalism can be distinguished in terms of the claims they embody about the kinds of innate mental faculties which must be attributed to learners. I claim, in particular, that both countenanced, in fact saw the need for attributing, some such faculties to learners, but that rationalists attributed to them a kind of innate faculty the existence of which empiricists denied.

It is clear that both empiricists and rationalists did attribute certain innate mental faculties to the learner. Locke attributed to human beings a 'faculty' or 'natural power' for distinguishing ideas, and held that this faculty 'is so absolutely necessary, that without it there could be no knowledge, no reasoning, no imagination, no distinct thoughts at all'. Hume described the principles which govern the workings of the imaginative faculties as certain 'original (i.e. innate) qualities of human nature'. And Mill claimed that faculties for perceiving similarities and differences between sensations 'are parts of our nature'.[76] This is the standard empiricist account of innate mental faculties. The rationalist account is in some respects similar. Descartes referred to the inborn dispositions of the faculty of the understanding; Leibniz to the soul's 'active power', and to

[75] See J. Searle, 'Chomsky's Revolution in Linguistics', reprinted in Harman, *On Noam Chomsky*; Graves *et al.*, 'Tacit Knowledge'; and Edgley, 'Innate Ideas'.

[76] See Locke, *An Essay* ii, p. 169; Hume, *A Treatise*, pp. 10–13; and Mill, *A System*, p. 44.

a readiness to receive ideas which is innate in our souls; and Whewell claimed that 'the acts of the mind are governed by certain laws', and mentioned the mental faculty by which sensations are transformed into ideas.[77]

On the other hand, it is also clear that rationalists attributed to the learner a kind of innate mental faculty the existence of which empiricists quite emphatically denied. In particular, rationalists attributed to the learner an inborn faculty for associating certain ideas prior to any experience of their connection, while empiricists denied the existence of any such faculty, claiming instead that all associative bonds between ideas arise solely from experience. Descartes and Leibniz attributed to human beings a kind of innate natural geometry, in virtue of which certain sensations are associated with certain ideas of distance.[78] Berkeley claimed, however, that these associations are formed entirely on the basis of experience.[79] Leibniz claimed that the view that the mind has certain innate faculties implies that these faculties must take the form of innate dispositions to associate ideas in certain ways rather than others.[80] Berkeley explicitly denied this, claiming instead that we are equally ready to associate any idea with any other idea. He held that experience alone determines which associative relations we come to perceive.[81]

Both empiricists and rationalists, then, attributed innate faculties to the learner, but they differed profoundly about the nature of these faculties. For the empiricist, the innate faculty for forming associations between ideas is initially unbiased. For the rationalist, this faculty is, on the other hand, initially biased in particular ways. Empiricists and rationalists can thus be distinguished in facultative, as well as in epistemic, terms. A facultative strategy for supporting linguistic rationalism could succeed then. Such a strategy would involve arguing that

---

[77] See Descartes, *Notes*, pp. 442–3; Leibniz, *A Discourse*, p. 331; and Whewell, *Inductive Sciences* i, pp. 27–37.

[78] See Descartes, *Optics*, p. 106; and Leibniz, *New Essays*, p. 136.

[79] Berkeley, *New Theory*, p. 9.

[80] Leibniz, *New Essays*, pp. 110–11.

[81] Berkeley, *New Theory*, p. 13.

empirical research about language acquisition suggests the existence of biased rather than unbiased innate associative faculties.

9   *Evidence Bearing on Linguistic Rationalism*

A standard mentalistic argument for linguistic rationalism has the following form. Language-users know, and therefore have acquired knowledge of, a grammar of their language. This grammar has certain characteristics such as the abstractness of certain of the elements and structural descriptions which it defines and the cyclicity of certain of the operations in terms of which such structural descriptions are defined. Given the kind of data available to language-learners a grammar with these characteristics could not be acquired by learning processes of a kind countenanced by empiricists. A grammar with these characteristics could be acquired, however, by learning processes of a kind countenanced by rationalists. The empiricist account of learning therefore fails, since it is, in particular, incapable of explaining the acquisition of the grammar which language-users are conjectured to know.[82]

The form of this argument is logically unexceptionable. Its force has nevertheless been disputed by opponents of linguistic rationalism such as Derwing. He claims, in particular, that this argument supports linguistic rationalism only if the grammar language-users allegedly know does in fact have those characteristics which are so troublesome from an empiricist point of view.[83] This is, of course, as yet an open empirical question, and, from a methodological point of view, a very difficult one to answer. A rather more general point nevertheless remains. The kinds of 'facts' which this standard argument invokes are highly 'theory-impregnated'. They are nothing like the 'basic facts' about which we might expect linguists to agree, whatever their theoretical views. For this reason, then, this standard

---

[82] See Chomsky, *Language and Mind*, pp. 44–5; and Katz, *The Philosophy of Language*, pp. 249–60.
[83] See Derwing, *Transformational Grammar*, pp. 46–7.

argument for linguistic rationalism can have nothing like the persuasive force which its advocates might wish it to have.

Arguments for linguistic rationalism based on the simulative and facultative strategies, however, need not depend on such highly theory-impregnated facts. The kinds of facts on which such arguments depend are much more like those described by the 'basic statements' about the truth of which linguists of different theoretical commitments might be expected to agree. An argument for linguistic rationalism based on the simulative strategy might, for instance, have the following form. The process of language learning has certain readily observable features such as characteristic ontogenetic sequences and over-generalization phenomena.[84] Given suitable input, the device E does not exhibit these behavioural features, while the device R does. Since E and R simulate the learning processes described by empiricists and rationalists respectively, the rationalist account of learning is thus to be preferred to the empiricist account. (A similar argument for linguistic rationalism based on the facultative strategy could also be constructed. And this argument too would depend only on facts about readily observable characteristics of the language learning process.) Since the non-mentalistic strategies for supporting linguistic rationalism rely on empirical facts of a less controversial kind than does the mentalistic strategy, I conclude that these non-mentalistic strategies are methodologically superior to the mentalistic one, and should be preferred to it, other things being equal.

A simulative strategy for supporting linguistic rationalism would succeed if we could show that the process of language acquisition has certain characteristics which are features of the behaviour of an R-like device simulating that process, but not of an E-like device. In fact, there does seem to be evidence to this effect.

Consider, for instance, the following facts about language

[84] See D. Slobin, 'Data for the Symposium', in D. Slobin, ed., *The Ontogenesis of Grammar*, London, 1974.

learning.[85] Even at the earliest stages of this process we find that (*a*) learners who can combine words to form *n*-word sequences do so only in a certain limited number of ways, despite the fact that the speech of adults in their environment contains a much greater variety of *n*-word combinations; and (*b*) the only combinations actually used by learners are those which, from an 'adult' point of view, express grammatical relations between their elements. Learners, for instance, might say *the house*, but not *of the*, despite the fact that both of these two-word sequences form subsequences of adult sentences such as *I opened the door of the house*.

It is clear that an *R*-like device simulating the process of language acquisition might exhibit behaviour of this kind. This would be the case, in particular, if *R* stored abstract representations in terms of which input data (in the form of sequences of words) were classified as instances of the various grammatical categories; and, in addition, stored relations defined only on those *n*-element combinations of grammatical categories which are themselves grammatical categories. Such a device might, for instance, classify input *the* as a Determiner and input *house* as a Noun, and might then combine *the* and *house* to form the output sequence *the house* in virtue of the fact that this sequence itself instances the grammatical category Noun Phrase.

On the other hand, it is also clear than an *E*-like device simulating the process of language acquisition would not exhibit behaviour of this sort. Since *E* begins the learning process unpredisposed in any way to form combinations of its input elements, and since the data available to it manifest many more combinations of these elements than are in fact grammatically constitutive, we would, at least at early stages, expect *E* to emit all *n*-element combinations for which it has evidence in its input data, and only after explicit correction of grammatically non-constitutive sequences gradually to converge on the behaviour which the actual language-learner exhibits at the very beginning of this process.

[85] See D. McNeill, 'Developmental Psycholinguistics', in F. Smith and G. Miller, eds., *The Genesis of Language*, Cambridge, 1966, pp. 45–8.

Since *R*-like devices do adequately simulate this aspect of language acquisition, while *E*-like devices do not, the former are obviously to be preferred to the latter as simulations of this process. And since these devices adequately represent rationalist and empiricist accounts of learning, the former of these is preferable to the latter on the basis of this kind of evidence. Linguistic rationalism is thus supported by this simulative argument. And this argument depends, empirically, only on relatively uncontroversial facts about language learning.

It is, moreover, clear that these same facts about language learning can also be invoked in an argument for linguistic rationalism which is based on a facultative strategy. This argument might have the following form. On the facultative interpretation, empiricists and rationalists were seen to differ primarily in their attitude towards the existence of innate pre-experiential associations between ideas of certain kinds. Rationalists claimed that associative biases mediate the learning process, while empiricists denied that this is so. As soon as language-learners begin to combine vocabulary items, they do so according to a strictly limited set of patterns. In particular, these patterns constitute only a very small subset of the set of *n*-word substrings observed by language-learners in the speech of their teachers. This suggests that these patterns are not, as empiricists would have to hold, complexes to which learners have associatively been conditioned, but instead reflect the pre-experiential associative relations between the grammatical categories which such combinations instance, as a rationalist might claim. The language-learner has a cognitive faculty, then, the existence of which was countenanced by rationalists, but not by empiricists. We must, then, prefer the rationalist account of learning to the empiricist account on these empirical grounds. Linguistic rationalism is thus supported by this facultative argument. And this argument depends, empirically, only on certain more or less uncontroversial facts about language acquisition.

I claim, then, that an empiricist theory of learning cannot be sustained since it fails to account for certain elementary and readily observable facts about language acquisition which a rationalist theory can account for. In particular, I claim that it is readily observable that language-learners impose linguistically constitutive hierarchical structure on the data available to them in the speech of their mentors, and that an empiricist theory cannot account for this fact since this structure is not 'observable' in that data and cannot, on this account, be held to be imposed on that data by the innate mental resources of the language-learner.

In this form, this claim has, however, recently been challenged by Sampson, who has outlined a more sophisticated empiricist theory of learning than that which I have so far considered. Sampson has argued that this theory in fact provides a better account of just the kinds of facts which I have invoked than does a rationalist theory.

Sampson's sophisticated empiricist theory of learning is based on Simon's account of the evolution of hierarchical structures. According to Simon, any gradually developed structure is (very) likely to be hierarchically organized since non-hierarchical structures are statistically much less likely to persist.[86] This account thus suggests that the products of human learning are themselves (very) likely to be hierarchically organized, even if the human learning process is not itself constrained by the kinds of innate predispositions to impose hierarchical structure which were countenanced by rationalists, but not by empiricists.

According to Sampson, then, it is unsurprising from an empiricist point of view that language-learners impose hierarchical structure on the data about their language which they encounter. Sampson claims, in particular, that 'Simon's thesis guarantees as a statistical certainty that ... the probability of [language-learners selecting] non-hierarchical grammars also compatible with their data before they master the data in the gradual [hierarchical] way is so remote as to be negligible ... the grammars internalized by children will be hierarchical ... despite the fact that nothing in the architecture

---

[86] See H. Simon, 'The Architecture of Complexity', in *The Sciences of the Artificial*, Cambridge, 1969.

of their minds makes non-hierarchical grammars unthinkable for them', as a rationalist account of language learning suggests.[87]

I believe that we can accept Sampson's claim that a sophisticated empiricist theory of learning can account for the fact that language-learners impose hierarchical structure on the data presented to them. But even Sampson's theory fails to account for the fact that language-learners impose a particular kind of hierarchical structure on that data. From an empiricist point of view, both *of the* and *the house* are possible subcomponents of a hierarchical (though not linguistically constitutive) representation of the sentence *I opened the door of the house*. From an empiricist point of view, then, one ought to expect the language-learner to entertain the hypothesis that the sequence *of the* is a meaningful constituent of the hierarchically organized sentence *I opened the door of the house*. But we have already seen that the language-learner does not entertain this hypothesis. Even Sampson's sophisticated empiricist account of learning seems, then, to be incapable of accounting for this kind of elementary fact about the language acquisition process. Even this account, then, must be rejected as a viable alternative to the rationalist account which Chomsky espouses.

In conclusion, I claim to have shown how to construct and successfully to deploy two non-mentalistic strategies for supporting linguistic rationalism. These results can also be taken to show that the bridge thesis is false, and that the validity of linguistic mentalism is thus irrelevant to that of linguistic rationalism. We can thus defend Chomsky's rationalist account of language learning without accepting his mentalistic account of linguistic competence.

In the next chapter, I discuss Chomsky's 'intellectualistic' account of intelligent behaviour.

---

[87] G. Sampson, *Making Sense*, Oxford, 1980, p. 172.

3

CHOMSKY'S INTELLECTUALISM

1 *Introduction*

In Chapter Two I rejected Chomsky's mentalistic claim that language-users 'know' the grammar of their language. I proposed to substitute for it the realist claim that a grammar describes the operations of the mental mechanisms which provide the basis for linguistic competence. On the other hand, I also argued in Chapter Two that Chomsky's rationalist account of language acquisition can be sustained. In this chapter, I will consider a Chomskian doctrine which is related both to linguistic mentalism and to linguistic rationalism. This is the doctrine of *linguistic intellectualism*, according to which linguistic behaviour is rule-guided rather than law-governed, since a grammar is a system of rules and not a system of natural laws. According to linguistic intellectualism, then, linguistic behaviour crucially involves interactions between language users and their environment which are best described in rational, computational terms, rather than in the strictly causal terms in which the behaviour, for instance, of atoms and planets is best described.

Chomsky espoused linguistic intellectualism when he claimed that a 'grammar is a system of rules and principles that determine the formal and semantic properties of sentences ... [which] is put to use, interacting with other mechanisms of mind, in speaking and understanding language'. In the same vein, Chomsky characterized a grammar as 'the underlying system of rules that has been mastered by the speaker-hearer and that he puts to use in actual performance'. Moreover, Chomsky explicitly contrasted his intellectualist approach with what I will call a naturalistic approach when he noted that the principles of a grammar 'are not laws of nature ... [but are instead] rules that are constructed by the mind in the course of language acquisition ... [which] can be violated', as natural laws cannot.[1]

Briefly and abstractly then, intellectualism is embodied in the claim that intelligent behaviour is to be explained in terms of agents' rational calculations, according to rules or maxims, in the light of their goals and their beliefs about the situation in which they find themselves. Intellectualism thus stands in sharp contrast to *naturalism*, according to which intelligent behaviour is to be explained causally, in terms of the structural properties of agents and their environments. (The contrast between these two doctrines will be spelled out in more detail in Section 2 below.)

Before discussing linguistic intellectualism, its background and its implications, I may perhaps first indicate its relations to the other main components of Chomsky's system of ideas.

The affinity between linguistic intellectualism and linguistic individualism is clear enough. It is an immediate implication of intellectualism, as opposed to naturalism, that intelligent behaviour is to be explained, just as individualism requires, in terms of agents' rational calculations in respect of their goals and beliefs.[2] Chomsky's advocacy of linguistic intellectualism is thus consistent with his advocacy of linguistic individualism, and provides an illustration of the unity of his system of ideas.

The affinity between linguistic intellectualism and linguistic mentalism should also be clear. Linguistic mentalism is, of course, merely a species of linguistic intellectualism. As opposed to linguistic naturalism and, in particular, to its behaviouristic variants, these two doctrines concur in implying that linguistic behaviour involves mental operations determined by the rules of the grammar which the language user has mastered and internalized. Mentalism merely adds to this account of linguistic behaviour the claim that these rules are known to the language-user who is said to have internalized and to use them. Chomsky's

---

[1] N. Chomsky, *Reflections on Language*, London, 1976, p. 28; *Aspects of the Theory of Syntax*, Cambridge, 1965, p. 4; and *Problems of Knowledge and Freedom*, New York, 1971, p. 33.

[2] See J. Watkins, 'Ideal Types and Historical Explanation', reprinted in J. O'Neill, ed., *Modes of Individualism and Collectivism*, London, 1973, p. 145.

advocacy of linguistic intellectualism is thus consistent with his advocacy of linguistic mentalism, and provides another illustration of the unity of his system of ideas.

Given my rejection of linguistic mentalism, and my interest in defending linguistic intellectualism, the relation between these two doctrines may seem to constitute an embarrassment for my account of Chomsky's system. In response to this suggestion, I may perhaps simply point out that one can reject linguistic mentalism without *ipso facto* undermining linguistic intellectualism precisely because the former thesis is a species of the latter. One can do this, moreover, without undermining the unity of Chomsky's system in other ways—again, precisely because this unity depends less on Chomsky's advocacy of linguistic mentalism than it does on his advocacy of the more general doctrine of linguistic intellectualism.

What remains to be shown, then, is the relation between linguistic intellectualism and linguistic rationalism. This relation is, in effect, constituted by the fact that empiricists tended, in a naturalistic way, to assimilate intelligent action to law-governed behaviour, whereas rationalists tended, in an intellectualist fashion, to claim that intelligent behaviour is based on rational calculations according to rules.[3] Good examples of these tendencies are easy enough to exhibit. On the one hand, Descartes claimed that the visual perception of distance is mediated by the individual's knowledge of geometrical rules. On the other hand, Berkeley claimed that the visual perception of distance is mediated by the laws which govern the association of tactile and visual ideas of distance.[4] Chomsky's advocacy of linguistic intellectualism is thus consistent with his advocacy of linguistic rationalism, and provides yet another illustration of the unity of his system of ideas.

2   *Intellectualism and Naturalism*

A recurring problem of considerable interest and importance in

[3]   See J. Margolis, *Persons and Minds*, Dordrecht, 1978, p. 108.
[4]   See R. Descartes, *Optics*, trans. P. Olscamp, Indianapolis, 1965, p. 106; and G. Berkeley, *An Essay Towards a New Theory of Vision*, in *Philosophical Works*, ed. M. R. Ayers, London, 1975, p. 9.

the philosophy and methodology of psychology is that of determining the appropriate or privileged theoretical vocabulary in terms of which explanations of human abilities and their manifestations in intelligent behaviour are to be formulated. In a related context, Aristotle had already said: 'The student of nature and the dialectician would define each of these differently, e.g. what anger is. For the latter would define it as a desire for retaliation or something of the sort, the former as a boiling of the blood and hot stuff round the heart.'[5] Here we already see in embryo the two main approaches which have subsequently been taken to this problem.

The naturalistic approach is reductionistic in the sense that it identifies the language within which it is appropriate to formulate theories of human abilities and intelligent behaviour with the language within which it is appropriate to formulate theories of non-intelligent dispositions and their manifestations. According to naturalism, theories of human abilities and intelligent behaviour should be formulated in a language of causal relations and causally mediated processes. What is involved in possessing a certain ability? According to naturalism, the presence of an individual with the requisite structural properties in a suitably structured environment causes those events by which the ability in question is manifested.

According to naturalism, then, we should explain human abilities and intelligent behaviour in terms of causal relations between individuals and their environments—in just the way, in fact, in which natural scientists explain the dispositions and behaviour of other non-intelligent entities.[6]

The intellectualist approach, on the other hand, is anti-reductionistic. While naturalists identify explanations of human abilities with explanations of natural dispositions, intellectualists claim that these phenomena are to be explained in terms of theories constructed in fundamentally different kinds of

---

[5] Aristotle, *De Anima*, trans. D. Hamlyn, Oxford, 1968, p. 4.

[6] On this account, behaviourism is a version of naturalism, according to which the internal structural properties of organisms are irrelevant in the causation of their behaviour.

languages.[7] While the language of causal relations and structural properties suffices for the formulation of theories of natural dispositions, only a language of rational relations can be adequate for the formulation of theories of human abilities. What is involved in possessing a certain ability? According to intellectualism, those who have this ability have it because they are capable of applying rules or maxims which indicate rational relations between means and ends. What is involved in manifesting this ability? According to intellectualism, individuals manifest an ability when they apply a rule or maxim to guide the behaviour by which this ability is manifested.

Intellectualists, then, propose to explain human abilities and intelligent behaviour in terms of the rational relations between actions guided by rules or maxims and the goals for the sake of which those actions were undertaken.

The continuing debate about these two doctrines has, of course, been responsive to a number of philosophical considerations of general importance. I will now introduce some of these considerations, partly by way of providing a historical and conceptual framework for my subsequent discussion of linguistic intellectualism.

Perhaps the single most important consideration in the debate about intellectualism is embodied in the fact that this doctrine appears to be responsive, whereas naturalism appears to be unresponsive to the deeply entrenched intuition that manifestations of human abilities display the rationality of the human agent—a rationality which strictly causal accounts of human behaviour simply fail to capture.

Historically, the force of this intuition appears to have motivated Plato's rejection of naturalism, and to have contributed to Descartes' explicit rejection of naturalism, and to

---

[7] When I characterize intellectualism as anti-reductionist, I ignore the reductionistic intellectualism, or panpsychism, of Leibniz, who proposed to explain natural dispositions, as well as human abilities, in an intellectualist fashion. See G. Leibniz, *Monadology*, in *Leibniz Selections*, ed. P. P. Wiener, New York, 1951, pp. 536–7 and 547.

Kant's more equivocal, but still basically anti-naturalistic position.[8]

Of course, naturalists also acknowledged the force of this intuition, and tried to find a place for it in their systems. Hobbes, for instance, espoused an apparently inconsistent congeries of doctrines related to this question. He advocated naturalism and rejected teleological explanations, but also recognized the importance of references to goals and practical maxims in the explanation of intelligent behaviour.[9] Hume too struggled with this intuition and tried to accommodate it to his naturalistic psychology. He claimed that intelligent behaviour is a causal consequence of mechanically operative instincts, but also noted that these instincts function in a way which, as we might now say, simulates the rational calculations postulated by intellectualists.[10] (Hume's strategy here will prove useful when I later attempt to construct a defensible modern version of intellectualism.) Hume also foreshadowed Ryle's approach to the problem of the rationality of intelligent human behaviour when he suggested that the distinction between intelligent and non-intelligent dispositions implies the need, not for distinct explanatory schemata, but rather for a criterion of demarcation. As long as we have some principled way of distinguishing these kinds of phenomena, we may, on Hume's account, explain both in a naturalistic way without violating our intuition that they nevertheless somehow differ.[11]

A second important consideration in the debate about intellectualism is embodied in the fact that it appears to be responsive, whereas naturalism appears to be unresponsive to the common-sense intuition that human abilities are exercised

---

[8] See Plato, *Phaedo*, in *The Dialogues of Plato*, trans. B. Jowett, Oxford, 1892, ii, pp. 116–18; and I. Kant, *The Critique of Practical Reason*, in *Kant's Critique of Practical Reason and Other Works on the Theory of Ethics*, ed. T. Abbott, London, 1909, p. 131.

[9] See T. Hobbes, *Leviathan*, ed. C. B. Macpherson, Harmondsworth, 1968, pp. 81, 87, and 95–6.

[10] See D. Hume, *An Enquiry Concerning Human Understanding*, ed. L. A. Selby-Bigge and P. H. Nidditch, Oxford, 1975, pp. 54–5.

[11] See D. Hume, *A Treatise of Human Nature*, ed. L. A. Selby-Bigge, Oxford, 1888, p. 55. See also G. Ryle, *The Concept of Mind*, Harmondsworth, 1973, p. 32.

freely, while manifestations of non-intelligent dispositions are causally necessitated. Intellectualists capture this intuition by requiring that these kinds of phenomena be explained in different ways, whereas naturalists appear to deny the possibility of freedom by proposing instead that intelligent human actions are to be explained in the same causal framework as is non-intelligent behaviour.

Like the problem of rationality, the problem of freedom has been an important issue in the historical debate between intellectualists and naturalists. Descartes, for instance, contrasted the freedom of intelligent human behaviour, for which he proposed an intellectualist explanation, with the causal necessity of mechanical behaviour, for which he proposed a naturalistic explanation. And for Kant, the problem of freedom was even more intimately connected with his intellectualist tendencies than was the problem of rationality.[12]

Naturalists, on the other hand, seem to have been forced to try to reduce our intuitions about freedom to epiphenomena of deeper, strictly causal processes. Hume, for instance, held that our intuitions about freedom depend on our ignorance of those causal factors which actually necessitate our behaviour. Hobbes, on the other hand, claimed that freedom consists, not in the absence of causal necessitation, but rather in the absence of external impediments to otherwise causally necessitated behaviour. Hobbes thought that the behaviour of non-intelligent and even inanimate entities could be free in this sense. And LaMettrie went even further, and claimed that the idea of freedom is itself nonsensical.[13]

A third important consideration in the debate between intellectualists and naturalists is embodied in relations between the methodological doctrines which they espoused and important and incompatible ontological doctrines. Intellectualism, then, is closely associated with ontological dualism, while naturalism

---

[12] See R. Descartes, *Principles of Philosophy*, in *The Philosophical Works of Descartes*, ed. E. Haldane and G. Ross, Cambridge, 1911, i, pp. 233–4; and Kant, *Practical Reason*, pp. 116–17.

[13] See Hume, *A Treatise*, pp. 312–13; Hobbes, *Leviathan*, p. 261; and J. de LaMettrie, *Man a Machine*, trans. G. Buddey and M. Calkins, LaSalle, 1912, pp. 133–4.

is closely associated with materialist monism. And while the precise nature of the relations between these ontological and methodological doctrines remains to be shown here, the historical and conceptual affinity between intellectualism and dualism, on the one hand, and naturalism and materialism, on the other hand, cannot easily be denied.

Certainly, materialism does seem to imply the viability of a naturalistic methodology, and to be incompatible with an intellectualist methodology. If all entities are entities of the same kind, then the behaviour of all entities ought to be explicable in the same kind of way. LaMettrie and Gassendi certainly drew this inference.[14] Moreover, intellectualism seems both to presuppose and to be implied by dualism. A dualism of substances suggests a dualism of explanations. Certainly, dualism and intellectualism were both features of Descartes' philosophy, and, among modern critics of intellectualism, Ryle has suggested that this was no mere accident.[15] Given the increasingly monistic philosophical climate since Descartes's time, the affinity between intellectualism and dualism has posed an increasingly serious problem for defenders of intellectualism.

A fourth important consideration in the debate between intellectualists and naturalists is embodied in the common-sense intuition that there is a distinction between voluntary and involuntary behaviour.

This intuition certainly forms part of the conceptual background to intellectualism. Intellectualists propose to capture it by offering intellectualist accounts of voluntary behaviour and naturalistic accounts of involuntary behaviour. Descartes, for instance, attempted to provide a naturalistic explanation of the (involuntary) circulation of the blood, and an intellectualist account of human understanding. In a similar spirit, Whewell claimed that it is appropriate to explain voluntary actions

---

[14] LaMettrie, *Man a Machine*, p. 143. See also P. Gassendi, 'Fifth Set of Objections', in Haldane and Ross, *Philosophical Works* ii, pp. 144–6.

[15] See R. Descartes, *Discourse on Method*, in Haldane and Ross, *Philosophical Works*, i, pp. 117–18. See also Ryle, *The Concept of Mind*, p. 34.

intellectualistically, while explaining involuntary behaviour in a naturalistic way.[16]

Naturalists also recognized the force of this intuitive distinction. Given their reductionistic policies, they were, of course, unable to capture it by proposing, as intellectualists did, to explain voluntary and involuntary behaviour in different kinds of ways. In this case too they were forced to deny the implications drawn by intellectualists from this intuitive distinction. LaMettrie, for instance, explicated this distinction in terms of the relative complexity of the uniformly causal processes underlying both voluntary and involuntary behaviour. And Hume acknowledged the force of our intuitions about this distinction, but claimed that our knowledge of both voluntary and involuntary behaviour is in each case limited to knowledge of the constant conjunction of behaviour with its causes, and that this intuitive distinction therefore does not compel us to adopt different strategies for explaining voluntary and involuntary behaviour.[17]

Traditional versions of intellectualism, then, are responsive to intuitions about the rationality of human behaviour, the freedom with which human abilities are exercised, naïve ontological dualism, and the distinction between voluntary and involuntary behaviour. Intellectualists propose to account for these intuitions by explaining intelligent human behaviour in terms of theories constructed in a language which differs from that in which it is appropriate to explain events in the natural world. As it is my aim here to construct and defend a modern (naturalistic) version of intellectualism, so too is it my hope that this version of intellectualism will also be responsive to these intuitions.

As I have just said, it is my intention here to construct a defensible modern version of intellectualism. I hope, in particular, to construct a version of intellectualism which is immune to Ryle's well-known criticisms of traditional versions

---

[16] See Descartes, *Discourse*, pp. 110–18; and W. Whewell, *The Philosophy of the Inductive Sciences*, London, 1967, i, pp. 612–15.

[17] See LaMettrie, *Man a Machine*, pp. 140–1; and Hume, *An Enquiry*, p. 66.

of this doctrine. Aside from the intrinsic interest of the problems involved, the construction of such a version of intellectualism is important in view of recent attempts to revive intellectualism in the face of Ryle's widely-accepted criticisms and in opposition to a long recent tradition of naturalistic psychology.

Attempts to revive intellectualism have, in particular, occurred in the context of recent work in linguistics. I have already mentioned Chomsky's intellectualist claim that a grammar is 'the underlying system of rules that has been mastered and internalized by the speaker-hearer and that he puts to use in actual performance'.

Furthermore, it is appropriate, at least initially, to develop an account of intellectualism against the background of Ryle's criticisms since Ryle's work has often been invoked in the debate about the currently intellectualist methodological orientation of linguistics. Cooper, for instance, refers to Ryle's well-known anti-intellectualist position in his criticism of Chomsky's doctrine of linguistic intellectualism. In particular, he follows Ryle in urging that

not all intelligent behaviour can require explanation in terms of using and applying rules and principles, since using and applying them are themselves intelligent activities which, according to the [intellectualist] legend, would therefore require explanation in terms of further rules and principles—and so on *ad infinitum*.[18]

My specific aim in this chapter, then, is to defend the intellectualist methodology of current linguistic research. And I will, for the reasons indicated, begin my discussion with an examination of Ryle's argument against intellectualism.

3   *Ryle's Criticism of Intellectualism*

I will here construct a (naturalistic) version of intellectualism, and attempt to show that it is immune to Ryle's criticisms of this doctrine. I will first reconstruct Ryle's major argument, and

[18]   D. Cooper, *Knowledge of Language*, London, 1975, p. 139. See also N. Malcolm, 'The Myth of Cognitive Processes', in T. Mischel, ed., *Cognitive Development and Epistemology*, New York, 1971, pp. 391–2; and G. Harman, 'Psychological Aspects of the Theory of Syntax', *Journal of Philosophy* lxiv (1967), p. 76.

show that it depends on a particular assumption about intellectualist theories of intelligent behaviour. I will then construct a naturalistic version of intellectualism, show that it does not satisfy the assumption on which Ryle's *reductio* argument is based, and is therefore unaffected by that argument. I will also show how this version of intellectualism is related both to classical versions and to Chomsky's doctrine of linguistic intellectualism.

Ryle holds that intellectualism is embodied in the claim that 'intelligent performance involves the observance of rules, or the application of criteria'.[19] According to a principle on which Ryle's anti-intellectualist argument especially depends, an intelligent action inherits its quality of intelligence from an ancestral intellectual action (of applying some rule) which is itself intelligently performed.[20] We can call this principle the *principle of inheritance*. Ryle's argument against intellectualism has the form of a *reductio ad absurdum*, which is, in turn, constituted by the threat of an infinite regress.

The regress arises in the following way. If we explain the occurrence of some overt intelligent action by postulating the performance of some covert intellectual action, as intellectualism requires, then, by the principle of inheritance, the overt intelligent action inherits its quality of intelligence, not from the performance *simpliciter* of that covert action, but rather from its intelligent performance. But in this case, this covert intellectual action must, by the principle of inheritance, in turn have inherited its quality of intelligence, which it passes on to the overt action which it guides, from the intelligent performance of some second-order covert intellectual action which guides the performance of the postulated first-order intellectual action. And so on *ad infinitum*.[21] Since an intellectualist explanation of intelligent behaviour in effect involves an infinite explanatory regress, such as explanation must be rejected.

Furthermore, it appears that this conclusion cannot be

---

[19] Ryle, *The Concept of Mind*, p. 29.
[20] Ibid., p. 31.
[21] Ibid., p. 32.

avoided by postulating the existence of a level of intellectual activity which is primitive, in the sense of being itself dependent on the performance of no higher-order intellectual activity. This is so because postulating primitive intellectual actions would halt the infinite explanatory regress only at the cost of implying that there are no overt intelligent actions. This obviously unacceptable implication arises in the following way. By the principle of inheritance, any action inherits its quality of intelligence from some anterior intellectual action. But the postulated primitive intellectual actions have inherited no such title to intelligence since they are, by hypothesis, dependent on no intellectual actions anterior to themselves. These primitive intellectual actions thus have no quality of intelligence to pass along, ultimately, to the overt actions in the guidance of which they are allegedly involved. These overt actions, then, cannot themselves be intelligent, since their quality of intelligence derives, on this account, from the intelligent performance of those intellectual actions by which they are allegedly guided.

Ryle's argument, then, does appear to provide a *reductio ad absurdum* of intellectualism. But it crucially depends on the principle of inheritance. An intellectualist explanation involves an infinite explanatory regress only if intellectualists must in fact explain all intelligent actions in an intellectualist fashion. And intellectualists must explain all intelligent actions intellectualistically only if they are committed to the principle of inheritance. If intellectualists need not be committed to the principle of inheritance then they can halt Ryle's regress by postulating primitive intellectual actions, and can do so, moreover, without being forced *ipso facto* to deny the existence of overt intelligent actions. It is clear, then, that Ryle's *reductio* argument depends on the assumption that intellectualists are perforce committed to the principle of inheritance. We can call this assumption *Ryle's assumption*.

Ryle himself appears to have believed that his assumption about the intellectualist's commitments was satisfied by classical versions of intellectualism. He claims, for instance, that 'the absurd assumption made by the intellectualist legend is that a performance of any sort inherits all its title to intelligence from some anterior internal operation of planning what to do'.[22] Ryle himself did not otherwise explicitly defend the claim that classical versions of intellectualism do satisfy his assumption. I will, however, now present three considerations which appear to show that Ryle's assumption about intellectualism was in fact correct. I will then use these considerations as a starting point for the construction of a version of intellectualism which does not satisfy Ryle's assumption and is therefore immune to the force of his *reductio* argument.

Versions of intellectualism which do not satisfy Ryle's assumption, because they do not involve commitment to the principle of inheritance, can postulate a level of primitive intellectual activity. But there are at least three reasons to suppose that any such version of intellectualism is unsatisfactory. (I will later suggest that these considerations do not provide *decisive* grounds for rejecting such a version of intellectualism.)

First, postulating primitive intellectual actions appears to imply that there is a distinction between those actions which require intellectualist explanations—namely, the overt and possibly some of the covert ones—and those which do not— namely, the primitive intellectual actions. But this distinction appears to be incompatible with the intellectualist claim that it is just the intelligent actions which require intellectualist explanations. For the postulated primitive intellectual actions are certainly intelligent, since they involve the application of just those rules, out of all of those available to the agent, which are in fact relevant to the attainment of his or her goals. Indeed, primitive intellectual actions must be intelligent in this sense if postulating their occurrence is to contribute to an explanation of the overt intelligent behaviour which they are alleged to guide. We can, in other words, postulate primitive intellectual actions only at the cost of creating a distinction between kinds

---

[22] Ryle, *The Concept of Mind*, p. 29.

of intelligent actions which seems to be indefensible in intellectualist terms.[23]

Second, if the occurrence of a postulated primitive intellectual action is, by hypothesis, not to be explained intellectualistically, then it is presumably to be explained naturalistically. But if the occurrence of a primitive intellectual action is to be explained naturalistically, then the intellectualist who postulates such an action has surely abandoned all but the pretence of providing a truly intellectualist account of intelligent behaviour. The explanation of intelligent behaviour implicit in this 'naturalistic' version of intellectualism has the following form. The agent has certain structural properties. The presence of an entity with such properties in a suitably structured environment causes just that primitive intellectual action which involves the application of a rule relevant to the attainment of the end the agent has in view. This rule guides the agent's behaviour in pursuit of this end. But the burden of this kind of explanation is surely borne not by its intellectualist, but rather by its naturalistic, component. On this kind of account, the fundamental relation between agents' environments and their overt intelligent actions is a causal and not a rational one. The intellectualist, in other words, appears to be free to abandon the principle of inheritance, and thus to postulate primitive intellectual actions, only at the cost of reducing intellectualism to a kind of naturalism.

Third, postulating primitive intellectual actions appears to render the intellectualist vulnerable to a plausible naturalistic criticism. If we concede that there are some intelligent actions which do not themselves require intellectualist explanations, as we do when we postulate primitive intellectual actions, then there is no principled reason to suppose, as intellectualists do, that overt intelligent actions themselves require intellectualist explanations.

If intellectualists abandon the principle of inheritance, they

[23] Ibid., p. 31. See also G. Harman, 'Reply to Arbini', *Synthese* xix (1969), p. 426; and T. Nagel, 'The Boundaries of Inner Space', *Journal of Philosophy* lxvi (1969), p. 457.

are free to postulate primitive intellectual actions, and can thus avoid Ryle's *reductio* argument against intellectualism. But the preceding considerations seem to show that intellectualists can abandon the principle of inheritance only at the allegedly unacceptable cost of being forced to accept a naturalistic version of intellectualism which has implications which appear to be as inimical to intellectualism as is the conclusion of Ryle's argument. I would like now to try to show, however, that a naturalistic version of intellectualism can be shown not to have implications which are intellectualistically unacceptable. I would now like to try to show, in other words, that there is an acceptable version of intellectualism which avoids Ryle's *reductio* argument by postulating primitive intellectual actions, and which also provides an intellectualistically acceptable account of the primitive intellectual actions which it postulates, and thus avoids the force of the three considerations against such a version of intellectualism which I have just adduced.

4 *Naturalistic Intellectualism*

The discussion in Section 3 showed, in effect, that there is a version of intellectualism which is immune to Ryle's *reductio* argument. According to this naturalistic version of intellectualism, intelligent behaviour is to be explained by postulating etiologically prior intellectual actions which involve applications of behaviour-guiding rules or maxims. On this account, some of the postulated intellectual actions involved in the etiology of overt intelligent actions are primitive in the sense that the applications of rules which they involve are causally determined, rather than themselves rule-guided.[24]

This version of intellectualism is clearly immune to Ryle's *reductio* argument. That argument depends, as we have seen, on the principle of inheritance. But naturalistic intellectualism in effect abandons the principle of inheritance when it

---

[24] This is more or less the standard modern version of intellectualism. For an influential treatment, see D. Dennett, 'Intentional Systems', *Journal of Philosophy* lxviii (1971). Dennett also anticipates the evolutionary modifications to this account which I propose.

recognizes the need to postulate a level of primitive intellectual activity. It is nevertheless arguable that this naturalistic version of intellectualism is not an acceptable alternative to versions of intellectualism which do incorporate the principle of inheritance, and which are therefore undermined by Ryle's *reductio* argument. This is so, in particular, because a naturalistic version of intellectualism appears to provide no adequate account of the rationality of the primitive intellectual actions which it postulates.

According to naturalistic intellectualism, intelligent agents perform just those primitive intellectual actions relevant to the attainment of their goals because they are entities with particular sets of internal structural characteristics. But such an account appears to suggest that the primitive intellectual actions in terms of which overt intelligent actions are explained are causally, rather than rationally, responsive to the situations in which agents act. In particular, such an explanation appears to be defective from an intellectualist point of view because it fails to provide an account of the rational character of the relation between agents' situations and the primitive intellectual actions which they perform in those situations. To provide such an account is, in fact, the fundamental problem facing those who wish, by adopting a naturalistic version of intellectualism, to immunize intellectualism against Ryle's *reductio* argument.

I believe that a solution to this fundamental problem can be developed on the basis of Popper's account of the evolution of intelligent abilities. I believe, in particular, that we can, with reference to evolutionary considerations, provide an account of the primitive intellectual actions posited by naturalistic intellectualists which shows how these actions are rationally, and not merely causally, responsive to the situation in which the agent acts. Such an account has the following form.

Individuals evolutionarily ancestral to the agent had structural characteristics which enabled them to perform a variety of actions, including intellectual actions, in pursuit of their goals, without causally necessitating them to perform any one of these actions in any particular situation. In Popper's terminology, the behaviour of these individuals was under the 'plastic control' of their structural characteristics and those of their environments.[25]

Some, but not all, of the intellectual actions which such individuals were able to perform were rationally relevant to the attainment of the goals they pursued, in the sense that these actions, but not the others, were actions the performance of which resulted in the attainment of the goals which these individuals pursued. Those individuals who habitually performed the intellectual actions which were in this sense rationally relevant to the attainment of their goals would have had an evolutionary advantage with respect to those of their fellows who did not habitually perform these actions.[26]

When a successful pattern of intellectual activity is established in an individual or in a group of individuals, whether by 'trial and error' or by 'conditioning', genetic mutations may occur which fix this pattern of behaviour by providing a physical-structural basis for it. As Popper points out in his discussion of the 'Baldwin effect', successful patterns of behaviour can influence the selection of genetically encoded structural characteristics which facilitate the 'automatization' of that behaviour.[27] Since the pattern of behaviour was itself evolutionarily advantageous, individuals in whom this pattern had genetically been fixed would themselves have an evolutionary advantage with respect to other individuals. A pattern of intellectual activity which is rationally relevant to attaining the goals of the organism could in this way become genetically fixed for organisms of this kind, and for their descendents.

Individuals for whose behaviour naturalistic intellectualists wish to offer an explanation in terms of primitive intellectual actions are, on this account, descended from individuals for whom a pattern of successful intellectual activity had become genetically fixed in the way described. Their specific inheritance from them is that set of structural characteristics which enable them to perform just those primitive intellectual actions which

[25] See K. Popper, *Objective Knowledge*, Oxford, 1972, pp. 149–50.
[26] Ibid., p. 245.
[27] Ibid.

are relevant to the attainment of their goals. They, of course, perform these primitive intellectual actions without themselves having any reasons for doing so. No higher-order rule guides their performance of these postulated primitive intellectual actions. But these actions are, on our Popperian account, rationally, and not merely causally, responsive to the situation in which they occur. The fact that agents perform these actions rather than others is a consequence of evolutionary factors, and, as Popper points out, evolutionary processes can 'simulate' processes of rational choice.[28] While agents do not themselves choose to perform just those postulated primitive intellectual actions which are relevant to the attainment of their goals, evolutionary processes have 'chosen' (i.e. selected) individuals who are structurally so constituted that the primitive intellectual actions which they perform are rationally adapted to the goals they pursue.

I think we may claim, then, that this Popperian version of naturalistic intellectualism does provide an account of the fact that agents perform just those primitive intellectual actions which are rationally relevant to the attainment of their goals. We may claim, in short, that this evolutionarily naturalistic version of intellectualism does account for the rationality of the postulated primitive intellectual actions and is therefore a coherent alternative both to naturalism *per se* and to those non-naturalistic versions of intellectualism which do incorporate the principle of inheritance and which are therefore subject to Ryle's *reductio* argument.

These Popperian considerations thus seem to undermine the claim that any version of intellectualism which rejects the principle of inheritance *ipso facto* collapses into a form of naturalism which can provide no account of the rational relation between the agent's situation and the action the agent performs in that situation. For we have shown that the naturalistic elements inherent in this version of intellectualism can themselves be treated in an intellectualist way. We have shown, in effect, how causal relations can simulate rational relations.

[28] Ibid., p. 267.

These Popperian considerations also perhaps suggest a way of undermining the claim that rejection of the principle of inheritance *ipso facto* commits the intellectualist to rejecting the principle that it is precisely the intelligent actions which require intellectualist explanations. In particular, these considerations show that naturalistic intellectualists need not abandon this principle of demarcation since they can, in fact, provide a kind of intellectualist explanation of the primitive intellectual actions which they postulate. On this account, intellectualists can explain the occurrence of these actions not in terms of agents' reasons for performing them, since this would induce an infinite regress, but rather in terms of the reasons for performing them which, as a result of evolution, agents incorporate in the form of structural characteristics. Such an explanation might be called quasi-intellectualist, since it is responsive to the problem of accounting for the rationality of primitive intellectual actions. At the same time, however, such an explanation is not threatened by an infinite regress, as a 'truly' intellectualist explanation might be, since the reasons invoked are embodied in agents as structural characteristics and not as practical maxims.

These considerations show, in short, that this evolutionarily naturalistic version of intellectualism is neither subject to Ryle's *reductio* argument (since it does not incorporate the principle of inheritance on which that argument depends), nor indistinguishable from naturalism *per se* (since it is, while naturalism is not, responsive to the rationality of intelligent actions).

I will later consider the relation between naturalistic intellectualism and other intuitions which have been important in the debate about intellectualism. Before doing so, though, I would first like to consider the relation between the naturalistic version of intellectualism here recommended and both linguistic intellectualism and classical versions of intellectualism.

The most striking feature of our version of intellectualism is embodied in the proposal to postulate the occurrence of primitive intellectual actions. This version of intellectualism may appear to differ in respect of this proposal from classical versions of intellectualism which, according to Ryle at least, reject the notion of primitive intellectual actions and propose instead to explain all intelligent actions in terms of etiologically prior intellectual actions.

This appearance is, however, deceptive. Classical intellectualists too seem to have rejected the principle of inheritance which Ryle attributed to them when he claimed that 'the absurd assumption made by the intellectualist legend is that a performance of any sort inherits all its title to intelligence from some anterior internal operation of planning what to do'.[29] In a related, epistemological context, Descartes proposed to halt a threatening regress of reasons for believing something to be the case by positing the existence of causal factors which operate in such a way as to provide conclusive grounds for belief. Indeed, Descartes even came close to proposing a biological account of the rational relevance of these postulated causal factors.[30] Leibniz also postulated primitive mental operations which, while rationally responsive to the agent's goals, are nevertheless employed in an instinctive way.[31]

It would thus seem that the naturalistic version of intellectualism has important affinities with classical versions of intellectualism, and that these versions might therefore be no more vulnerable to Ryle's criticism than is the naturalistic version.

There are also some striking affinities between naturalistic intellectualism and the linguistic intellectualism advocated by Chomsky and his colleagues. Advocates of linguistic intellectualism recognize, for instance, that the force of Ryle's *reductio* argument can be avoided only by rejecting the principle of inheritance. We can easily see that linguistic intellectualists recognize the need to reject the principle of inheritance if we examine the model of intelligent behaviour which both

---

[29] Ryle, *The Concept of Mind*, p. 32.

[30] See Descartes, *Principles*, p. 236; and *Meditations on First Philosophy*, in Haldane and Ross, *Philosophical Works*, i, p. 197.

[31] See G. Leibniz, *New Essays Concerning Human Understanding*, trans. A. Langley, New York, 1896, p. 87.

Chomsky and Fodor, among others, have recommended—the simulation of that behaviour by a suitably programmed computer.[32]

We might, of course, explain the overt, input-output behaviour of a machine simulating intelligent behaviour by reference to the practical maxims which are stored as its programme. But we would not usually attempt to explain its covert behaviour, of applying these maxims, by reference to applications of practical meta-maxims which guide the applications of those practical maxims which we posit to explain the machine's overt behaviour. Rather, we would explain this postulated covert activity in terms of the physical–structural characteristics of the machine and its causally mediated interactions with its environment. We would, in other words, halt a threatening regress of programs by abandoning the principle of inheritance and instead explaining the machine's primitive covert behaviour in a naturalistic way—in the same way, in fact, as the naturalistic intellectualist proposes to halt Ryle's regress of intellectual actions.[33]

Naturalistic and linguistic intellectualism also concur in recognizing that the principle of inheritance can be rejected without *ipso facto* abandoning the project of providing at least a kind of intellectualist explanation of postulated primitive intellectual activity. Again, consideration of the analogy between computer simulation of intelligent behaviour and the explanation of such behaviour which is provided by naturalistic intellectualism is revealing.

We might explain the primitive covert behaviour of a computer in a naturalistic way, but might also explain this behaviour, and especially its rational relevance to the problem which the computer has been programmed to solve, by pointing out that the computer was designed, by its constructor, to engage in just that primitive activity which is in fact relevant to

---

[32] See N. Chomsky, *Language and Mind*, New York, 1972, pp. 191-2; and J. Fodor, *Psychological Explanation*, New York, 1968. ch. 4.

[33] See Chomsky, *Reflections*, p. 71; and J. Fodor, *The Language of Thought*, New York, 1975, p. 74, n. 14.

the solution of problems which it has been programmed to solve. Likewise, the naturalistic intellectualist proposes to rationalize the primitive intellectual activity involved in human problem-solving by pointing out that human beings were 'designed' by evolution, which simulates the role of a creator, to function in a way appropriate to the realization of their ends.[34]

Naturalistic intellectualism of the kind recommended here differs from linguistic intellectualism, however, in emphasizing the role of evolutionary considerations in harmonizing naturalistic and intellectualist elements of an adequate intellectualist account of intelligence. The possibility of invoking evolutionary considerations in this context seems not to have been considered by linguistic intellectualists. Indeed, Chomsky himself characterizes evolutionary explanations of intelligent behaviour in a way which suggests that he sees little interest in pursuing this line of inquiry.[35] I hope that the use to which I have put these Popperian considerations will dispel notions of this kind.

I think that we may conclude here, then, that there is a version of intellectualism which is internally coherent and which is, as well, immune to Ryle's *reductio* argument, and that this naturalistic version of intellectualism has affinities both with classical and with linguistic versions of that doctrine.

I will now consider the relation between naturalistic intellectualism and ontological questions which were significant in traditional discussions of intellectualism and naturalism.

5 Ontology and Intellectualism

I will here consider the problem of specifying the conditions under which naturalistic intellectualism is compatible with materialist monism. We can call this problem the *compatibility problem*. There are at least three reasons why such an exercise is important.

First, it is important in view of the widespread claim that

<hr>

[34] See Popper, *Objective Knowledge*, p. 267.
[35] See Chomsky, *Language and Mind*, pp. 96–7; and *Reflections*, p. 59.

intellectualism, in any form, presupposes, and thus stands or falls with the viability of a dualistic ontology. As we have seen, this claim was an important feature of the historical debate about classical versions of intellectualism. More recently, Ryle has also endorsed this claim, suggesting that intellectualism is plausible precisely to the extent to which we 'are wedded to the [dualistic] dogma of the ghost in the machine'.[36]

Second, this exercise is important in view of the fact that many prominent linguists have explicitly committed themselves to a materialist ontology. Chomsky, for instance, refers to the mind as a 'biological structure' and to the 'properties of the mind that underlie the acquisition of language' as 'biological properties of the organism'.[37]

Third, such an exercise is important since it is desirable to show, if possible, that naturalistic intellectualism is ontologically neutral between materialist monism and dualism. It is therefore important to ask whether there is a version of materialism with which naturalistic intellectualism is compatible. (It is presumably obvious that naturalistic intellectualism is compatible with ontological dualism.)

Before addressing the compatibility problem in some detail, it will be useful to introduce some terminology.

According to naturalistic intellectualism, explanations of intelligent behaviour employ two distinct kinds of locutions. M-locutions have the form: 'x is the application of a practical maxim or rule R'. P-locutions have the form: 'x is a causal interaction between an individual with structural properties S and an environment E'. According to all versions of intellectualism, M-locutions are ineliminable, in favour of P-locutions, in explanations of intelligent behaviour.

If naturalistic intellectualism were ontologically neutral, then it would be possible to interpret M-locutions in either of two distinct ways. (a) We might interpret M-locutions as referring to irreducibly mental events. Given the fact that ineliminable P-locutions can only be interpreted as referring to

[36]   Ryle, *The Concept of Mind*, p. 32.
[37]   Chomsky, *Reflections*, pp. 7 and 155.

physical events, this interpretative policy would yield a dualistic interpretation of naturalistic intellectualism. (*b*) We might, on the other hand, interpret *M*-locutions as referring to physical events. This interpretative policy would yield a materialist interpretation of naturalistic intellectualism.

The compatibility problem can now be posed more sharply in the form of a question. Is naturalistic intellectualism coherent if its *M*-locutions are interpreted as referring to physical events?

It will perhaps be clear that the compatibility problem has no positive solution if *reductionism* is implied by materialism. We can easily see that this is so.

According to reductionism, any law of any special science such as intellectualist linguistics can be reduced to a law of some primary physical science in the following way. Let the statement 'All Ψ_is are Ψ_js' express a law of some special science. Reductionism then implies that the following two conditions obtain. (i) There are bridge laws of the forms 'All Ψ_is are Φ_ms' and 'All Ψ_js are Φ_ns', which express contingent event identities. According to these bridge laws, in other words, every event which satisfies a certain linguistic description, for instance, also (contingently) satisfies a certain physical description. (ii) The formula 'All Φ_ms are Φ_ns' expresses a law of physics.[38]

If materialism implies reductionism, then there could be no coherent materialist interpretation of naturalistic intellectualism. If it is the case that the laws of intellectualist linguistics are reducible in this way to the laws of physics, which involve only *P*-locutions, then it is not the case, as intellectualism implies, that any explanation of intelligent linguistic behaviour necessarily employs *M*-locutions. The reducibility of linguistic laws to physical laws makes it possible to eliminate *M*-locutions from explanations of intelligent behaviour without loss of empirical content or explanatory power. And this possibility is incompatible with the intellectualist claim that such *M*-locutions are ineliminable in such contexts. There is thus no

[38] See Fodor, *The Language of Thought*, pp. 11–12.

coherent materialist interpretation of intellectualism if materialism implies reductionism. If we are to provide a positive
solution to the compatibility problem, then, we must try to
show that materialism does not imply reductionism.

Fodor has recently constructed an argument which is alleged
to show that materialism does not imply reductionism. Fodor's
argument has the following form.

(*a*) The laws of every science are formulated in particular
theoretical vocabularies, which are distinguished by their stocks
of 'natural kind predicates'. Not every predicate is a natural
kind predicate of every science. For instance, the predicate 'is
a monetary transaction' is not a natural kind predicate of
physics, though it may be a natural kind predicate of economics.
The natural kind predicates of a particular science are, in short,
those predicates which appear in the laws of that science.[39]

(*b*) Reductionism implies that every natural kind predicate
of every special science is coextensive with a natural kind
predicate of some primary physical science. This is so because
reductionism implies the existence of bridge laws which express
the contingent identity of events referred to in the laws of a
special science with events referred to in the laws of physics.[40]

(*c*) According to materialism, every event referred to by
every natural kind predicate of every science is a physical event.
Even if we assume the truth of materialism, however, it is not
the case that the natural kind predicates of the special sciences
are coextensive with those of physics. This is so because the
physical events which, according to materialism, are denoted by
the natural kind predicates of the special sciences may have
virtually nothing in common from a physical point of view.[41]
These events, in other words, may have quite varied descriptions in terms of the natural kind predicates of physics. But in
this case, the bridge laws demanded (and promised) by
reductionism may identify events satisfying a natural kind
predicate of some special science with events satisfying a

---

[39] See Fodor, *The Language of Thought*, pp. 13–14.
[40] Ibid., p. 14.
[41] Ibid., 15–16.

(perhaps quite large) disjunction of physical natural kind predicates. These bridge laws, in other words, may be statements of the form 'Every Ψ is a Φ_1 or a Φ_2 or ... a Φ_k', where Ψ is a natural kind predicate of the special science and each Φ-predicate is a natural kind predicate of physics. But a disjunction of natural kind predicates is not itself a natural kind predicate, since such a disjunctive predicate does not figure in the laws of the primary physical science.[42]

(*d*) But reductionism implies that the natural kind predicates of the special sciences are coextensive with the natural kind predicates of physics. Reductionism is therefore false, even if materialism is true. Materialism, then, does not imply reductionism. There may therefore be coherent materialist interpretations of intellectualist theories of linguistic behaviour, for instance.

If Fodor's argument is sound, the materialist interpretation of intellectualism preferred by prominent linguistic intellectualists such as Chomsky may in fact be a coherent interpretation. There is in this case a positive solution to the compatibility problem.

Of course, if Fodor's argument is not sound, then the position of those linguistic intellectualists, such as Chomsky, who are also materialists may well be philosophically incoherent. I hasten to add, however, that this fact, if such it be, does not in itself undermine the intellectualist *research strategy* of Chomsky and his associates. While it may well be true that the *M*-locutions favoured by intellectualist linguists are in principle eliminable from adequate explanations of intelligent behaviour, the use of such locutions in such explanations may still heuristically be justified. For one thing, explanations of intelligent behaviour involving un-eliminated *M*-locutions may well be the only kinds of explanations currently available, and such explanations may, in any event, provide greater 'insight' into the bases of intelligent behaviour than would be provided by reductionistic explanations in physical terms. For another thing, such explanations may be heuristically useful, or even

---

[42] Ibid., pp. 20-2.

necessary, in providing a basis from which explanations in strictly physical terms might subsequently be constructed.

I claim, in short, here to have shown that even if there is no philosophically coherent interpretation of intellectualism if materialism is true, the preferred research strategy of intellectualists may still in these circumstances be defensible.

6 *Intentionality and Intellectualism*

I would now like to consider the extent to which naturalistic intellectualism is responsive to the intuitive distinction between voluntary and involuntary behaviour. I will also consider the extent to which Chomsky's version of linguistic intellectualism is responsive to this distinction.

I have already indicated the importance for classical versions of intellectualism of the naive intuitive distinction between voluntary and involuntary behaviour. I noted, in particular, that this distinction was taken by classical intellectualists to provide something like a criterion of demarcation between those phenomena which are most appropriately explained in intellectualist terms and those which are most appropriately explained in naturalistic terms. I might now point out that a similar proposal has been central to recent discussions of intellectualism as well. Taylor, for instance, implicitly adopted this demarcation criterion when he suggested that 'the "automatic" behaviours are the ones ... which can most plausibly be accounted for in mechanistic terms ... [while] more plastic behaviours ... involve intelligence in judging their appropriateness and in adapting means to the end'.[43] Mischel, Nagel, and Fodor, among others on both sides of the debate about intellectualism, have also endorsed versions of this criterion.[44]

Given the importance for intellectualism of the intuitive distinction between voluntary and involuntary behaviour, we

---

[43] C. Taylor, 'The Explanation of Purposive Behaviour', in R. Borger and F. Cioffi, eds., *Explanation in the Behavioural Sciences*, Cambridge, 1970, p. 74.

[44] See T. Mischel, 'Language Learning and Innate Knowledge', in S. Brown, ed., *Philosophy of Psychology*, London, 1974, p. 178; Nagel, 'The Boundaries', p. 457; and Fodor, *Psychological Explanation*, p. 87.

must now consider whether naturalistic versions of intellectualism can properly be responsive to this distinction.

The naturalistic version of intellectualism recommended here provides a naturalistic explanation of the occurrence of those primitive intellectual actions which provide the basis for overt intelligent actions. Given the intellectualist demarcation criterion, this account thus suggests that naturalistic intellectualists propose to treat these postulated primitive intellectual actions as involuntary, rather than voluntary, behaviour. But this appears in turn to suggest that naturalistic intellectualism may not, after all, be responsive to the distinction between voluntary and involuntary behaviour. In proposing, in effect, that the basis for voluntary intelligent action is provided by a capacity for involuntary primitive intellectual activity, naturalistic intellectualism may appear to reduce voluntary action to an effect of involuntary behaviour.

Thomas Nagel in effect drew attention to this problem in his discussion of Fodor's (naturalistic) version of intellectualism. Noting that Fodor admitted 'the relevance of a notion like [voluntary] performance at the terminal level of overt behavior', Nagel asked why Fodor refused to admit the relevance of this notion 'at the [covert] level of integration that makes a complex performance possible'.[45] Nagel can, I think, be understood as asking here whether Fodor's version of intellectualism does not reduce voluntary action to involuntary behaviour by implying, in particular, that the latter provides the basis for the former.

Nagel's question is, of course, related to the question which gives force to Ryle's *reductio* argument. Can intellectualists posit primitive intellectual actions, which are to be explained naturalistically, without blurring the distinction between distinct kinds of actions? In the case of Ryle's argument, it is alleged, in effect, that naturalistic intellectualists blur the distinction between rational and non-rational actions. In the case of Nagel's argument, it is alleged, in effect, that naturalistic

[45] Nagel, 'The Boundaries', p. 457.

intellectualists blur the distinction between voluntary and involuntary behaviour. The problem in both cases is that of reconciling any version of intellectualism which rejects the (generalized) principle of inheritance with the existence of important intuitive distinctions. In the case of Ryle's argument, it is alleged that intellectualists can account for the intuitive distinction between rational and non-rational actions only if they accept a principle of the inheritance of rationality. In the case of Nagel's argument, it is apparently alleged that intellectualists can account for the distinction between voluntary and involuntary actions only if they accept a principle of the inheritance of intentionality. We can say that this latter allegation is embodied in *Nagel's assumption*.

Naturalistic intellectualists of course reject Nagel's assumption. In fact, no coherent version of intellectualism could incorporate this assumption. Any version of intellectualism which did incorporate this assumption would be threatened by an infinite regress of voluntary actions, just as it would be threatened by an infinite regress of rules or maxims if it accepted Ryle's principle of inheritance. The question which remains, then, is whether naturalistic intellectualists can reject Nagel's assumption without *ipso facto* undermining their (tacit) claim to provide a principled account of the distinction between voluntary and involuntary behaviour.

According to naturalistic intellectualism, we should explain a voluntary action by positing the occurrence of involuntary primitive intellectual behaviour of a kind which is relevant to the guidance of that action. Naturalistic intellectualism nevertheless does not blur the distinction between voluntary and involuntary behaviour. While the primitive intellectual events which are alleged to guide overt voluntary behaviour are involuntary, rather than voluntary, the behaviour which they guide may itself be voluntary. An agent chooses, but is not determined, to perform an action of a certain kind. This choice 'triggers' those involuntary intellectual activities which guide the performance of the action in question. The action is voluntary, a matter of causally undetermined choice; but it is based on that involuntary primitive intellectual activity which the agent, as a result of evolution, is causally determined to engage in when a choice of this kind has been made.

Having in this way disposed of Nagel's problem, I will now suggest that the version of naturalistic intellectualism recommended here has certain affinities in this regard both with classical versions of intellectualism and with linguistic intellectualism.

As I have already pointed out in my discussion of Ryle's argument, classical intellectualists were aware of the various kinds of infinite regress which might tend to threaten their account of intelligent behaviour, and also seemed to realize that this account could be protected from such threats only by positing some sort of primitive intellectual activity. In the present context, this realization was embodied for classical intellectualists in their proposal to account for voluntary performances by postulating capacities for involuntary behaviour of relevant kinds. This proposal emerges particularly clearly in Descartes's discussion of the interaction of mind and body in the human performance of overt voluntary actions. Given that the mind directs the performance of such actions, it does so, according to Descartes, by causing the body to perform involuntary actions which are relevant to the execution of that performance.[46] When a person wishes, for instance, to observe a distant object, this volition is 'translated', at the interface between mind and body, into that series of involuntary physical actions which disposes the eye in a particular and relevant way. According to Descartes, it would be empirically incorrect to suppose that these physical activities are themselves voluntary performances. The person whose behaviour we explain in these terms did not, after all, wish to undertake this series of actions; he or she wished, rather, to see a particular object.[47] In another context, Descartes proposed to explain our voluntarily

[46] See R. Descartes, *The Passions of the Soul*, in Haldane and Ross, *Philosophical Works*, i, pp. 347 and 351.
[47] For criticism of Descartes's position which resembles Nagel's criticism of Fodor's position, see B. Spinoza, *Ethics*, trans. R. Elwes, New York, 1969, pp. 244–7.

exercised capacity for constructing theories about the world in terms of our capacity involuntarily for recognizing the truth of our clear and distinct ideas about the world.[48] Leibniz also claimed that this capacity for understanding was based on a capacity involuntarily for drawing certain kinds of inferences.[49] Classical versions of intellectualism appear, then, to embody a solution to Nagel's problem which is quite similar to the one I have here provided. And this fact can, in turn, be taken to show that naturalistic and classical versions of intellectualism have strong affinities of a kind not normally noticed by commentators on intellectualism.

That these same affinities exist between naturalistic intellectualism and linguistic intellectualism is also clear. They are manifested, for instance, in Chomsky's claim that a language, which is used in a voluntary way, is, however, 'created anew in each individual by operations which lie beyond the reach of will or consciousness'—i.e. by operations which are carried out involuntarily during the process of language acquisition.[50]

In this section, then, I have argued that we can undermine the claim that naturalistic intellectualism implies a reduction of voluntary to involuntary behaviour and therefore blurs the important intuitive distinction between these kinds of behaviour. In the next section, I will ask whether naturalistic intellectualism is responsive to the intuition that intelligence is freely exercised, rather than causally determined.

7 Freedom and Intellectualism

I have already mentioned the significance which advocates of intellectualism attribute to the intuition that, in certain things at least, human beings act freely. Classical intellectualists believed that this intuition is incompatible with a purely naturalistic account of intelligent human behaviour. I will here try to show, however, that naturalistic intellectualism is also responsive to this intuition.

---

[48] See Descartes, *Principles*, p. 236.
[49] See Leibniz, *New Essays*, p. 87.
[50] Chomsky, *Reflections*, p. 4.

There appear to be two main senses in which intelligent behaviour might be said to be free. (*a*) Intelligent behaviour might be free in the sense that it is completely undetermined, or, at least, radically underdetermined, by any rational or causal factors. (*b*) Intelligent behaviour might be free in the sense that it is not blindly determined in the way in which the non-intelligent behaviour of atoms and planets appears to be. Intelligent behaviour might, in other words, be free in the sense of being determined, at least partially, by characteristics of the individual who engages in it, rather than being determined, as non-intelligent behaviour is, entirely by external relations between objects. The notion of freedom in this second main sense can further be explicated in terms of two subsidiary notions. (i) Intelligent behaviour might be free in the sense that it is not determined solely by the structure of the agent's external environment. Intelligent behaviour, in other words, might be free in the sense of depending on the agent's own internal structural characteristics. (ii) Intelligent behaviour might be free in the sense that it depends on laws created by agents themselves—laws to which they submit themselves, rather than merely blindly obeying, as they blindly obey the natural laws to which they are subject and which they do not themselves create.

It is apparent that freedom in sense (*a*) corresponds roughly to freedom in the sense which Hume derided as illusory when he claimed that 'liberty, when opposed to necessity, not to constraint, is the same thing with chance; which is universally acknowledged to have no existence'.[51] Likewise, freedom in senses (*b* i) and (*b* ii) corresponds, closely and crudely, respectively, to freedom in Kant's two senses—to freedom in the 'psychological' and 'transcendental' senses.[52]

No scientific psychology could, I think, be responsive to the existence of freedom in the sense of chance. To say that intelligent behaviour is free even in the sense of being radically

---

[51] Hume, *An Enquiry*, p. 96.
[52] See Kant, *Practical Reason*, p. 190.

underdetermined by any causal or rational factors is, in effect, to acknowledge the impossibility of discovering any true laws or rules which govern or guide that behaviour. This observation expresses, I think, the force of Hume's objection. For he felt that we are able to discover laws about the intelligent behaviour of human beings.[53] In any event, with respect to freedom in this sense, neither naturalism nor intellectualism could hope to be responsive. They are on a par in this respect. Both naturalistic and intellectualist accounts of human behaviour are possible only if human behaviour is not free in this sense; neither can account for this kind of freedom, if such there should be.

Naturalism and intellectualism are furthermore at least potentially on a par with respect to the possibility of freedom in the 'psychological' sense. Intellectualism acknowledges this possibility when it acknowledges the role of individuals' goals and practical maxims, as well as their external environments, in determining their behaviour. Likewise, all non-behaviouristic versions of naturalism acknowledge this possibility when they acknowledge the role of individuals' internal structural characteristics in determining their behaviour.

Classical intellectualism and naturalism diverge, however, with respect to the possibility of freedom in the 'transcendental' sense. In acknowledging the role of practical maxims in guiding agents' behaviour, intellectualism in effect acknowledges that such behaviour is at least partially determined by laws, embodied in the practical maxims, which individual agents may themselves have constructed. Naturalism, on the other hand, appears not to be· responsive to the possibility of freedom in this transcendental sense. According to naturalism, intelligent behaviour is determined by laws of nature, not by laws which agents themselves may have constructed and submitted themselves to. While agents might discover the laws which govern their behaviour, just as they might discover other kinds of natural laws, they do not, on this naturalistic account, submit

---

[53] See Hume, *An Enquiry*, pp. 84–5.

themselves to them, but are, rather, blindly governed by them, just as they are blindly governed by the law of gravitation, for instance.

From these considerations we can conclude, then, that free-dom in the transcendental sense may pose a problem for naturalistic versions of intellectualism, just as it does for naturalism *per se*. For such versions of intellectualism of course incorporate naturalistic, as well as intellectualist, assumptions about the etiology and nature of intelligent human behaviour.

Among prominent linguistic intellectualists, Chomsky appears to believe that his basically naturalistic version of intel-lectualism is responsive to the possibility of freedom in the transcendental sense. According to Chomsky, the rules of a grammar are constructed by the individuals whose behaviour they guide.[54] And this account suggests, I think that Chomsky believes that linguistic behaviour is transcendentally free; that it is determined by rules which language users themselves construct. On the other hand, Chomsky also seems to recognize what I think naturalistic intellectualism itself implies—that language users do not freely submit themselves to the linguistic rules which they themselves construct, but are, rather, causally determined to construct them in the way they do. According to Chomsky, 'the language learner has no "reason" for acquiring the [rules of his] language; he does not choose to learn and cannot fail to learn under normal conditions'.[55]

The question which remains, then, is this. Can naturalistic intellectualism of the kind Chomsky espouses be responsive to the possibility of transcendental freedom, as Chomsky believes it can, if it implies that individuals are caused to construct and apply those practical maxims which guide their behaviour, as Chomsky also recognizes it does?

My strategy in answering this question will, in effect, be essentially the Popperian strategy already here so much invoked. I will argue, in effect, that there is a sense in which individuals with a capacity for intelligent behaviour submit

---

[54] See Chomsky, *Reflections*, pp. 39 and 131.
[55] Ibid., p. 71.

themselves to, rather than merely being blindly governed by, those practical maxims which guide their intelligent behaviour.

According to naturalistic intellectualism, applications of primitive practical maxims are causal consequences of interactions between individuals and their environments. It is for this reason that we might say that the individual is blindly determined to apply these maxims and that the behaviour which they guide thus is not transcendentally free. At the same time, however, the fact that individuals' primitive intellectual behaviour is blindly determined in this way is itself a consequence of the evolutionary history of the species to which the individuals belong. In particular, this fact is a consequence of the fact that the practical maxims which are primitive for the agent in question were freely constructed by organisms evolutionarily ancestral to the agent. For these ancestral organisms, action in accordance with these maxims was transcendentally free. For these organisms did construct these maxims for themselves and did submit themselves to them, rather than merely obeying them blindly.

Furthermore, evolution has merely resulted in the automatization of the construction and application of such maxims. It has simply made these processes causally dependent on appropriate environmental circumstances. While action in accordance with these maxims is not, strictly speaking, transcendentally free for contemporary agents for whom these intellectual actions are primitive, we might say that action in accordance with these maxims is transcendentally free for the species to which the agent belongs, and is, therefore, free in some derived sense for that agent. If we accept the Popperian idea that individuals 'telescope' into their internal, causally efficacious structures a capacity for performing, in a merely psychologically free way, those transcendentally free actions of their evolutionary ancestors, then we might say that their performance of these actions simulates the transcendental freedom with which their ancestors performed them.

I think, in short, that naturalistic intellectualism is in some extended sense responsive to the possibility of transcendental freedom. In fact, I think that the sense in which this is true is a substantial one. Naturalistic intellectualism captures the intuition that each of the practical maxims in an agent's repertoire is itself the product of the transcendentally free problem-solving behaviour of the agent's ancestors, even though the agent may freely construct very few of the maxims which guide her or his intelligent behaviour.

I will now discuss the relation between linguistic intellectualism and Chomsky's claim that the grammar of a language is 'mentally represented' by users of that language.

8   *Representationalism and Intellectualism*

Chomsky claims that language users 'mentally represent' the grammar of their language.[56] We can call this claim *linguistic representationalism*. I will here consider the relation between this claim and Chomsky's version of intellectualism. This exercise is important, I think, partly because there is a certain amount of confusion about the appropriate interpretation for Chomsky's representationalist claim. In order to provide a background for my discussion, I will, then, first consider four ways in which this claim has been interpreted. I will then single out two of these interpretations, and argue that one of them is, while the other is not, compatible with linguistic intellectualism.

We find in the literature about linguistic representationalism four interpretations of that thesis.

(*a*) Harman has drawn attention to the possibility of providing what I will call a tautological interpretation of linguistic representationalism. He says:

There is a trivial sense in which, in learning a language, one forms a representation of the rules of the grammar of the language. We can trivially let the principle of representation be this: a person *p* at time *t* represents grammar *g* if and only if, at *t*, *p* knows the language for which *g* is the grammar.[57]

---

[56]   See Chomsky, *Language and Mind*, p. 18.
[57]   G. Harman, 'Review of *Language and Mind*', reprinted in G. Harman, ed., *On Noam Chomsky*, Garden City, 1974, p. 214.

This interpretation of representationalism is tautological in view of its equivalence to the claim that an empirically adequate grammar of a language describes the linguistic competence of users of that language. And this latter claim is itself tautological on the standard account of the relation between grammars and theories of linguistic competence.

(*b*) Stich has noted the possibility of providing what I will call a minimal interpretation of linguistic representationalism, which, he says, 'amounts merely to the claim that a grammar describes a certain ability of a speaker and that some internal mechanism or another underlies this ability'. Stich also claims that representationalism is, on this interpretation, an 'utterly trivial' thesis.[58] But minimal representationalism is, clearly, not nearly so trivial a thesis as is tautological representationalism, since tautological representationalism is, while minimal representationalism is not, compatible with behaviouristic theories of linguistic competence, which eschew reference to internal mechanisms. Even though minimal representationalism is a metaphysical thesis in Popper's sense, it may still avoid triviality by influencing the development of non-behaviouristic theories of linguistic competence.

(*c*) Stich has also noted the possibility of providing what he calls a 'substantive' and what I will call a weak interpretation for linguistic representationalism, according to which 'a grammar is internally represented only if there is some interesting isomorphism between the structure of the grammar and the structure of the mechanism which accounts' for the user's linguistic competence.[59] On this interpretation, then, a grammar may be taken as describing the structures and processes which provide the basis for language use. Clearly, this interpretation is logically stronger than the minimal interpretation, since the former is, while the latter is not, compatible with the claim that an empirically adequate grammar does not necessarily

[58] S. Stich, 'Competence and Indeterminacy', in D. Cohen and J. Wirth, eds., *Testing Linguistic Hypotheses*, Washington, 1975, p. 97.
[59] Ibid., p. 98.

describe the mechanism which provides the basis for linguistic competence.

(*d*) Putnam has, in effect, drawn attention to the possibility of providing what I will call a strong interpretation for linguistic representationalism. Putnam says:

A digital computer is a device which stores its own program and which consults its program in the course of a computation. It is not at all necessary that the brain be a digital computer in this sense. The brain does not, after all, have to be reprogrammed as an all purpose digital computer does. (One might reply that learning is 'reprogramming'; but Fodor is talking about the program for learning, not about what is learned: and this program might be stored as the brain's structure, not as a code.)[60]

The significance of Putnam's remarks lies, I think, in the implicit suggestion that there is a distinction between claiming, on the one hand, that a grammar is mentally represented in the sense that it is embodied in certain neural structures, and claiming, on the other hand, that a grammar is mentally represented in the sense that an encoding of it is stored in memory and consulted during linguistic performance. The strong interpretation of linguistic representationalism is, then, embodied in the latter of these claims.

The distinction between weak and strong representationalism of course tends to be disguised by the fact that even strongly represented grammars will be embodied in some physical structure, just as the program for a computer is, in effect, embodied in the physical structure of the memory cores in which it is stored.[61] This distinction can nevertheless be sharpened, perhaps, by appealing to an analogy.

[60] H. Putnam, 'What is Innate and Why', unpublished manuscript.
[61] My claim to this effect may seem perverse to those who recognize a sharp distinction between a computer's 'hardware' and its 'software'. But I claim that no such sharp distinction can be sustained. A computer has certain hardware characteristics because it has been constructed in a particular way from certain component parts which have particular characteristics. One characteristic of 'programmable' computers is that the variety of computationally relevant physical states which they can assume is not completely determined by their hardware characteristics. In fact, programming such a computer in effect involves selecting one such state from the set of states consistent with the computer's hardware characteristics. But the means by

Consider the relations, first, between a Turing machine *M* and its machine table *T*, and second, between a universal Turing machine *U* which is simulating *M* and the machine table *T* of *M*. The following facts seem clear. The machine table *T* describes the structure of the machine *M*, but does not describe the structure of the machine *U*, which is described by its own distinct machine table. However, an encoding of the machine table *T* is stored on its input tape by the universal machine *U*, but not by the machine *M* which *T* describes.[62]

I claim that a weakly represented grammar bears the same relation to the 'mind' in which it is represented as the machine table *T* does to the machine *M*, while a strongly represented grammar bears the same relation to the 'mind' in which it is represented as the machine table *T* does to the universal machine *U* which is simulating *M*. On the basis of this analogy, I will now attempt to show that Chomsky's intellectualism is compatible only with strong, and not with weak representationalism. There are, I think, at least two arguments which are relevant here.

The first such argument depends on a distinction drawn by Quine between rule-fitting and rule-guided behaviour. According to Quine, fitting is a matter of true description, but guiding is a matter of cause and effect.[63] It should be clear that intellectualism involves the claim that the rules of a grammar of a language guide, rather than merely fit, the behaviour of users of that language. But in this case, it follows more or less directly that these rules must be strongly represented by language users. To see this, we can invoke the analogy we have constructed.

which such a selection is effected do not differ in any philosophically interesting way from the means by which the hardware characteristics of this device were selected by its constructors. In one case, the range selected is wide and more or less permanently fixed. In the other case, the range selected is narrow and easily alterable. But the existence of these differences provides no adequate warrant for the claim that there is a deep and conceptually significant distinction between the two cases. In each case, we determine (to the relevant extent) a range of physically possible states of the device consistent with the computational properties we want it to have.

[62] See M. Minsky, *Computation: Finite and Infinite Machines*, Englewood Cliffs, 1967, ch. 7.

[63] See W. V. Quine, 'Methodological Reflections on Current Linguistic Theory', reprinted in Harman, *On Noam Chomsky*, pp. 104-5.

The relation between the behaviour of a Turing machine M and its machine table T is one of true description, but not one of cause and effect. On the other hand, the relation between the behaviour of the universal Turing machine U, which is simulating M, and the machine table T of M is one of cause and effect, but not one of true description of the internal operations of U. In view of our analogy, it now follows that only a strongly represented grammar could be said to guide the behaviour of language-users who mentally represent it, and, therefore, that only strong representationalism is consistent with the doctrine of linguistic intellectualism which Chomsky espouses.

The second argument depends on Cooper's suggestion that linguistic intellectualism implies that language-users consult the rules of their mentally represented grammars.[64] To see that this suggestion implies the dependence of linguistic intellectualism on strong representationalism, we can again appeal to our analogy. There is, then, a perfectly straightforward, if metaphorical, sense in which the universal Turing machine U, which is simulating the machine M, consults the machine table T of M: U 'scans' the encoding of T which appears on its input tape. On the other hand, there is no obvious sense in which the machine M itself consults its own machine table T during its computational operations (which are, of course, described by T). Given our analogy, it now follows that a mentally represented grammar could be consulted by language-users, as intellectualism requires, only if that grammar were strongly, and not merely weakly, represented. It follows, then, that intellectualism presupposes strong representationalism, just as I have claimed.

In this chapter, I have tried to construct a version of intellectualism which is immune to Ryle's *reductio* argument, and is responsive to intuitions about human freedom and the intentionality of intelligent human behaviour. The naturalistic version of intellectualism which I have developed here incorporates certain Popperian assumptions about the evolution of

---

[64] See Cooper, *Knowledge of Language*, pp. 42–53.

human intelligence. I have also tried to show that this version of intellectualism has strong affinities both with classical versions of intellectualism, and with the doctrine of linguistic intellectualism which Chomsky advocates. If the version of intellectualism presented here does provide a coherent alternative both to naturalism and to versions of intellectualism which are subject to Ryle's critical arguments, then I think I may claim to have shown that the version of linguistic intellectualism advocated by Chomsky is also defensible.

In the next chapter, I will consider Chomsky's account of human creativity.

4

CHOMSKY'S LIMITATIONISM

1 Introduction

Chomsky has long been concerned with human creativity, particularly as it may be manifested in everyday language use. His account of creativity has recently begun to receive a substantial amount of critical attention.[1] It is my aim in this chapter to offer a sympathetic analysis of Chomsky's account of creativity. I will be particularly concerned to consider Chomsky's *limitationist* claim that biologically fixed innate cognitive faculties 'set limits on human intellectual development'—limits within which human creativity is manifested.[2]

Before considering, developing, and defending Chomsky's characteristically limitationist account of human creativity, it will, perhaps, first be useful to consider the relations between this account and other important elements in his system of ideas.

As we shall shortly see in some detail, Chomsky developed his characteristic account of true human creativity on the basis of his observations about the 'creativity' which he detected in ordinary language use. In fact, Chomsky has distinguished two senses in which language use might be said to be creative. First, he sees a kind of creativity manifested in the *productivity* of language—in the ability of language-users to produce and to understand sentences which are new to their experience.[3] Second, he sees a kind of creativity manifested in the *Cartesian creativity* of language use—in language-users' ability to produce sentences which are appropriate to, though not determined by,

[1] See for instance B. Den Ouden, *Language and Creativity*, Lisse, 1975; G. Sampson, *Liberty and Language*. Oxford, 1979; G. Sampson, *Making Sense*, Oxford, 1980; and M. Drach, 'The Creative Aspect of Chomsky's Use of the Notion of Creativity', *Philosophical Review* lxxxx (1981).

[2] N. Chomsky, *Reflections on Language*, London, 1976, p. 123.

[3] See N. Chomsky, *Current Issues in Linguistic Theory*, The Hague, 1964, p. 8.

the context in which they are employed.[4] Given this distinction, we can now easily see how Chomsky's claims about creativity cohere with other philosophically significant components of his total system of ideas.

As we have already seen, Chomsky's observations about linguistic productivity played a crucial role in the development of his subjectivistic account of linguistic phenomena. His subjectivistic claim that a language 'has no existence apart from its mental representation' was, after all, invoked to explain the productivity of ordinary language use.[5] There is, then, a clear and straightforward connection between Chomsky's linguistic subjectivism and his account of the creativity which is manifested in the productivity of ordinary language use.

There is also a close connection between Chomsky's account of creativity and his characteristically mentalistic account of linguistic competence. Indeed, Chomsky suggested that the mentalistic claim that language-users 'know' the grammar of their language provides the basis for explaining linguistic productivity.[6] There is, then, a clear connection between Chomsky's mentalism and his account of the creativity which is manifested in linguistic productivity. Of course, I have already suggested that such a mentalistic account of linguistic competence cannot be sustained and must instead be replaced by a realist account. But it is clear, I think, that a realist account of the kind I recommend and which Chomsky himself accepts is dictated by facts about linguistic productivity, even if a mentalistic account of the kind Chomsky prefers is not. An adequate explanation of linguistic productivity does seem to involve the realist supposition that language-users stand in some kind of psychological relation to the grammar of their language.[7] There is, then, a close connection between Chomsky's account of creativity and the realist account of linguistic competence

---

[4]   See N. Chomsky, *Language and Mind*, New York, 1972, p. 100.

[5]   Ibid., p. 95.

[6]   See N. Chomsky, *Aspects of the Theory of Syntax*, Cambridge, 1965, p. 8.

[7]   L. Hutchinson, 'Grammar as Theory', in D. Cohen, ed., *Explaining Linguistic Phenomena*, Washington, 1974, p. 45.

which he accepts and by which his preferred mentalistic account must, I think, be replaced.

In view of the relation between Chomsky's account of creativity and his realist (or mentalistic) account of linguistic competence, there is also a close connection between his views on creativity and his individualistic conception of language. Certainly, Chomsky's individualistic account of linguistic phenomena is dictated by his psychologically realistic claims about grammars. If a mentally represented grammar provides the psychological basis for productive language use, then it is natural to suppose, as Chomsky does, that linguistics 'is a subfield of psychology'.[8] Chomsky's linguistic individualism is, in other words, dictated by his realism, which, in turn, is dictated by his views about linguistic productivity.

There is also a close connection between Chomsky's account of creativity and his intellectualist claim that linguistic behaviour is rule-guided rather than law-governed. Certainly, the Cartesian creativity of ordinary language use and, in particular, the fact that language-users typically produce sentences 'independently of detectable stimulus configurations' suggest that linguistic behaviour cannot be treated as a law-governed phenomenon.[9] Chomsky's linguistic intellectualism, then, seems to have been dictated by his observations about the (Cartesian) creativity which is manifested in ordinary linguistic behaviour.

Finally, there is also a close connection between Chomsky's limitationist account of creativity and his characteristically rationalist account of human learning. In particular, his rationalist claim that language acquisition is possible only because the language-learner is innately equipped with a schema which defines the set of possible languages is the source of his characteristic claim that true human creativity is itself possible only because there are limits on the kinds of cognitively or aesthetically significant objects which human beings can construct or understand.[10] Chomsky's linguistic rationalism is,

---

[8] Chomsky, *Reflections*, p. 160.
[9] Chomsky, *Language and Mind*, p. 100.
[10] Ibid., p. 89 n. 19; and Chomsky, *Reflections*, p. 123.

in short, reflected in his characteristically limitationist account of true creativity.

There are, then, clear and significant relations between Chomsky's limitationist views on creativity and other important elements in his system of ideas. These relations, then, provide further illustrations of the unity of his system.

2 *Linguistic Creativity and True Creativity*

Chomsky's characteristic account of true human creativity is coherent with, and can be illuminated by considering, an account of the creativity which he detects in ordinary linguistic phenomena. Of course, Chomsky does distinguish true human creativity from the creativity which may be manifested in everyday linguistic behaviour.[11] Nevertheless, Chomsky has also suggested, with appropriate qualifications, that the linguistic phenomena which he calls creative may provide evidence for the existence of creativity in the more usual sense, as well as providing a simplified and thus more perspicuous model in terms of which we might come better to understand the phenomenon of true creativity.[12] Although I will mainly be concerned here to analyse, elaborate, and defend Chomsky's account of true creativity, it will thus be useful first to consider his account of linguistic creativity.

It is important to note at the outset, however, that Chomsky has in fact applied the term 'creative' (and its cognates) to linguistic phenomena in two apparently distinct, but in fact related, ways. Indeed, it has been suggested that Chomsky's two-fold use of this notion reveals a deep confusion on his part.[13] I believe that this suggestion is incorrect, but it is nevertheless important to sound a cautionary note here. In his discussions of linguistic creativity, Chomsky may sometimes appear to stress different aspects of this phenomenon.

In his earliest extensive discussion of the foundations of linguistics, Chomsky drew attention to a characteristic of

---

[11] See N. Chomsky, *Cartesian Linguistics*, New York, 1966, p. 27.
[12] See N. Chomsky, *For Reasons of State*, London, 1973, pp. 174 and 185.
[13] See Drach, 'The Creative Aspect', p. 63.

human linguistic competence which he later called 'the central fact to which any significant linguistic theory must address itself'.[14] In that earlier discussion, Chomsky noted that the typical language-user 'has observed [only] a certain limited set of utterances of his language, [but can] on the basis of this finite linguistic experience ... produce an indefinite number of new utterances which are immediately acceptable to other members of his speech community'.[15] Chomsky later used the phrase 'the "creative" aspect of language' to refer to the characteristic he had so described.[16] We can say that language-users who produce (or understand) sentences which are new to their experience manifest their linguistic *productivity*.[17]

In the present context, it is important to note that Chomsky believes that we can explain the productivity of ordinary language use. According to Chomsky, we can explain how language-users are able to produce and to understand novel sentences by supposing that they have mastered 'a grammar, which is a system of rules for pairing semantic and phonetic interpretations' of the sentences of their language.[18] Since the grammar of a language provides a procedure for constructing interpretations for all of the acceptable word-sequences of that language, language-users who have mastered such a grammar are, according to Chomsky, able to employ it to provide interpretations for both the familiar and the novel sentences of their language.[19]

It is furthermore interesting to note that Chomsky believes that we can also explain the acquisition of the ability to use language productively. Language-learners are able to acquire this ability because, according to Chomsky, they are innately equipped with a schema for constructing grammars of the

[14] Chomsky, *Current Issues*, p. 7.
[15] N. Chomsky, *The Logical Structure of Linguistic Theory*, New York, 1975, p. 61.
[16] Chomsky, *Current Issues*, p. 8.
[17] See Chomsky, *Language and Mind*, p. 92 n. 21.
[18] N. Chomsky, 'Recent Contributions to the Theory of Innate Ideas', *Synthese* xvii (1967), p. 4.
[19] See Chomsky, *Language and Mind*, p. 100.

various human languages.[20] According to Chomsky, such a schema 'characterizes' and thus delimits 'the class of potential languages'.[21] On this account, then, language-learners are able to construct a grammar for their language, on the basis of quite fragmentary data about that language, because they are genetically 'programmed' with the capacity to construct grammars of the relevant kind—and, thus, only of that kind. In the present context, Chomsky's account of linguistic productivity is of interest primarily because of his suggestion that it is possible to acquire the ability to use language productively because there are biologically fixed limits on the kinds of grammars which human beings can master in the usual way. The significance of this suggestion in this context will emerge shortly.

Chomsky's discussion of linguistic productivity does not, however, exhaust his analysis of the creativity he detects in ordinary language use. He has also drawn attention to other characteristics of ordinary language use which perhaps more clearly manifest creativity in something like the normal sense. Chomsky refers, then, to 'the "creative" aspect of language use' as something which, he says, manifests itself in language-users' ability to produce and to understand 'an indefinite number of expressions which are new to [their] experience', and to do so 'on the appropriate occasion, despite their novelty, and independently of detectable stimulus configurations'.[22] We can say that language-users who produce novel sentences in a way which is appropriate to, though not determined solely by, the circumstances of their use manifest their *Cartesian creativity*.[23]

In the present circumstances, it is interesting to note that Chomsky believes that the Cartesian creativity of ordinary

---

[20] See Chomsky, *Language and Mind*, p. 89 n. 19.

[21] Ibid., p. 88.

[22] Ibid., pp. 11 and 100.

[23] As Chomsky himself has pointed out, Descartes and others working in his tradition drew attention to the significance of just those aspects of language use which, according to Chomsky, manifest the 'creativity' of ordinary language use. (See Chomsky, *Cartesian Linguistics*, pp. 3 ff.) It is thus appropriate to use the phrase 'Cartesian creativity' to refer to these aspects of language use.

language use is now, and is always likely to remain, beyond the range of scientific explanation.[24] It is, in this context, also interesting to note that Chomsky nevertheless believes that it may be possible to characterize some of the mechanisms which make the Cartesian creativity of ordinary language use possible.[25] In particular, it is clear that language-users' ability to manifest their Cartesian creativity presupposes their ability to manifest their linguistic productivity. The ability to produce novel sentences which are appropriate to, though not solely determined by, the context of their production clearly depends on the ability simply to produce novel sentences. And since language-users' ability simply to produce novel sentences is, according to Chomsky, dependent on their mastery of a grammar of their language, their Cartesian creativity must like-wise depend on their mastery of such a grammar.[26] In short, language-users' Cartesian creativity is possible, according to Chomsky, only because they have mastered and can employ a grammar of their language.

As I have already indicated, Chomsky's account of true human creativity, as it might be manifested, for instance, in science and the arts, is coherent with, and could in fact be inferred from, his speculations about linguistic productivity and the Cartesian creativity of ordinary language use. Of course, Chomsky distinguishes what he calls 'the problem of normal creativity', as it might be manifested in the Cartesian creativity of ordinary language use, from what he refers to as 'the general problem of true creativity, in the full sense of this term'.[27] Chomsky points out, then, that one 'would not refer to an act as "creative" simply on the basis of its novelty and independence of identifiable drives or stimuli'.[28] According to Chomsky,

[24] See N. Chomsky, *Rules and Representations*, Oxford, 1980, p. 24.

[25] See Chomsky, *Language and Mind*, p. 103.

[26] Of course, the supposition that language-users have mastered such a grammar does not, on Chomsky's account, suffice to explain users' Cartesian creativity, since this supposition does not show how users produce utterances which are appropriate to, but not determined by, their situation.

[27] N. Chomsky, 'Human Nature: Justice versus Power', in F. Elders, ed., *Reflexive Water*, London, 1974, p. 152; and *Cartesian Linguistics*, p. 16.

[28] Chomsky, *Cartesian Linguistics*, p. 84 n. 30.

'true "creativity" in a higher sense ... implies value as well as novelty'.[29]   Nevertheless, Chomsky clearly sees a relation between the phenomenon of true creativity and that of normal (Cartesian) creativity. True creativity, like normal creativity, is taken to involve novelty, appropriateness to context, and unpredictability in terms of external stimuli. Moreover, Chomsky claims that true creativity, like the creativity of ordinary language use, 'is predicated on', but not of course exhaustively explainable in terms of, 'a system of rules and forms, in part determined by intrinsic human capacities'.[30] Furthermore, Chomsky's claim that the acquisition of a capacity for Cartesian creativity depends on the availability to the language-learner of a restrictive schema for the construction of grammars is reflected in a characteristically limitationist thesis about true creativity. Chomsky suggests, then, that the possibility of true human creativity depends on the fact that 'other [innately based] cognitive systems too set limits on human intellectual development, by virtue of the very structure which makes it possible to construct rich and comprehensive systems of belief and knowledge'.[31] According to Chomsky, then, we may be genetically 'programmed' with the capacity to construct certain kinds of scientific theories and aesthetically significant objects. The fact that human beings are programmed in this way makes creativity possible in the scientific and aesthetic domains according to Chomsky, but it also sets limits on the possible range of truly creative human activities.

On Chomsky's account, then, true human creativity involves novelty, appropriateness to context, unpredictability in terms of environmental circumstances, and value. Chomsky furthermore claims that true creativity 'takes place within—presupposes, in fact—a system of constraints and governing principles'.[32] We can call this claim the *limits thesis*, since it posits limits on true

---

[29]   Chomsky, *Cartesian Linguistics*, p. 27.
[30]   Chomsky, *Reflections*, p. 133.
[31]   Ibid., p. 123.
[32]   Chomsky, *For Reasons of State*, p. 183.

human creativity.[33] As Chomsky himself has noted, versions of the limits thesis were also characteristically advanced by aesthetic theorists working in the German Romantic tradition.[34] Because this feature of Chomsky's account of creativity has provoked at least one critic of that account to maintain that 'Chomsky has misappropriated the term "creative"', I will concentrate here and in what follows on this feature of Chomsky's account.[35] Indeed, it is especially important to focus our attention in this way because, as Chomsky himself has pointed out, the 'image of a mind, initially unconstrained, striking out freely in arbitrary directions, suggests at first glance a richer and more hopeful view of human freedom and creativity' than that implicit in his own account of creativity within the limits set by our innate cognitive capacities.[36]

In what follows, then, I intend to present and develop a general account of true human creativity within the framework of which it would be coherent to claim, as Chomsky does, that true human creativity takes place within, and is only possible in virtue of the existence of, innate limits on human cognitive capacities.

3 The Nature of Creativity

I suggested at the conclusion of the preceding section that Chomsky's characteristic account of creativity might be, and has indeed been taken to be, incompatible with some of our basic settled beliefs about creativity. To determine whether

[33] It is interesting to note that the limits thesis is too schematic to be subject to direct empirical refutation and is therefore metaphysical in the (non-pejorative) Popperian sense. According to the limits thesis, there are systems of beliefs and objects of aesthetic value which human beings must fail to find intelligible or which they must be unable to construct. But the limits thesis does not specify which systems of beliefs or objects of value are inaccessible to human intelligence in this way. The limits thesis is therefore consistent with every claim that some particular system of beliefs or object of value is accessible to human intelligence. No such claim can refute the limits thesis. I will try to show in Sections 7 and 8, however, that the limits thesis, like most metaphysical claims, can indirectly be criticized and evaluated.

[34] See Chomsky, *Cartesian Linguistics*, p. 23.

[35] Sampson, *Liberty and Language*, p. 106.

[36] N. Chomsky, *Problems of Knowledge and Freedom*, New York, 1971, pp. 49-50.

this is indeed the case, we must first consider what it is that we do (or are alleged to) believe about human creativity. Then, in Sections 5 and 6 below, I will attempt to show that a general account of creativity which incorporates Chomsky's fundamental limitationist claims is in fact consistent with our basic settled beliefs about creativity.

The most widely noted characteristic of the created product is its *novelty*. This fundamental characteristic has, in fact, been described in a number of different ways.

First, the created product is sometimes held to be novel in the sense that no method or set of rules or recipe available to the producer before its production could have sufficed to determine the activities of that producer. Kant, for instance, characterized creative genius 'as a talent for producing that for which no definite rule can be given; it is not a mere aptitude for what can be learnt by a rule'. Likewise, Koestler suggested that 'the problems which lead to original discoveries are precisely those which cannot be solved by any familiar rule of the game'. And Tomas claimed that we do not 'congratulate an artist for being creative [simply] because he was able to obey rules that were known before he painted his picture or wrote his novel or poem'.[37] On this view, then, the created product is novel in the sense that the activities involved in its production were not determined solely by pre-existent rules or methods.[38]

Second, the created product is sometimes held to be novel in the sense that we could not, before its production, have

---

[37] I. Kant, *Critique of Judgment*, trans. J. H. Bernard, New York, 1951, pp. 150–1; A. Koestler, *The Act of Creation*, London, 1964, p. 209; and V. Tomas, 'Creativity in Art', in V. Tomas, ed., *Creativity in the Arts*, Englewood Cliffs, 1964, p. 98.

[38] To avoid confusion, it is important, I think, to distinguish here between rules which do determine, and those which merely guide or limit productive activities. Behaviour-guiding rules need not be behaviour-determining, since the guidance they provide may merely define a range of possible behaviour without determining which behavioural event within that defined range actually occurs. Given this distinction, I want to suggest, then, that we interpret the account of the novelty of the created product here at issue as requiring that the production of that product not be determined in this sense by antecedently available rules. On this view, then, it is thus consistent with this account of the novelty of the created product that production of that product be guided or limited by antecedently available rules. And who would want to insist that this is not a genuine possibility? Is the poet who works within a framework of certain (behaviour-guiding) metrical conventions *ipso facto* uncreative?

predicted what characteristics it would have. Sampson, for instance, suggested that 'it is intrinsic to the notion of creativity that the nature of creative acts cannot be predicted [but] can only be described after the event'. Similarly, Rothenberg and Hausman claimed that 'the specific natures [of created products] cannot be predicted from a knowledge of their antecedents'.[39] On this view, then, the created product is novel in the sense that its characteristics could not have been predicted on the basis of antecedent knowledge about the circumstances of its production.

Third, the created product is sometimes held to be novel in the sense that it is different in kind from previously created products in the same domain. 'To be creative', according to Sampson, 'is to produce something which falls outside the class of any set of principles that might have been proposed to account for previous examples'. Or as Briskman proposed, 'really outstanding creative achievements have a habit of breaking, in important ways, with the tradition out of which they emerged'.[40] On this view, then, the created product is novel in the sense that it is incompatible with any set of standards which could have been inferred from previous creative practice in the same domain. (I will later argue that this account of the novelty of the created product cannot be sustained in its full generality.)

A second widely noted characteristic of the created product is its *exemplariness*. It has frequently been said in this regard that the created product can serve as a model for the production of, or sets standards for the evaluation of, future (possibly non-creative) productions in the same domain. Kant, for instance, claimed that created products 'must be models, i.e. exemplary [and] must serve as standards or rules of judgement for others'. And Koestler suggested that true creativity results in the 'invention of a new recipe' which can be used by

[39] Sampson, *Liberty and Language*, p. 105; and A. Rothenberg and C. Hausman, 'The Creativity Question', in *The Creativity Quest*, Durham, 1976, p. 23.

[40] Sampson, *Liberty and Language*, p. 105; and L. Briskman, 'Creative Product and Creative Process in Science and the Arts', *Inquiry* xxii (1980), p. 96.

others.[41] On this view, then, a product is creative only if (or only to the extent to which) it can serve as a model for others.

Finally, it has been suggested that the created product is an appropriate, but non-random, response to the circumstances of its production. Briskman, for instance, claimed that 'one of the most striking features about [created] products is their appropriateness, the "internal connection" which exists between these products and the backgrounds against which they emerge'. And Hausman has insisted that the creative process, far from being merely random, 'must include critical attentive effort that is relevant to the new structure that issues from the process'.[42] On this view, then, a product is creative only if, or only to the extent to which, it is an appropriate and non-random response to the circumstances in which it is produced.

In short, our basic settled beliefs about true human creativity appear to be these. The created product is novel, exemplary, and appropriate to the demands of the situation in which it is produced. The creative process, on the other hand, is neither random nor fully determined by antecedent rules or recipes. I take these basic beliefs as a tentative 'factual basis' against which to evaluate any account of true human creativity. In Section 5 below, I will present such an account. In Section 6, I will instantiate this general account in the form of an account of creativity which incorporates Chomsky's fundamental limitationist claims about true human creativity, and will there attempt to show that such an account of creativity is consistent with our basic settled beliefs about this phenomenon. Before doing so, though, I must first introduce considerations which are preliminary to the construction of a general account of human creativity.

4   *Constraints on Problem-Solving*

In developing a general account of true human creativity which incorporates Chomsky's basic limitationist claims about this

---

[41] Kant, *Critique of Judgment*, p. 151; and Koestler, *The Act of Creation*, p. 380.
[42] Briskman, 'Creative Product', p. 98; and C. Hausman, *A Discourse on Novelty and Creativity*, The Hague, 1975, p. 42.

phenomenon, I will adopt and adapt Briskman's suggestion that 'a scientific or artistic product is [creatively] valuable insofar as it constitutes or incorporates a solution to a problem'.[43] In order adequately to develop this suggestion, it will be useful first to consider the nature of problems in a bit more detail than Briskman himself does.

Nickles has recently suggested that problems 'cannot even be formulated, cannot exist, in the absence of rational constraints on their solution'. According to Nickles, 'these constraints . . . are not just there in the problem situation: together they largely define the problem and give it structure'.[44] A scientific problem, for instance, might be defined by constraints which require that the desired theoretical product constitute an explanation of some particular class of phenomena, that it be consistent with a particular theoretical and metaphysical framework, and with known relevant facts, and that it embody certain methodologically desirable features. In short, Nickles has suggested, in effect, that every problem can be defined by a system of constraints of the kind just illustrated. By developing Nickles's suggestion to this effect, we can, I think, construct a typology of kinds of problems which will be useful in explicating Briskman's suggestion that the created product 'constitutes or incorporates a solution to a problem'.

According to Nickles, the constraints which define a particular problem 'implicitly specify the range of acceptable [solutions, and thus] normally provide a heuristic guide or directive' for problem-solvers.[45] It is clear that the sets of constraints which define various problems can provide varying degrees of heuristic guidance in this sense.

(*a*) Some problems are defined by constraints which are *determinative*, in the sense that these constraints actually provide procedures for constructing adequate solutions for the

---

[43] Briskman, 'Creative Product', p. 95.

[44] T. Nickles, 'Can Scientific Constraints be Violated Rationally?', in T. Nickles, ed., *Scientific Discovery, Logic, and Rationality*, Dordrecht, 1980, p. 288; and Nickles, 'Scientific Discovery and the Future of Philosophy of Science', in Nickles, op. cit., p. 26.

[45] Nickles, 'Scientific Discovery', p. 37.

problems in question. In effect, an algorithm is available for the solution of such *routine* problems. For example, multiplication problems in elementary arithmetic are routine in this sense. Constraints on such problems define an algorithm, a procedure which can be applied mechanically to generate adequate solutions to these problems.

(*b*) Some problems are defined by constraints which are merely *limitative*, in the sense that these constraints do not provide procedures for constructing adequate solutions, but do implicitly specify necessary and sufficient conditions for such solutions. In effect, a solution-recognition procedure is available for such *well-defined* problems. A solution-candidate which satisfies the constraints on such a problem is *ipso facto* an adequate solution of that problem.[46] For example, the problem of theorem-hood is well-defined in this sense in many formal systems. Although there are necessary and sufficient conditions for the adequacy of proposed proofs of theorem-candidates in such systems, there are, in these systems, no mechanical procedures which can be employed to find (or to 'generate') proofs meeting these conditions for arbitrary theorem-candidates. Of course, a problem which is well-defined with respect to a given set of constraints may be transformed into a routine problem upon the discovery of suitable additional constraints.

(*c*) Some problems are defined by constraints which are merely *eliminative*, in the sense that they do not provide procedures for constructing adequate solutions, but do specify necessary (but not sufficient) conditions for adequate solutions. In effect, a solution-evaluation procedure is available for such *partially defined* problems. Although a solution-candidate which does satisfy the constraints on such a problem is not necessarily an adequate solution, a solution-candidate which fails to satisfy these constraints is *ipso facto* an inadequate solution. For example, design problems of many kinds may be partially defined in this sense. The architect's problem in designing a house may be constrained by financial considerations,

---

[46] See H. Simon, *Models of Discovery*, Dordrecht, 1977, p. 161.

peculiarities of the site, the cost and availability of materials, the building code, etc. These constraints specify necessary conditions for the adequacy of the design. But they do not specify sufficient conditions. Indeed, it may be impossible to specify sufficient conditions in this kind of context. Of course, a problem which is partially defined with respect to a given set of constraints may be transformed into a well-defined problem upon the discovery of suitable additional constraints.

(*d*) Some problems are defined by constraints which are merely *tentative*, in the sense that adequate solutions of such problems require the violation of one or more of these constraints. Clearly, constraints on such *radical* problems are not even eliminative. However, to say that the constraints on a radical problem are merely tentative is not to suggest that the solution of such a problem is totally unconstrained. An adequate solution to a radical problem must satisfy some of the constraints which initially defined that problem. Otherwise, of course, such a 'solution' would be a solution to quite a different problem. But radical problems are difficult, of course, precisely because the problem-solver does not and cannot beforehand know which of the initially defining constraints must be violated in order to obtain an adequate solution.[47] For example, many scientific problems are radical in this sense. It may be impossible, for instance, to accommodate certain facts to a given theory in accordance with acceptable methodological practices (e.g. in a non-*ad hoc* way). In this case, the problem of understanding certain phenomena may well be soluble only if we reject one (or more) of the prior constraints on this problem—only, for instance, if we revise the theory or reject certain of the facts or relax certain standards of methodological practice. Of course, a problem which is radical with respect to a particular set of constraints may be transformed into a partially defined problem when the problem-solver does discover which of these constraints must be violated in order to obtain an adequate solution.

---

[47] See Briskman, 'Creative Product', p. 101.

(*e*) Some problems appear to be defined by constraints which are quite *trivial*, in the sense that they do not, even tentatively, specify even necessary conditions for adequate solutions. Such *improvisational* problems appear to be quite common in the aesthetic domain.[48] The only initial constraints on adequate solutions to such problems appear to be those inherent in the medium within which such solutions are to be sought.[49] Of course, as they interact with their medium, problem-solvers gradually build up a system of constraints on their further activities: constraints implicit in the emerging product.[50] 'Constraints on his further choices then simply derive', according to Harrison, 'from what he may come to see as consistent or inconsistent with how he has already acted'.[51] Free improvisation in jazz performance is an example of an aesthetic activity which involves an improvisational problem in this sense.

Two features of this typology of problems are worth noting. First, this typology has the form of a hierarchy. A routine problem is thus *ipso facto* well defined, but not vice versa; a well-defined problem is *ipso facto* partially defined, but not vice versa; etc. Second, the 'rank' of a problem in this hierarchy is not absolute or fixed. Rather, the 'rank' of a problem is a function of the set of constraints in terms of which it is defined on some particular occasion. A problem which is, for instance, partially defined with respect to a particular set of constraints may be transformed into a well-defined problem upon the discovery of suitable additional constraints. (I think that it is reasonable to say, at least informally, that the problem remains the same in such cases. What changes is our knowledge about it, and about the methods required for its solution.)

Given this hierarchy of problems, we are, I think, now in a better position to develop Briskman's suggestion that creativity

---

[48] See E. Vivas, 'Naturalism and Creativity', in Tomas, *Creativity in the Arts*, p. 92.

[49] See Hausman, *A Discourse*, p. 61.

[50] See Tomas, 'Creativity in Art', p. 108.

[51] A. Harrison, *Making and Thinking*, Hassocks, 1978, p. 160.

is manifested in problem-solving. I attempt to do so in the next section.

5 Creativity as Problem-Solving

I have already mentioned Briskman's suggestion that the created product 'constitutes or incorporates a solution to a problem'. Given the typology of problems outlined in the previous section, we are now in a position to give a general account of creativity along the lines implicit in Briskman's suggestion.

As a first approximation to a fuller account, I would like to suggest that creativity is a matter of degree, and that the degree of creativity manifested in a particular product is inversely proportional to the 'strength' of the constraints on the problem for which that product is a solution. This is, I think, a plausible suggestion.

Clearly, no creativity is exhibited when an individual uses an available algorithm to solve a routine problem, the defining constraints on which are, as we have seen, of maximal strength. Of course, intelligence is required to apply the relevant algorithm in an appropriate way to the problem at issue.[52] But few, I think, would dispute the claim that the product which results from applying the relevant algorithm to a routine problem is not a created product. Using a reliable mechanical procedure for solving a problem is, it seems, the very antithesis of creative behaviour.

Clearly, some creativity may be exhibited when individuals solve a well-defined problem, the defining constraints on which are, as we have seen, weaker than those which define a routine problem. Of course, individuals who solve such a problem behave in a merely intelligent and non-creative fashion when they employ the available solution-recognition procedure to test the adequacy of the various solution-candidates which they may have constructed. This is so, of course, because such a procedure for determining the adequacy of proposed solution-candidates is a reliable mechanical procedure. We might say, then, that a

[52] Ibid., pp. 71–3.

non-routine problem consists of two sub-problems—the 'generation' of solution-candidates, and the evaluation of proposed solution-candidates—and that in the case of well-defined problems, the availability of a solution-recognition procedure renders the second of these two sub-problems a routine problem.[53] Given the unavailability in this case of a reliable mechanical procedure for 'generating' adequate solution-candidates, however, problem-solvers must themselves discover these in a way which is not determined by the constraints which define their problem. And it is in this, I think, that the creativity of their efforts consists.

I hope that it is clear that similar remarks could be made about the locus and degree of creativity which must be exhibited if the problem-solver is to solve a partially-defined, radical or improvisational problem.

In short, then, I propose, as a first approximation, that a product is creative (*ceteris paribus*) just to the extent to which the constraints which define the problem for which it is a solution fail to determine the process by which that product is produced. I believe that I have indicated how this proposal accounts for and explicates common and well-founded intuitions about the relative degrees of creativity which are characteristic of various created products. The strength of the constraints which define a particular problem is one factor, then, in determining the degree of creativity characteristic of products which are solutions for that problem.

But a second factor is also important in determining the degree of creativity characteristic of a particular product. Recall my suggestion, in Section 4, that the 'rank' of a problem in the hierarchy of problems is not fixed, but can instead be transformed by the discovery of additional relevant constraints. Now consider two individuals confronting the same problem, defined in terms of the same set of initial constraints. The first individual solves this problem and, in doing so, discovers a hitherto unknown reliable mechanical procedure which can be

[53] See A. Newell *et al.*, *The Processes of Creative Thinking*, Santa Monica, 1959, p. 14.

brought to bear on problems of this general kind. The second individual, on the other hand, also solves this problem, but does so in an *ad hoc* way, without discovering the reliable mechanical procedure in question. It is clear, I think, that we would want to say that the first individual was more creative than the second individual. For the second individual merely solved the particular problem with which both he and the first individual were concerned, while the first individual solved this problem and also made a contribution, in effect, to the solution of other problems of the same general kind. Her contribution consists, of course, in the discovery of additional, hitherto unknown constraints on this problem. I would like to suggest, then, that the degree of creativity characteristic of a particular product also depends on the extent to which the production of that product results in the discovery of constraints on solutions to the problem which it solves which were unknown before its production.

As a second approximation, then, I would like to suggest that the degree of creativity characteristic of a particular product depends on two factors. First, it depends on and varies inversely with the 'strength' of the constraints which initially defined the problem for which it is a solution. And second, it depends on and varies directly with the degree to which the production of the product reveals the existence and relevance of constraints on the problem for which it is a solution which were hitherto unknown: a discovery which, of course, has the effect of increasing the 'strength' of the constraints which define the problem in question (and others of its kind).

One further complication to the schema is required. I think that it is important to distinguish kinds, as well as degrees, of creativity. In particular, I think it is useful to distinguish between subjective creativity and intersubjective creativity. The contrast between these kinds of creativity emerges clearly, I think, if we consider the possibility that an individual might act creatively, in some sense, even in solving a problem for which an algorithm has been discovered. For such an individual might not know even of the existence of the algorithm in question. And for an individual in this position, the constraints taken into account in formulating and trying to solve such a problem are of less than maximal 'strength'. Such an individual needs, in some sense, to be just as creative as were those individuals who solved problems of this kind before anyone had discovered the algorithm in question. I would like to suggest, then, that the degree of subjective creativity exhibited by individuals in solving a problem depends on the 'strength' of those constraints which they actually take into account in formulating that problem. Of course, we would not, I think, want to say that ignorant individuals of the kind described make a creative contribution to the tradition of enquiry within which their problem falls. For this reason, then, I would like to suggest that the degree of intersubjective creativity characteristic of a product depends on the 'strength' of the constraints on the problem for which it is a solution which would be taken into account by an ideally rational and well-informed participant in the tradition of enquiry within which that problem falls.

Three remarks about this distinction are in order here:

First, it should be noted that degrees of subjective creativity are characteristic of problem-solvers, while degrees of inter-subjective creativity are characteristic of products. Two interesting consequences follow from this difference. First, it is clear that an individual may exhibit a high degree of subjective creativity in producing a product which itself has a low degree of intersubjective creativity. Second, it is also clear that two individuals who solve the 'same' problem may exhibit different degrees of subjective creativity. For the version of the problem solved by one individual may be more highly constrained than the version solved by the other individual.

Second, it is important, I think, to define the degree of creativity which is characteristic of a product in the inter-subjective terms suggested, and not in terms of constraints which could be said 'objectively' to define the problem for which that product is a solution. Consider the individual who provides an *ad hoc* solution for a problem of a kind for the solution of which an algorithm is later discovered. Surely, we would want to say that such an individual solved the problem in a creative way. But given that it is timelessly true, if it is ever true, that the constraints which 'objectively' define this problem are of maximal 'strength', the solution proposed is, therefore, objectively quite uncreative. Since this characterization is intuitively unacceptable, the degree of creativity characteristic of a created product is thus best determined as a function of the intersubjective constraints which define the problem for which that product is a solution.

Third, when we speak of the 'true creativity' characteristic of the greatest aesthetic and scientific achievements, it is clear that we are referring to the intersubjective creativity of the created products which constitute those achievements, and not to the subjective creativity of the individuals whose achievements these products are. And this, I think, is as it should be.[54] Of course, it should be clear from my definitions that an individual who produces a product which manifests a high degree of intersubjective creativity *ipso facto* manifests a high degree of subjective creativity. For the constraints which subjectively define a problem can be 'weaker' but not 'stronger' than those which intersubjectively define that problem. Highly creative products are thus *ipso facto* the products only of highly creative individuals. And this too, it seems clear, is as it should be.

On my account, then, the degree of creativity characteristic of a particular product is a function, first, of the 'strength' of the constraints which initially and intersubjectively define the problem for which that product is a solution, and second, of the increment, if any, in the 'strength' of these constraints which results from the discovery, during the process of production, of intersubjectively 'novel' constraints on problems of this general kind.

In the next section, I will attempt to incorporate Chomsky's characteristically limitationist claims about creativity into the general account of creativity so far developed. I will also

---

[54] See Briskman, 'Creative Product', p. 89.

attempt to show that the resulting account of creativity is indeed compatible with those basic settled beliefs about this phenomenon which I outlined in Section 3.

6 *Creativity within Limits*

As I have already pointed out, Chomsky's most interesting claims about creativity are embodied in the limits thesis, according to which there are biologically determined and fixed limits on the scientific theories and aesthetically significant objects which human beings can creatively produce and find intelligible.

Given the general account of creativity recommended here, we can reformulate the limits thesis in what will, I hope, be a revealing way. To say, in terms of this account, that there are limits on human creativity is to say, in effect, that there are limits on the kinds of problems which human beings can formulate and solve. And this in turn entails that there are limits on the kinds of constraints in terms of which human beings can define problems which are humanly soluble.

Of course, on my account of creativity, there is nothing mysterious about the claim that creativity takes place within limits. This claim follows directly from the suggestion that created products are solutions to problems, and that problems are defined by constraints which set limits within which the production of created products takes place. But the fact, if such it be, that creativity is constrained in this way suggests only that creativity takes place within the *local* limits set by the constraints which define the particular problems for which created products are solutions. However, the limits thesis appears to entail the existence of limits on creativity which are not merely local in this way. In this section, then, I will try to show that the general account of creativity which I recommend is consistent with the existence of those *global* limits on creativity the existence of which the limits thesis entails. I will also try to show that the resulting limitationist account of creativity is consistent with our basic settled beliefs about this phenomenon.

It is important to notice that the claim that there are global limits on human creativity entails that there is a biologically fixed set of constraints in terms of which human beings can define humanly soluble problems. This claim does not, however, entail either that every member of this fixed set is a defining constraint on every humanly soluble problem, or that there are fixed 'core constraints' on every humanly soluble problem. (There are fixed 'core constraints' on every humanly soluble problem if there is a subset of the fixed set of problem-defining constraints which is common to every such problem.) Indeed, the limits thesis is clearly compatible with the possibility that every humanly-soluble problem is defined by a distinct subset of the fixed set of problem-defining constraints. This thesis is only inconsistent with the claim that there are no limits on the kinds of constraints in terms of which humanly soluble problems can be defined. Of course, the limits thesis offers no characterization of this fixed set of problem-defining constraints. It is, as I have already remarked, a metaphysical thesis about human creativity.

In fact, it is reasonable to assume, as Chomsky himself does, that the fixed set of problem-defining constraints posited by the limits thesis is at least partially ordered with respect to the accessibility of its members.[55] On this account, then, we would expect the subset of problem-defining constraints which limit and guide general human problem-solving at some time t to differ from the subset of constraints which limit and guide problem-solving at some other time t'.

Indeed, it is interesting to ask how human beings might gain access to problem-defining constraints to which they had not previously had access. I would like to suggest that this occurs as a consequence of attempts to formulate and to solve those problems which can be defined in terms of currently available constraints. Of course, problems which are intersubjectively radical at a given time are likely to be especially salient in the process of discovering constraints which were intersubjectively

---

[55]   See N. Chomsky, *Language and Responsibility*, Hassocks, 1979, p. 65.

unavailable before that time. This is so, of course, because radical problems are, as we have already seen, problems which can be formulated, but cannot be solved in terms of a given set of constraints. To solve such a problem, it is necessary to violate some of the constraints by which it was initially defined. And the problem-solver who does successfully discover which of these initially-defining constraints must be violated might in this way discover new, more abstract constraints which are consistent both with the solution of the radical problem at issue and with the solution of those problems which had previously been formulated and solved in terms of the more specific constraints the inadequacy of which this radical problem revealed. Indeed, on this account, it is appropriate to say that the problem-solver discovers, rather than invents or creates, previously unknown constraints. According to the limits thesis, all of the problem-defining constraints in principle available to human problem-solvers are, in effect, latent in the innate cognitive faculties which mediate human problem-solving. In short, creators, on this account, merely gain access to potential constraints on their productive activities with which they were, in a sense, already biologically endowed.

I believe, then, that we can appropriately interpret Chomsky's limits thesis as entailing the claims (*a*) that there is a biologically fixed and partially ordered set of problem-defining constraints in terms of which every humanly soluble problem can be formulated, and (*b*) that human beings progressively gain access to the remoter elements of this ordered set through their attempts to solve the problems which they can formulate in terms of the constraints to which they have already gained access. Creativity, in these terms, takes place within the global limits defined by this set of constraints, but at the same time may involve the violation of those local limits in terms of which particular problems are defined at some given stage of human intellectual development. What remains to be shown, of course, is whether such a limitationist account of creativity is compatible with those basic settled beliefs about creativity which I discussed in Section 3.

I will now try to show that the account of globally limited creativity which I have developed here is compatible with the basis settled belief that the created product is novel.

(*a*) On one account, the created product is held to be novel in the sense that no antecedently available recipe or set of rules could have sufficed to determine the production of that product. Now it may appear that the limitationist account of creativity developed here is in fact incompatible with this claim. For this account appears to entail the claim that recipes or rules are always antecedently available, if they are ever available, in the sense that they are always latent in the biologically fixed innate problem-solving faculties which we attribute to human beings in accordance with this account. In other words, it is a consequence of this account of globally limited creativity that the biologically fixed set of constraints in terms of which every humanly soluble problem can be formulated is a feature of the innate intellectual endowment of every normal human being and is therefore always at least potentially available to limit and guide the problem-solving behaviour of human beings.

This appearance of incompatibility is deceptive. As we have already seen, it is independently important to recognize a distinction between the intersubjective antecedent availability and the objective antecedent existence of problem-defining constraints. But it is clear that the account of globally limited creativity recommended here entails only the objective antecedent existence, and not the intersubjective antecedent availability, of those rules or recipes which do guide the production of created products. As we have seen, constraints which are on this account always antecedently existent are not *ipso facto* always antecedently available, in the intersubjective sense, as constraints on actual human problem-solving activities. But in this case, of course, there is no incompatibility between the claim that created products are novel in the sense under discussion, and the claim that human creativity takes place within global limits of the kind at issue. For created products are novel in this sense only in the sense that their production could not have been determined by rules or recipes which were antecedently available in the intersubjective sense.

Notice, furthermore, that Chomsky's limitationist account of creativity does not entail the claim that all humanly soluble problems are objectively routine. It does, of course, entail the claim that all humanly soluble problems are definable in terms of constraints drawn from a biologically fixed set of constraints. But the subset of this set in terms of which a given humanly soluble problem can objectively be defined need not be determinative in strength. This point only strengthens my claim that Chomsky's limitationist account of creativity is consistent with the claim that created products are novel in the sense at issue. If the constraints which define a problem (even objectively) are not determinative in strength, then it is trivially true that no antecedently available set of rules could have sufficed to determine the production of a product which solves that problem.

(*b*) On a second account, the created product is held to be novel in the sense that some at least of its characteristics are unpredictable. Now it may appear that the account of globally limited creativity developed here is incompatible with this claim. This account appears, in particular, to entail the claim that, before the discovery of the relevant algorithm, solutions for objectively routine problems were creative, despite the fact that knowledge of this algorithm would have enabled us to predict the characteristics of the products which constitute these solutions. In other words, it might seem that we could predict the characteristics of intersubjectively creative solutions to objectively routine problems if we knew the content and structure of the biologically fixed set of problem-defining constraints which are on this account attributed to human beings.

But, of course, it is no part of the account of globally limited creativity developed here that we could antecedently know the content and structure of this fixed set of constraints. Indeed, it is a feature of this account that human beings obtain knowledge about the content and structure of this set only as a by-product of their creative problem-solving activities. In other words, the characteristics of created products are on this account predictable, when they are predictable at all, only with respect to knowledge about the fixed set of problem-defining constraints which is obtained as a result of, and is thus unavailable before, the production of that product.

(*c*) On a third account, the created product is held to be novel in the sense that it is incompatible with any set of standards which could have been inferred from previous creative practice in the same domain. Now it may appear that the account of globally limited creativity is in fact incompatible with this claim. This account appears, in particular, to entail the claim that the individual who solves a well-defined or partially defined problem in fact produces a product which is creative to some degree. But such a product is not, of course, incompatible with (all) antecedently available standards, since these standards are, in effect, set by the limitative or eliminative constraints which define the problem for which such a product is a solution.

The account of globally limited creativity recommended here thus appears to diverge at this point from our basic settled beliefs about the novelty of created products. I do not think, however, that this is a defect of this limitationist account of creativity. I think that we have independent reasons to suppose that this basic settled belief cannot be sustained in its full generality.

Consider the individual who succeeds in proving a new theorem in a particular formal system. Assume that this formal system is one in which the theorem-proving problem is well-defined, but non-routine. Assume, in other words, that a proof-checking algorithm is, while a proof-finding algorithm is not, available for this formal system. It is clear, I think, that we would want intuitively to say that the proof discovered by such an individual is a created product. And we can, of course, say just that if we accept the account of creativity recommended here. Products which are solutions for non-routine but well-defined problems are to some degree creative on that account.

But we could, of course, say no such thing were we to accept, in its full generality, the requirement that the created product be incompatible with antecedently available standards in the relevant domain of enquiry. For the proof in question obviously is, and indeed must be, compatible with antecedently available standards which determine the validity of proposed proofs in the formal system in question. Since my account is, while the requirement at issue is not, compatible with our intuitions about this kind of case, I conclude that we must limit the applicability of this requirement. It is thus no defect of the limitationist account of creativity developed here that it is incompatible, at least in some cases, with the requirement that created products be incompatible with antecedently available standards.

I will now try to show that the account of globally limited creativity developed here is compatible with the basic settled belief that the created product is exemplary. Indeed, this account shows how it is possible for created products to be exemplary in an intersubjective and not merely in an objective sense. I showed in Section 5 that the created product is exemplary in the sense that (or, to the extent to which) its production reveals the existence of previously unknown constraints on problems of the kind which it solves. But I did not there show how it is possible for individuals to recognize and to identify the particular ways in which a created product is exemplary in this sense. Sometimes, of course, the created product reveals particular previously unknown constraints in a straightforward and explicit way, as when it has the form of a recipe or set of rules for solving problems of a certain kind— problems which could previously be solved only in an *ad hoc* way. But this need not always be the case, and indeed rarely is so in the aesthetic domain in particular, where the novel constraints which a product reveals have to be inferred from the characteristics of that product. Of course, the inference required in such cases is easily accounted for if we assume, as we can on the limitationist account of creativity, that every normal individual has access, in principle, to a common and biologically fixed set of problem-defining constraints. Individuals who recognize that a creator has gained access to previously unknown problem-defining constraints are, on this account, able to do so because they too are capable of gaining access to such constraints. It is for this reason, then, that created products can be exemplary in the required intersubjective sense.

Finally, I think it can be shown that the account of globally limited creativity developed here is compatible with the basic settled belief that the created product is an appropriate and non-random response to the circumstances of its production. Indeed, the created product is an appropriate response to the situation in which it is produced, on this account, in just the sense in which a solution to a problem is an appropriate response to the situation in which the problem is posed. Likewise, the created product is a non-random response to the situation in which it is produced, on this account, because that situation involves constraints on the problem for which that product is a solution—constraints which guide the production of that product in a non-random way.

In short, I believe that it is fruitful to embed Chomsky's limits thesis within the general account of true human creativity which I developed in Section 5. Within the framework defined by that account, the limits thesis can be interpreted as entailing the claim that every humanly soluble problem can be formulated in terms of constraints drawn from a biologically fixed and partially ordered set of constraints which are, in principle, available to guide human beings in their problem-solving activities. I also believe that I have shown that this integrated, limitationist account of creativity is compatible with those of our basic settled beliefs about creativity which provide a 'factual basis' against which to test any general account of creativity. In the next section, I will consider some objections to this account of globally limited creativity.

7 Objections to Limitationism

In the previous section, I tried to show how Chomsky's characteristically limitationist claims about true human creativity could be embedded in a general account of creativity, according to which created products are solutions to certain kinds of problems. I suggested, in particular, that Chomsky's limits thesis could be interpreted as entailing the claim that there are biologically fixed limits on the kinds of constraints in terms of which humanly soluble problems can be defined. In this section, I will consider a number of objections to this claim.

I have, in effect, already considered and rejected one fundamental objection to the account of globally limited creativity which has been developed here. In the previous section, I rejected the suggestion that this account is incompatible with those basic settled beliefs about creativity which can be taken to constitute a tentative 'factual basis' with which any adequate account of creativity must be compatible. Nevertheless, there are other plausible objections to this account, though I believe that they too can be met.

Sampson has presented three major arguments which are alleged to undermine the account of globally limited creativity which Chomsky advocates and which I have developed in more detail here. The first of these arguments is general, while the other two involve more specific claims.

(a) Sampson's major general objection to Chomsky's account of true creativity is based on his claim that we regard 'the production of novel works of art, or new scientific theories, as "creative" activities because of the fact that, at any given time, it is impossible to delimit the range of potential future products of these activities'.[56] And this claim, according to Sampson, flatly contradicts Chomsky's limitationist claim that creativity 'takes place within . . . a system of constraints' or global limits.

According to Sampson, it is possible to defend the notion of creativity which he recommends, and which he sees as inconsistent with Chomsky's account of creativity because language 'gives us some of the most striking positive evidence that Man is creative in the richer sense' which Sampson prefers.[57] Before considering Sampson's two specific arguments to

[56] Sampson, *Liberty and Language*, p. 105.
[57] Ibid., p. 212.

this effect, however, I would first like to consider in a bit more detail Sampson's own notion of creativity, and some of his general critical remarks about Chomsky's limitationist account of creativity.

According to Sampson, 'acts which are truly creative cannot, by definition, be predicted'; to suppose otherwise involves the *scientistic* assumption that 'all human phenomena can be analysed by the scientific method'. Sampson claims that Chomsky's account of creativity is indeed scientistic in this sense since 'when we ask what Chomsky means when he calls men creative, he turns out to refer to [their] ability to behave in conformity to certain fixed, rigorous rules'.[58] Two remarks are in order here.

First, it apparently follows from Sampson's claims here that he takes behaviour which conforms to rules to be behaviour which can *ipso facto* be predicted. But I do not see that rule-conforming behaviour is *ipso facto* predictable behaviour. As I have already pointed out, it is useful to distinguish between rules which determine and rules which merely guide behaviour. The tactical rules with which a chess-playing computer is programmed may determine its responses at any given point in the game; they may determine which of the moves which is possible at that point is actually made. Knowledge of the rules which thus determine the behaviour of the computer would enable us, then, to predict that behaviour. Rule-determined behaviour may well be predictable behaviour. But the rules of chess—as opposed to tactical rules for playing chess—are not behaviour-determining in this way. Of course, the rules of chess guide the behaviour of the chess player by implicitly defining, at any given point in the game, a range of possible moves. But conformity merely to the rules of chess does not suffice to determine which of these possible moves is actually made. Knowledge of the rules which thus guide, but do not determine, the behaviour of the chess player does not enable us to predict that behaviour. Rule-guided behaviour may well be unpredictable

<hr />

[58] Ibid., pp. 107–8.

behaviour. It seems, then, that Sampson is wrong to suggest that behaviour in conformity to rules is *ipso facto* predictable behaviour.

Second, Sampson's characterization of Chomsky's account of creativity is a grossly unsympathetic one. It is of course true that Chomsky has said that the language-user's ability to produce and understand novel utterances manifests a kind of creativity. It is also of course true that Chomsky has suggested that this ability can be accounted for by supposing that the language-user has mastered a system of rules. But Chomsky has never suggested, and has in fact consistently denied, that the behaviour by which this 'creative' ability is manifested is predictable behaviour. If 'scientism' involves the supposition that all human behaviour is predictable, then Chomsky cannot rightly be accused of scientism simply because he has suggested that linguistic creativity is manifested in rule-guided behaviour. As we have already seen, Chomsky has explicitly insisted that linguistic behaviour is not rule-determined behaviour, that it is not predictable behaviour, and that it is not, therefore, uncreative behaviour in at least one of the senses in which Sampson characterizes behaviour as uncreative.

My last remarks in fact suggest another difficulty in interpreting Sampson's account of creativity. While it is true that Sampson characterizes creative behaviour as unpredictable behaviour ('by definition'), it is also true, as we have already seen, that he characterizes creative activities in terms of our inability 'to delimit the range of potential future products of these activities'. It is clear that these two characterizations of creativity are not equivalent. Behaviour the range of which is delimited, whether by rules or by laws, need not be predictable behaviour, since the relevant rules or laws may merely delimit a range of possibilities without determining which of these possibilities will be realized in any particular situation. Of course, behaviour which is predictable is *ipso facto* behaviour the range of which is delimited; and behaviour the range of which is not even delimited is *ipso facto* unpredictable. What these considerations suggest, then, is that Sampson's characterization of creative behaviour in terms of its unpredictability must be interpreted as dependent on his more fundamental characteriz-ation of creative behaviour as behaviour the potential range of which it is impossible to delimit. For the latter characterization implies, but is not implied by, the former. Chomsky can thus consistently claim that creative behaviour is both unpredictable and delimited in its range of possibilities. And Sampson cannot, therefore, refute Chomsky's limitationist account of creativity merely by establishing that creative behaviour is unpredictable; he must instead establish that the range of creative possibilities in a particular domain cannot be delimited. I shall now try to show that Sampson's examination of the semantic aspect of language use succeeds in establishing merely that semantically creative behaviour is unpredictable and thus fails to undermine Chomsky's account of creativity.

Sampson presents two major specific arguments, both of which concern aspects of human semantic behaviour, which are intended to show that Chomsky's limitationist account of human creativity cannot be sustained.

(*b*) Sampson distinguishes 'among the grammatical sequences of words, those which are "sensical" . . . from those which are nonsensical', and claims that 'it is with respect to sensicality . . . that language-use is creative . . . [in the sense that] there will be no specifiable limits on the ways in which the usage of various communities may differ'. According to Sampson, semantic creativity in this sense involves 'render[ing] sensical some word-sequences which were previously grammatical but non-sensical'.[59]

Let us consider one of Sampson's examples of this kind of semantic creativity. According to Sampson, the sentence 'HORSELESS CARRIAGES TRAVEL RAPIDLY was non-sensical in 1700 but is a mere truism today'.[60] What does Sampson mean when he says that this sentence 'was nonsensical in 1700'? The answer to this question is, I am afraid, not entirely clear. Sampson does explicitly claim that this sentence

---

[59] Sampson, *Liberty and Language*, pp. 118-9.
[60] Ibid., p. 119.

'was not just *false* at the earlier date', and he elsewhere characterizes another nonsensical sentence as one which 'could not
possibly be true'.[61] But this characterization is not very helpful.
If the sentence *Horseless carriages travel rapidly* was nonsensical
in 1700 in the sense that it 'could not possibly be true', then
how has this sentence become today a 'mere truism'? Possibly,
Sampson means to suggest that a nonsensical sentence is one
which could not possibly be true so long as the meanings of
its component expressions are held constant, and that nonsensical sentences become sensical (or vice versa) when meaning-
change of a relevant kind occurs. But this suggestion seems to
be refuted by Sampson's own discussion of this example. He
says, in particular, that this sentence 'was *nonsensical*, provided
. . . that HORSELESS is understood to mean "not designed to
be harnessed to a draught animal" (as it did when HORSELESS
CARRIAGE became a common phrase)'—i.e. as it did when the
sentence *Horseless carriages travel rapidly* became a 'mere
truism'.[62] Apparently, then, Sampson does not consider
meaning-change to be necessary in order to render sensical
'word-sequences which were previously grammatical but nonsensical'.

Let us begin again, momentarily ignoring Sampson's explicit
account of nonsensicality. I am not myself certain that the
intuitive distinction between sense and nonsense can be explicated in any simple or satisfactory way. A number of distinct
factors seem to interact in giving rise to whatever intuitions we
may seem to have about this distinction. So, while I shall
propose an alternative to Sampson's account of this distinction,
I do not suggest that this alternative account adequately
explicates the intuitive distinction. Nevertheless, while my
account of this distinction is stipulative, rather than explicative,
it will, I think, serve as an adequate basis for interpreting and
evaluating Sampson's argument.

I thus suggest that we draw the sensical/nonsensical distinction
in the following way. At any given time, there are sentences

[61] Sampson, *Liberty and Language*, p. 119.
[62] Ibid.

which are accepted, by a person or a population, as obviously and unproblematically true, and which, in virtue of their logical and evidential relations to other sentences, could not be taken to be false without undermining in a radical way the belief system of the person or population in question. Let S be the conjunction of the sentences which report these 'core beliefs'. A nonsensical sentence, then, is one which is inconsistent with S, while a sensical sentence is one which is consistent with S. On this account, then, a sentence which is nonsensical is one which could not possibly be taken to be true, so long as the conjunction S is accepted as true. A sentence which is non-sensical in this sense may become sensical if and when the 'core beliefs' with which it is inconsistent are themselves abandoned or revised in some appropriate way.

Actually, I am inclined to suppose that my stipulative account of the sensical/nonsensical distinction would be acceptable to Sampson; that he may indeed merely have chosen an unfortunate form of words ('could not possibly be true') with which to express ideas about nonsensicality which are approximately those made explicit here. I have two reasons for supposing this. First, Sampson endorses recent critical discussions of the distinction between analytic and synthetic sentences, and my explicit stipulative account of the sensical/nonsensical distinction is loosely derived from these discussions.[63] Second, my account easily enables us to reconstruct some of Sampson's own remarks about the nonsensicality of particular sentences. For instance, Sampson claims that the sentence 'COLOURLESS GREEN IDEAS SLEEP FURIOUSLY makes no sense', and the reasons he adduces for this claim are these: 'ideas have no visual appear-ance and do not sleep, nothing can be both colourless and green', etc.[64] In terms of the account of nonsensicality which I recommend, we can easily reconstruct these considerations in the following terms. The sentence in question is nonsensical because we (or, at least, for just those who) have 'core beliefs' which are inconsistent with this sentence—namely, the beliefs

---

[63] Ibid., pp. 125-6.
[64] Ibid., p. 118.

that there is nothing which is both colourless and green, that ideas have none of the characteristics which are associated with visual perception, etc. So I think that my account of non-sensicality might reasonably be supposed to be an account which should be acceptable to Sampson.

Let us suppose, then, that the nonsensical sentences for a particular population at a given time are just those sentences which are inconsistent with the 'core beliefs' of the population at that time. It follows, then, that Sampson's claim that there can, 'with respect to sensicality . . . be no specifiable limits on the ways in which the usage of various communities may differ' entails the claim that there can be no specifiable limits on the ways in which the 'core beliefs' of various communities may differ.[65] But, in fact, it is on just this issue that Chomsky's limitationist account of creativity does diverge from Sampson's views, as Sampson rightly suggests. For Chomsky has, in effect, suggested that there are limits on the range of possible systems of 'core beliefs'. He has said, for instance, that the innate cognitive faculties which make it possible for individuals to acquire systems of common sense and theoretical beliefs 'involve fixed and highly restrictive schemata' of a kind which 'sharply constrain the class of humanly accessible' systems of beliefs.[66] According to Chomsky, then, there may be a biologically fixed range of possible systems of 'core beliefs'; systems of 'core beliefs' can, on Chomsky's account, differ only within the limits defined by this biologically fixed range.

Now Sampson appears to attempt to refute Chomsky's position on this question by suggesting that it entails the claim that 'the borderline between analytic and synthetic sentences should be . . . clear'. And this claim, according to Sampson, is false, since 'grammatical sentences are continually shifting across [this borderline] as our knowledge grows'.[67] But does Chomsky's position really entail the existence of a sharp analytic/synthetic distinction? I do not think that it does.

---

[65] Sampson, *Liberty and Language*, pp. 118–9.
[66] Chomsky, *Reflections*, pp. 154 and 25.
[67] Sampson, *Liberty and Language*, p. 126.

In line with our interpretative policy, let us redefine the analytic sentences as those which report the 'core beliefs' current in some population. In this case, Chomsky's limitationist account of human intellectual capacities implies the existence of a sharp general distinction between analytic and synthetic sentences if and only if it implies the existence of a set of 'common core beliefs'—a set of beliefs which is common to every possible system of 'core beliefs'. Certainly, the existence of such 'common core beliefs' would imply the existence of a sharp general distinction between analytical and synthetic sentences—at least on the interpretation accepted here. Those sentences reporting 'common core beliefs' would be analytic in the sense that they would always be taken to be true, by any human population, whatever other sentences were accepted as true by such a population. On the other hand, there could be no sharp general analytic/synthetic distinction if such a set of 'common core beliefs' did not exist. If there are no 'common core beliefs', then any possible belief can either be or not be a 'core belief' in some possible system of human beliefs. But in this case, any sentence reporting a belief can shift across the borderline between analytic and synthetic, and there can consequently be no sharp general distinction between these kinds of sentences. But Chomsky's limitationist account of human intellectual capacities does not, of course, imply the existence of a set of 'common core beliefs'. The claim that there are limits on possible systems of beliefs does not entail the claim that each such system must share certain beliefs with every other such system. The claim that there are limits on systems of human beliefs is consistent with the claim, which Chomsky actually endorses, that there may be no beliefs which are common to every possible system of beliefs. There is, then, no merit to Sampson's claim that Chomsky's limitationist account of creativity implies the existence of a sharp general distinction between analytic and synthetic sentences.

I have already suggested that Sampson's discussion of semantic creativity succeeds in establishing, not that there are no limits on semantic creativity, but merely that semantically creative behaviour is unpredictable. It is, I think, clear that semantically creative behaviour of the kind under discussion is unpredictable behaviour. Sampson is clearly right when he suggests that 'it is not possible to predict a division of the grammatical sentences into sensical and nonsensical'.[68] But the unpredictability of semantically creative behaviour of this kind is entirely consistent with Chomsky's limitationist claim that such behaviour 'takes place within . . . a system of constraints'. Knowledge of such a system of constraints would enable us to predict that semantically creative behaviour will be confined to a range of possibilities defined by those constraints. Such knowledge would not, however, enable us to predict which particular possibility within the given range will be realized in response to the various cognitive pressures operative at some particular time. As Chomsky himself has said, 'to foresee the achievements of great artists or the future discoveries of science . . . seems a hopeless quest'.[69]

Sampson's discussion of the creativity involved in 'render[ing] sensical sentences which were previously grammatical but nonsensical' has not, in short, established that Chomsky is wrong to claim that 'fixed and highly restrictive schemata [may] sharply constrain the class of humanly accessible' systems of beliefs.

(*c*) Sampson claims that 'there is no telling what properties will be seized on to extend the applicability [of a word] from those phenomena which have previously been [designated by that word] to novel phenomena needing to be named'. The kind of semantic creativity which is involved in extending the applicability of a word is, then, apparently understood by Sampson to involve no limits. According to Sampson, there is 'no fixed stock of simple concepts, from which we can pick out a few as criterial for the use' of a given word.[70]

Presumably, the alternative to Sampson's position here is expressed by Chomsky when he says that 'new entities are

---

[68] Sampson, *Liberty and Language*, p. 119.
[69] Chomsky, *Language and Responsibility*, p. 76.
[70] Sampson, *Liberty and Language*, p. 127.

assigned correctly to a "sort" and designated by a sortal predicate just in case they share [with other entities already designated by the sortal predicate] the "essential properties" [of the sort], whatever they are'.[71] For it appears to follow from this claim that there are limits beyond which we cannot appropriately extend the applicability of a given word—at least without changing the meaning of that word. These limits are, apparently, determined by the 'essential properties' of the 'natural kind' designated by the word in question. (I hasten to add that Chomsky has stressed that the properties of individuals or of 'natural kinds' are 'essential', on his account, only relative 'to the systems of language and commonsense understanding'.[72])

What sort of evidence does Sampson present to show that he is right and Chomsky is wrong about the kind of semantic creativity which is involved in extending the applicability of a word to cover novel phenomena? Sampson's evidence is, in fact, derived from Wittgenstein's discussion of games. According to Sampson, Wittgenstein's discussion shows that we 'may confidently predict that the word GAME will in future be used for things different in kind from any of our contemporary games, but we cannot predict what features of these novel things will cause them to be called games'.[73]

I do not think that Sampson's position here can be sustained. It apparently follows from Sampson's Wittgensteinian account of semantic creativity that we might creatively extend the range of the word *game* to cover some novel activity simply because that activity shares with some other activity, already called a game, some property which this activity itself need not share with all of the other activities also already called games, and which, indeed, it need share with none of these other activities. But if this is the way in which semantic creativity of this kind works, then we ought appropriately to be able to call nearly everything a game. There are an immense number of properties which are characteristic of many activities which are not

---

[71] Chomsky, *Reflections*, p. 45.
[72] Ibid., p. 46.
[73] Sampson, *Liberty and Language*, p. 127.

currently called games, each of which is characteristic of at least one activity already called a game. It follows from Sampson's account, then, that we ought rightly to be able to regard each of these other activities as a game.

But, surely, this cannot be the case. Tennis and conversation, to adapt one of Sampson's own examples, both involve turn-taking. But is conversation rightly to be regarded as a game? Of course, Sampson might urge that conversation can meta-phorically be regarded as a game, and, as indeed he does, that 'there is no difference other than a difference of degree between literal and metaphorical usage'.[74] This is a plausible suggestion, but it founders, I think, on the fact that metaphorical usage can be stretched to the breaking point. It is not always illuminating to call something a game simply because it shares a property with some activity already regarded as a game. And this fact tells against Sampson's account of the kind of semantic creativity involved in extending the usage of a word.

I think that Sampson is wrong, then, to suggest that there are no limits on the ways in which the usage of a particular word can creatively be extended. Chomsky is probably right to suggest that the ways in which we can creatively extend the usage of a word are limited by our beliefs about the 'essential properties' of the 'natural kind' designated by that word.

Of course, Sampson further objects to such an account that it entails the existence of 'a sharp distinction between analytic and synthetic sentences'—i.e. because those sentences would be analytic (i.e. true in virtue of the meanings of their component expressions) which attribute to the exemplars of a particular 'natural kind' any of the 'essential properties' of that kind.[75] Can this objection in fact be sustained? I do not think that it can. As Chomsky has urged, the 'essential properties' of a 'natural kind' are relative to our evolving systems of common sense and scientific beliefs. We might thus discover, for instance, that a property which we had taken to be an 'essential property' of a given 'natural kind' is not, in fact, characteristic of all

---

[74] Sampson, *Liberty and Language*, p. 129.
[75] Ibid., p. 128.

exemplars of that kind. But in this case, there can be no sharp general analytic/synthetic distinction because a sentence which was analytic before such a discovery becomes (synthetically) false after such a discovery. Notice, furthermore, that this possibility does not entail that there are no limits on the ways in which the usage of a word can creatively be extended. For the result of such a discovery as I have described is a *change*, not an extension, of usage. (Wittgenstein's argument does not, after all, depend on the possibility that we might, without any reference even to 'family resemblances', simply come to use a word in a different way.) The possibility that there are limits on creative *extensions* of word usage is thus consistent with the possibility that there is no sharp general distinction between analytic and synthetic sentences.

Sampson is quite right, of course, to stress that semantic creativity of the kind in question does involve unpredictability. But knowing beforehand the limits on possible creative extensions of the usage of a given word would not enable us to predict the characteristics of those things which will come to be regarded as the kind of thing which are rightly designated by the word in question. Anything which is correctly designated by a particular 'sortal predicate' will have an immense number of properties which are not, according to our way of thinking, 'essential' to the 'natural kind' designated by that predicate. And we cannot predict which of these 'non-essential' properties some novel thing, rightly designated by the predicate in question, will have. Furthermore, given the possibility of meaning-change, it may even be impossible correctly to predict that the denotata of a given word at a given time will share with the denotata of that word at other times any 'essential properties'. Chomsky's limitationist account of this kind of semantic creativity is thus consistent with the claim that it involves unpredictability in this sense.

Sampson's discussion of the kind of creativity involved in extending the usage of a word has not, in my view, established that Chomsky is wrong to claim that there may be limits on such extensions of word-usage. This kind of semantic creativity does appear to involve unpredictability, but of a kind which is consistent with Chomsky's analysis, and which cannot be shown to entail Sampson's claim that 'there is no telling what properties will be seized on to extend the applicability' of a given word.

In short, I think I may claim here to have established that Sampson's discussion of creativity does not show that we must reject Chomsky's claim that true creativity 'takes place within . . . a system of constraints'. Sampson's discussion merely establishes that creativity involves unpredictability of a kind which is consistent with Chomsky's limitationist account of creativity.

I will now consider somewhat more briefly three additional objections to Chomsky's limitationist account of creativity.

(*d*) It might be suggested that an account of creativity which incorporates the limits thesis entails an inherently implausible *preformationist* account of human creativity, according to which 'plans' for all of the products which human beings will ever create are somehow performed in the genetic endowment of human beings.[76]

Such an account as the one developed here does of course entail the claim that every created product is a solution to a problem which can be defined in terms of constraints drawn from a biologically fixed and innate set of constraints. There may be a sense, then, in which it is appropriate to say that a theory of globally limited creativity entails the claim that the constraints in terms of which every humanly soluble problem can be defined are preformed in the innate mental endowment of human beings. But it does not follow from this claim that the 'plans' for products which are solutions for problems definable in terms of such preformed constraints are themselves preformed in any interesting sense. 'Plans' for products are specified by combinations of elements of the preformed set of constraints, and there is no reason to believe that these combinations are preformed in the innate mental endowment of

---

[76] See Sampson, *Making Sense*, p. 2.

human beings. There is, then, no merit to the suggestion that an account of creativity which incorporates the limits thesis entails a preformationist view of human creativity.

(*e*) It might be suggested that a theory of globally limited creativity entails an inherently implausible *historicist* account of human creativity, according to which the production of created products is merely a manifestation of the historically inevitable unfolding of human consciousness, in which human will and intention play no causally efficacious role. This suggestion is, of course, closely related to the previous objection, since a historicist account of human creativity is simply a kind of preformationist account. But in this case, of course, this second objection may have no more merit than the first.

Of course, Chomsky has suggested that language acquisition is a process in which the human will plays no causally efficacious role.[77] And as I have already pointed out, there are close affinities between Chomsky's account of true human creativity and his account of language use and acquisition. But in this case, it might be natural to suppose that his limitationist account of creativity does have historicist (and therefore preformationist) implications.

But this supposition cannot in fact be sustained. Whatever the merits of Chomsky's 'historicist' account of language acquisition, there is no reason to suppose, and Chomsky himself does not suppose, that the analogy between language acquisition and creative problem-solving is perfect.[78] The analogy breaks down, in particular, for the following reason. It may be reasonable to suppose that human beings are evolutionarily pre-adapted to the problem of language acquisition. And in this case, of course, we might expect language acquisition to proceed in the automatic, reflexive and unwilled way which is characteristic of those problem-solving activities for which organisms have been pre-adapted. (Imprinting is a good example of reflexive problem-solving in situations to which organisms have been pre-adapted.) But there is, of course, no reason to

---

[77] See Chomsky, *Rules and Representations*, pp. 11 and 33.
[78] See Chomsky, *Reflections*, p. 144.

suppose, and a limitationist account of creativity does not entail, that human beings are pre-adapted in this way to most of the problems which they can formulate and solve. Indeed, we can adapt Koestler's distinction between problem-solving in 'natural' and in 'artificial' environments to make this point.[79]

Most of the problems which human beings can pose and solve in a creative way arise in situations which are biologically 'artificial', in the sense that situations of this kind were not causally implicated in the selection of those characteristics which are biologically innate for the species. And as Koestler points out, it is only in the case of problems which arise in biologically 'natural' environments that we can expect the pre-adaptation which enables problem-solving to proceed in a reflexive and unwilled way. Of course, our limitationist account of creativity does entail that human beings are biologically pre-equipped with intellectual resources which can be brought to bear on those problems which they can formulate and solve. But the fact that human beings may be pre-equipped in this way is not equivalent to their being pre-adapted in the way at issue. The fact that human beings are pre-equipped to solve certain kinds of problems does not, then, imply that they are capable of solving these problems in a merely reflexive and unwilled way. There is, then, no merit to the suggestion that a limitationist account of creativity entails a historicist view of human creativity.

(*f*) It might be suggested that our account of globally limited creativity is incompatible with an evolutionary account of human intellectual capacities. It is a consequence of a limitationist account of creativity of the kind developed here that human beings are biologically pre-equipped for solving problems which arise in biologically 'artificial' environments. But natural selective forces can, by definition, make themselves felt only in those environments which are 'natural' for any given species. It appears, then, that there can be no evolutionary explanation of the alleged fact that human beings are biologically pre-equipped

[79] See Koestler, *The Act of Creation*, pp. 608–9.

to solve certain kinds of problems which arise in biologically 'artificial' environments.

This appearance is, however, deceptive. For an evolutionary account of biologically innate characteristics does not entail that each such characteristic is itself the direct product of natural selective processes. Some of the biologically innate characteristics of organisms are clearly indirect by-products of evolutionary processes which resulted in the direct selection of other characteristics with which they were, in effect, 'linked'. An innate human capacity for problem-solving in biologically 'artificial' environments may be an indirect evolutionary consequence, then, of evolutionary processes which resulted in the selection of some other characteristic. Indeed, this appears to be Chomsky's own view of the matter.[80] There is, then, no merit to the suggestion that a limitationist account of creativity is incompatible with an evolutionary account of human intelligence.

I believe, in short, that the account of globally limited creativity developed here on the basis of Chomsky's views is immune to those apparently plausible objections which I have just considered. In the next section, I will consider some arguments in support of such an account of creativity.

8 *Arguments for Limitationism*

In this section, I will outline and evaluate a number of arguments which are alleged to support Chomsky's characteristically limitationist account of true human creativity. Before examining these arguments, it is important to note that none of them is intended to provide logically conclusive grounds for Chomsky's characteristic claims about globally limited creativity. Rather, each appears to have the form of a formally invalid 'inference to the best explanation'. I will thus not be concerned to point out what is, in any event, obvious—that each of these arguments is formally invalid.

(*a*) Chomsky has claimed that, without global constraints on

---

[80] See Chomsky, *Rules and Representations*, p. 100.

human problem-solving, 'we have arbitrary and random behaviour, not creative acts'.[81] From this claim, we can in fact infer an argument in support of the account of globally limited creativity developed here. This first argument might be taken to have roughly the following form. Creative behaviour is not merely random behaviour. Creative behaviour, if globally constrained, would not be merely random behaviour. Therefore, creative behaviour is globally constrained.

Two remarks about this argument are in order here. First, in insisting that creative behaviour is not merely random behaviour, Chomsky is, of course, merely endorsing a view, which, as I showed in Section 3, is widely and I think rightly accepted. Second, it is, at least, not obvious that this argument does satisfy the requirements on an 'inference to the best explanation'. We certainly appear to be able to warrant the claim that creative behaviour is not merely random behaviour on grounds which are logically weaker and less contentious than those invoked in Chomsky's argument. This is so, in particular, because the existence of merely local constraints on human problem-solving would appear to suffice to ensure that creative behaviour is not merely random behaviour; and because the possibility that there are local constraints on creative human problem-solving is consistent with the possibility that there may be no global constraints of the kind posited by Chomsky's limitationist account of creativity. Although it is true that globally constrained behaviour is non-random behaviour, this fact does not seem to warrant even an ampliative inference to Chomsky's characteristically limitationist claim that creativity presupposes a system of global constraints on human problem-solving.

(*b*) Chomsky has claimed that 'it is conceivable that the persistent failure [to explain human behaviour] is to be explained on the grounds that the true theory is beyond our cognitive reach'.[82] From this claim, we can in fact infer a second argument in support of the account of globally limited

[81] Chomsky, *Reflections*, p. 133.
[82] Chomsky, *Language and Responsibility*, p. 69.

creativity which has been developed here. Such an argument, then, apparently has something like the following form. Human beings have persistently failed to solve problems of a certain kind. If human problem-solving were globally constrained, then human beings would persistently fail to solve problems of certain kinds—namely, those which could not be solved in terms of the constraints in terms of which all humanly soluble problems can be formulated. Therefore, human problem-solving is globally constrained.

Some remarks about this argument are in order here. It is clear that the claim that human problem-solving is globally constrained does not by itself entail the claim that there are problems which, because they are humanly insoluble, human beings have persistently failed to solve. To derive this latter claim, we need, in addition, to assume that human beings have actually posed some of the problems which would be insoluble were there global constraints on their problem-solving activities. And to determine the truth of this assumption, we need, of course, to know which of the problems which human beings have posed or could pose are indeed humanly insoluble in the relevant sense. And in the context of the present argument, we certainly cannot assume that the humanly insoluble problems are or include those which human beings have persistently failed to solve. For this assumption would beg just the question here at issue—namely, are there humanly insoluble problems, as an account of globally limited creativity suggests? Furthermore, this account itself provides no a priori specification of the kinds of problems which are humanly insoluble, since it is, as I have already pointed out, a metaphysical thesis, according to which there are some, unspecified problems which are humanly insoluble. In other words, since we do not have independent reasons for supposing that problems which human beings have persistently failed to solve are humanly insoluble, we have no real evidence that there are humanly insoluble problems, and, therefore, no compelling reason to posit global limits on human problem-solving in order to explain the persistent failure of human beings to solve problems of various kinds. It would seem, then, that this second argument cannot be used to warrant even an ampliative inference to Chomsky's characteristic thesis that human problem-solving is globally limited.

(*c*) Chomsky has claimed that the constraints on scientific inquiry, for instance, 'must be special and restrictive, or it would be impossible for scientists to converge in their judgments on particular explanatory theories'.[83] From this claim, it appears that we can infer a third argument for the account of globally limited creativity which I have here derived from Chomsky's remarks on this subject. Such an argument might have roughly the following form. Problem-solvers working in a particular domain do converge in their judgements about the merits of particular problem-solutions. If human problem-solving were globally constrained, then such convergence in judgements would occur. Therefore, human problem-solving is globally constrained.

Some remarks about this argument are in order here. It might seem that this argument is subject to the same kind of objection which undermined the first argument we considered. That is, it might seem that we can warrant the claim that problem-solvers converge in their judgements on logically weaker and less contentious grounds than those which are invoked in the argument outlined above. In particular, it might seem that we can warrant this inference merely by supposing that there are local constraints on problem-solving in particular domains, and by pointing out that problem-solvers working in these domains will converge in their judgements about the merits of particular problem-solutions in so far as they know about and share a commitment to those local constraints.

But this argument cannot, I think, be undermined in this way. This is so, in particular, because the existence of merely local constraints on problem-solving in a particular domain would not suffice to explain the fact that problem-solvers working in that domain converge in their judgements about the

---

[83] Chomsky, *Reflections*, p. 24.

particular ways in which some created products are exemplary. As I have already pointed out, a created product is exemplary only if (or only to the extent to which) it 'reveals' the existence and relevance of constraints on problems of the kind for which it is a solution which were unknown before its production. To explain convergent judgements about the exemplariness of a created product, it will, therefore, not suffice to suppose that problem-solvers derive these judgements from their shared knowledge about those merely local constraints which antecedently defined the problem for which that product is a solution. The constraints the existence and relevance of which are revealed in an exemplary product are, by definition, not among those in terms of which the problem for which that product is a solution was antecedently defined. However, we can explain convergent judgements about the exemplariness of a created product if we assume that every human problem-solver has access, in principle, to a common and partially ordered set of biologically fixed constraints on human problem-solving. Judgements about exemplariness can converge, on this assumption, because problem-solvers share a capacity to gain access to elements in this set of constraints to which they had not previously had access. If problem-solvers do converge in their judgements about exemplariness, then we may have good grounds for supposing that human problem-solving is globally, and not merely locally, constrained.

(*d*) An account of human creativity which incorporates the limits thesis appears to be warranted on general biological grounds. The limits thesis is entailed by a *generalized limits thesis*, according to which, for every organic species, there are biologically fixed limits on the constraints in terms of which problems soluble by members of that species can be defined. And the generalized limits thesis of course entails a variant of the limits thesis for each non-human species. But it would, I think, be plausible to claim that many, if not all, of these variants could in fact easily be verified. And in this case, it must, I think, also be plausible to suppose that the limits thesis is itself true, though, of course, unverifiable. For it would surely be very odd indeed if human beings were the only organisms whose problem-solving capacities were not limited in some way.

Of course, it might be suggested that human beings are sufficiently different from other organic species for continuity considerations of this kind not to apply in this case. In particular, it might be suggested that the ability to use propositional languages differentiates human beings from other organisms, and provides a basis for their unlimited creative powers. But this suggestion cannot, I think, be sustained. Even if it is true that only human beings have a capacity to use propositional languages, and even though it also seems obvious that such a capacity would be associated with quantum differences in problem-solving capacities, it does not follow from these claims that human problem-solving capacities are unlimited. A capacity to use a propositional language does not ensure a capacity for unlimited problem-solving, as we can easily see by considering any propositional language which is based on a very simple vocabulary. In such a language, many problems cannot even be formulated, let alone solved. Of course, it might be suggested that human languages have vocabularies which, while limited at any given time in their expressive possibilities, can be enriched in ways which seem to have no natural limits. But, as I have already shown in my discussion of Sampson's objections to limitationism, it does not seem plausible to suppose that human languages do have infinitely enrichable vocabularies of the kind required. There is, then, no reason to suppose that a human capacity to use propositional languages suggests that human beings, unlike other organisms, are not inherently limited in their problem-solving capacities. I thus think that it is reasonable to suppose that continuity considerations do warrant acceptance of an account of creativity which incorporates Chomsky's limits thesis.

In summary, I believe that there are at least two arguments which support Chomsky's characteristically limitationist account of human creativity. I suggest, then, that it is reasonable to suppose, as Chomsky claims, that human problem-solving capacities are limited by biologically fixed and innate cognitive faculties.

In this chapter, I have considered, elaborated, and defended Chomsky's characteristic limitationist account of human creativity, according to which human creativity 'takes place within—presupposes, in fact—an [innately based] system of constraints and governing principles'. This completes my detailed discussion of Chomsky's characteristic philosophical commitments.

CONCLUSION

CHOMSKY'S LIBERTARIANISM

FROM the analysis of Chomsky's system of ideas presented here, we can now tentatively construct a systematic, if abstract, account of linguistic phenomena. The picture which emerges has a number of important features. First, human languages are social institutions the characteristics of which depend on the characteristics of the individuals by whose behaviour, beliefs, and dispositions they are constituted. More radically, languages themselves are epiphenomenal. They do not exist, either as social or as abstract Platonic entities. They are, rather, theoretical constructions which are grounded in the linguistic capacities of individual human beings. Second, despite their epiphenomenal character, languages serve as vehicles for the expression of thought and as means for effecting co-ordinated social action. Individuals succeed in communicating because (or just when) they are able to effect a co-ordination in the linguistic means which they use to express their thoughts. Third, individuals in a community are able to effect a co-ordination in the linguistic means which they use to express their thoughts, despite potentially great diversity in prior experience, because there are strong innate constraints on the kinds of grammars which they can acquire. Given these constraints, individuals with radically different prior experiences (within a certain range) will acquire grammars which are sufficiently similar to permit mutual intelligibility. Fourth, language use cannot adequately be treated as a form of law-governed behaviour. It must instead be seen as a creative, but rule-guided activity. The rules of their grammar guide the linguistic behaviour of the individual language users, but that behaviour is not determined (or, at least, is radically under-determined) by the circumstances in which it occurs.

Human linguistic phenomena, then, are constituted by individual human beings, freely and creatively expressing their thoughts by linguistic means which are co-ordinated with those employed by their interlocutors in virtue of the fact that individuals share a highly structured innate propensity to construct certain kinds of grammatical systems.

In fact, this account of linguistic phenomena contains elements of, or provides the basis for abstracting to, a general theory of human nature, as Chomsky himself recognizes.[1] Thus, we might say that Chomsky's account of linguistic phenomena reveals that human beings have a capacity for free, causally undetermined, and creative activity which is nevertheless intelligible to others because all human beings share innate propensities which, under suitable circumstances, induce the development in each individual of standards of intelligibility which are similar to those which develop in other individuals. (As Chomsky himself remarks, this abstract account of human nature resembles that developed by Kant, Rousseau, Humboldt and those influenced by them.)[2]

Of course, theories of human nature have long played an important role in political thinking, as Chomsky himself again recognizes.[3] He says in this regard: 'Social action must be animated by a vision of a future society, and by explicit judgments of value concerning the character of this future society. These judgments must derive from some concept of the nature of man.'[4] By way of conclusion, then, I would like to consider some ways in which Chomsky's theory of human nature, as derived from his account of linguistic phenomena, might be relevant to the problem, as Chomsky puts it, of 'creating social forms that will be more conducive to the satisfaction of human needs'.[5] I will divide my brief discussion of this question into two parts. First, I will review Chomsky's own explicit remarks on this subject. Second, I will try to show how Chomsky's

[1] See N. Chomsky, *For Reasons of State*, London, 1973, p. 176.
[2] Ibid., p. 177.
[3] Ibid., p. 170.
[4] Ibid., p. 183.
[5] Ibid., p. 149.

account of linguistic phenomena can be recruited to provide insight into a fundamental problem in the libertarian 'vision of a future society' which he endorses.

Chomsky's political views are libertarian and socialist. He says in this regard: 'The problem of "freeing man from the curse of economic exploitation and political and social enslavement" remains the problem of our time. As long as this is so, the doctrines and revolutionary practice of libertarian socialism will serve as an inspiration and a guide.'[6] According to Chomsky, libertarian socialism derives its specific 'vision of a future society' from 'deeper assumptions about the human need for liberty, diversity, and free association'.[7] And these assumptions appear, in turn, to rest on a still deeper assumption: that, as Humboldt said, 'the true end of Man ... is the highest and most harmonious development of his powers to a complete and consistent whole'.[8]

On this account, then, the organizing principle for political theory is embodied in the claim that the ideal social order is one in which 'free men can create and inquire, and achieve the highest development of their powers'.[9] From this principle, Chomsky derives a libertarian and socialist account of the ideal social order by invoking a number of subsidiary assumptions. For instance, Chomsky apparently endorses Bakunin's claim that the ideal social order is a libertarian one because liberty is 'the unique condition under which intelligence, dignity and human happiness can develop and grow'.[10] And he apparently opposes both private ownership and state control of the means of production on the grounds that 'man will not be free to develop his potentialities to the fullest' until these forms of control have been replaced by 'free and voluntary associations of producers'.[11] According to Chomsky, then, the social order of libertarian socialism (or anarcho-syndicalism) is best adapted

---

[6] See N. Chomsky, *For Reasons of State*, p. 166.
[7] Ibid., p. 157.
[8] Ibid., p. 177.
[9] Ibid., p. 182.
[10] Ibid., p. 155.
[11] Ibid., pp. 162 and 159.

to ensure the satisfaction of 'the fundamental human need . . . for spontaneous initiative, creative work, solidarity, [and the] pursuit of justice'.[12]

This, then, is Chomsky's 'vision of a future society'. I have suggested that this vision is related to an account of human nature which can be abstracted from Chomsky's account of linguistic phenomena. What, then, is the nature of this relation?

According to Chomsky, it is possible that 'the study of language might . . . offer an entering wedge, or perhaps a model, for an investigation of human nature that would provide the grounding for a much broader theory of human nature'.[13] And what of relevance to such a broader theory can the study of language be expected to reveal? According to Chomsky,

in its essential properties and the manner of its use, [language] provides the basic criterion for determining that another organism is a being with a human mind and the human capacity for free thought and self-expression, and with the essential human need for freedom from external constraints of repressive authority.[14]

The human capacity for language use, and, in particular, for Cartesian creativity in language use, provides evidence, in other words, that human beings have a capacity for 'free and creative action within the framework of a system of [self-imposed] rules'.[15] And the fact that creativity in language use takes place within innately determined limits undermines the radically authoritarian account of human nature according to which 'man is an infinitely malleable, completely plastic being . . . [who is therefore] a fit subject for the "shaping of behavior" by the state authority, the corporate manager, the technocrat, or the central committee'.[16]

In short, Chomsky's discussion of the relation between the theory of language and the politically relevant theory of human nature focuses on the Cartesian creativity of language use. In

---

[12]   Ibid., pp. 162 and 159.
[13]   Ibid., p. 176.
[14]   Ibid., p. 174.
[15]   Ibid., p. 185.
[16]   Ibid., p. 184.

conjunction with the normative assumption that 'the true end of Man . . . is the highest and most harmonious development of his powers', Chomsky's claim that the Cartesian creativity of language use reveals that human beings have an innately-based 'capacity for free thought and self-expression' suggests a 'vision of a future society' in which 'the fundamental human need . . . for spontaneous initiative [and] creative work' is recognized.

This, then, is the relation which Chomsky himself sees between his theory of language and his 'vision of a future society'. I believe that it is also possible, however, to detect another way in which Chomsky's account of linguistic phenomena might contribute to the development and defence of the theory of political relations which he favours.

As I have already pointed out, Chomsky claims that 'man will not be free to develop his potentialities to the fullest' until forms of social control and economic management based on relations of authority have been replaced by 'free and voluntary associations of producers'. Chomsky, then, envisages as an ideal a social order in which individual behaviour is effectively co-ordinated in the absence of political authority. Of course, it has often been suggested that it is impossible to constitute a social order in the absence of relations of political authority.[17] But I believe that we can in fact recruit certain elements of Chomsky's account of linguistic phenomena to show how a social order based on 'free and voluntary associations' might be possible.

The fundamental theoretical problem for the libertarian political theory which Chomsky endorses is that of showing how it is possible, in the absence of political authority, for human beings to converge in their judgements and sentiments and so constitute a community, rather than a bare, unco-ordinated collection of individuals. Ritter, for instance, says in this regard: 'Anarchist individuality and community are patently discordant. . . . Developed individuals, in all their anarchist delineations, tend to become detached by virtue of

---

[17] See P. Winch, 'Authority', reprinted in A. Quinton, ed., *Political Philosophy*, Oxford, 1967.

their self-assertion from their fellow humans.'[18] And Peters in effect poses this same problem from another perspective. He says:

Men perform predictably in relation to each other and form what is called a social system to a large extent because they accept a system of rules which are infinitely variable and alterable by human decision. Such systems can be maintained only if there is general acceptance of procedural rules which lay down who is to originate rules, who is to decide about their concrete application to concrete cases, and who is entitled to introduce changes.[19]

Indeed, Peters's remarks promise to be most helpful in formulating this fundamental problem in a precise way. For they suggest that it is possible for individuals to constitute a community only if most members of a group accept the authority of some of their number to formulate, interpret, and alter the rules which enable individuals to co-ordinate their behaviour. And this suggestion is, of course, uncongenial to libertarians like Chomsky, who claim, in effect, that relations of authority are not necessary to constitute a social order.

I would like here briefly to sketch a solution to this fundamental problem which is based on the Chomskian account of linguistic phenomena with which we have been concerned. I will first outline a Chomskian model of the linguistic community and suggest that it exhibits that community as one in which co-ordination is effected in the absence of relations of authority. I will then suggest that this result can be generalized to show how it is possible to constitute a dynamically co-ordinated social order in the absence of political authority.

A linguistic community is a group of individual language-users. It is constituted as a community because (or to the extent to which) each member of the group employs linguistic means for the expression of thought which are sufficiently similar to the means employed by other members of this group so that mutual intelligibility is possible. A linguistic community, in

---

[18] A. Ritter, *Anarchism*, Cambridge, 1980, p. 137.
[19] R. S. Peters, 'Authority', in Quinton, *Political Philosophy*.

other words, is constituted in virtue of the fact that the linguistic dispositions of each of its members are co-ordinated with those of other members. How, then, is the co-ordination of linguistic dispositions itself effected?

Of course, it might be suggested that the co-ordination of linguistic dispositions which is necessary to constitute a linguistic community is possible only if some language-users accept the authority of others to determine the correlations between sounds and meanings which provide the basis for linguistically mediated communication.[20] But Chomsky's analysis of linguistic phenomena suggests another account of how this co-ordination might be achieved. This analysis suggests, in particular, that linguistic dispositions are co-ordinated because individuals' dispositions arise as a result of an interaction between their (possibly unique) linguistic experience and strong innate constraints on the kinds of linguistic dispositions which they can acquire. Indeed, these innate constraints are so restrictive, on this account, that individuals with radically different linguistic experience will (within certain limits) develop systems of linguistic dispositions which sufficiently resemble each other to make mutual intelligibility possible. On this account, then, the co-ordination of linguistic dispositions is effected by a kind of pre-established harmony between the innately-based linguistic capacities of distinct individuals. It does not depend on the linguistic 'authority' of certain members of the linguistic community.

And neither does the achievement of a dynamic linguistic co-ordination depend on the authority of certain individuals in a particular community to introduce and to enforce changes in the system of shared linguistic dispositions. On this account, language change is co-ordinated because (or to the extent to which) each member of the linguistic community is independently predisposed to react in the same way to the introduction of novel patterns of usage.[21]

[20] See Winch, 'Authority', pp. 99–100.
[21] See F. D'Agostino, 'Ontology and Explanation in Historical Linguistics', *Philosophy of the Social Sciences* xv (1985).

I claim, in short, that this Chomskian account of the linguistic community exhibits it as a group the linguistic dispositions of the members of which converge, in the absence of (linguistic) authority, in a way which makes mutual intelligibility possible. On this account, convergence of linguistic dispositions occurs because each individual is independently predisposed to develop a system of linguistic dispositions which does provide a basis for linguistic behaviour which is intelligible to his or her interlocutors. Mutual intelligibility between interacting individuals is ensured, in short, because each individual has an innately-based 'interest' in communication and an innately-based capacity to develop a system of linguistic dispositions which will enable this interest to be satisfied.

I believe that this account of the relation between linguistic 'individuality' and linguistic 'community' may in fact provide the basis for a solution, in outline at least, of the fundamental problem for libertarian political theory. I suggest, then, that the judgements and sentiments and interests of individuals can converge in the way which is required if a community is to be constituted because (or to the extent to which) individuals have an innately-based 'interest' in co-ordinating their judgements and sentiments and interests with those of those with whom they interact, and an innately-based capacity to achieve this co-ordination. (Of course, the plausibility of this solution depends on the plausibility of those auxiliary assumptions which need to be invoked to account for the fact, if such it be, that human beings have generally failed to achieve this kind of co-ordination—whether in the presence or in the absence of relations of political authority. However, we might suggest, not implausibly I think, that this kind of co-ordination often has not been realized because external 'co-ordinating' political authority has usually served the narrow self-interest of privileged groups in a community at the expense of those deeper, innately based 'interests' which all individuals share and which, if unimpeded and undistorted by political authority, might have effected the co-ordination which political authority could not itself succeed in effecting.)

In conclusion, then, I believe that Chomsky's distinctive account of human linguistic phenomena may, as he himself has suggested, provide a politically relevant model of the human condition. His account of language is explicitly libertarian in its emphasis on the Cartesian creativity of language use. And it is implicitly libertarian in the anti-authoritarian account of the convergence or co-ordination of human interests and sentiments which can, I think, legitimately be abstracted from it.

BIBLIOGRAPHY

ARBINI, R., 'Comments on Linguistic Competence and Language Acquisition', *Synthese*, vol. 19 (1969).

ARISTOTLE, *De Anima*, trans. D. Hamlyn (Oxford: Oxford University Press, 1968).

AYER, A. J., *The Problem of Knowledge* (London: Macmillan, 1956).

BACH, E., 'Structural Linguistics and the Philosophy of Science', *Diogenes*, no. 31 (1965).

BERKELEY, G., *An Essay Towards a New Theory of Vision*, in *Philosophical Works*, ed. M. R. Ayers (London: Dent, 1975).

BEVER, T., 'The Psychology of Language and Structuralist Investigations of Nativism', in G. Harman, ed., *On Noam Chomsky* (Garden City: Doubleday, 1974).

BICKERTON, D., 'The Structure of Polylectal Grammars', in R. Shuy, ed., *Sociolinguistics: Current Trends and Prospects* (Washington: Georgetown University Press, 1973).

BLOOMFIELD, L., *Language* (London: Allen & Unwin, 1935).

——, 'A Set of Postulates for the Science of Language', in M. Joos, ed., *Readings in Linguistics I* (Chicago: University of Chicago Press, 1966).

BRISKMAN, L., 'Creative Product and Creative Process in Science and the Arts', *Inquiry*, vol. 22 (1980).

CHOMSKY, N., *Aspects of the Theory of Syntax* (Cambridge: MIT Press, 1965).

——, *Cartesian Linguistics* (New York: Harper & Row, 1966).

——, *Current Issues in Linguistic Theory* (The Hague: Mouton, 1964).

——, *For Reasons of State* (London: Fontana, 1973).

——, 'Human Nature: Justice versus Power', in F. Elders, ed., *Reflexive Water* (London: Souvenir Press, 1974).

——, *Language and Mind* (New York: Harcourt Brace Jovanovich, 1972).

——, *Language and Responsibility* (Hassocks: Harvester Press, 1979).

——, 'Linguistics and Philosophy', in S. Hook, ed., *Language and Philosophy* (New York: New York University Press, 1969).

——, *The Logical Structure of Linguistic Theory* (New York: Plenum Press, 1975).

——, *Problems of Knowledge and Freedom* (New York: Pantheon Books, 1971).

CHOMSKY, N., 'Recent Contributions to the Theory of Innate Ideas', *Synthese*, vol. 17 (1967).

——, *Reflections on Language* (London: Temple Smith, 1976).

——, *Rules and Representations* (Oxford: Basil Blackwell, 1980).

——, *Syntactic Structures* (The Hague: Mouton, 1957).

—— and KATZ, J., 'What the Linguist is Talking About', *Journal of Philosophy*, vol. 71 (1974).

COHEN, L. J., 'Some Applications of Inductive Logic to the Theory of Language', *American Philosophical Quarterly*, vol. 7 (1970).

COOPER, D., 'Innateness: Old and New', *Philosophical Review*, vol. 81 (1972).

——, *Knowledge of Language* (London: Prism Press, 1975).

CULLER, J., *Saussure* (London: Fontana, 1976).

D'AGOSTINO, F., 'Chomsky on Creativity', *Synthese*, vol. 58 (1984).

——, 'Individualism and Collectivism: The Case of Language', *Philosophy of the Social Sciences*, vol. 9 (1979).

——, 'Knowledge of Language', *British Journal for the Philosophy of Science*, vol. 28 (1977).

——, 'Language, Creativity and Freedom', *Philosophy of the Social Sciences*, vol. 14 (1984).

——, 'Ontology and Explanation in Historical Linguistics', *Philosophy of the Social Sciences*, vol. 15 (1985).

——, 'Rethinking Transformational Linguistics', *British Journal for the Philosophy of Science*, vol. 27 (1976).

——, Review of J. Katz, *Language and Other Abstract Objects, Australasian Journal of Philosophy*, vol. 61 (1983).

DANTO, A., 'Methodological Individualism and Methodological Socialism', in J. O'Neill, ed., *Modes of Individualism and Collectivism* (London: Heinemann, 1973).

——, 'Semantical Vehicles, Understanding, and Innate Ideas', in S. Hook, ed., *Language and Philosophy* (New York: New York University Press, 1969).

DENNETT, D., 'Intentional Systems', *Journal of Philosophy*, vol. 68 (1971).

DEN OUDEN, B., *Language and Creativity* (Lisse: Peter de Ridder Press, 1975).

DERWING, B., *Transformational Grammar as a Theory of Language Acquisition* (Cambridge: Cambridge University Press, 1973).

DESCARTES, R., *Discourse on Method*, in *The Philosophical Works of Descartes*, vol. 1, ed. E. Haldane and G. Ross (Cambridge: Cambridge University Press, 1911).

—, *Meditations on First Philosophy*, in *The Philosophical Works of Descartes*, vol. 1, ed. E. Haldane and G. Ross (Cambridge: Cambridge University Press, 1911).

—, *Notes Directed Against a Certain Programme*, in *The Philosophical Works of Descartes*, vol. 1, ed. E. Haldane and G. Ross (Cambridge: Cambridge University Press, 1911).

—, *Optics*, trans. P. Olscamp (Indianapolis: Bobbs-Merrill, 1965).

—, *The Passions of the Soul*, in *The Philosophical Works of Descartes*, vol. 1, ed. E. Haldane and G. Ross (Cambridge: Cambridge University Press, 1911).

—, *Principles of Philosophy*, in *The Philosophical Works of Descartes*, vol. 1, ed. E. Haldane and G. Ross (Cambridge: Cambridge University Press, 1911).

DRACH, M., 'The Creative Aspect of Chomsky's Use of the Notion of Creativity', *Philosophical Review*, vol. 90 (1981).

DUMMETT, M., 'What is a Theory of Meaning', in S. Guttenplan, ed., *Mind and Language* (Oxford: Oxford University Press, 1975).

EDGLEY, R., 'Innate Ideas', in G. Vesey, ed., *Knowledge and Necessity* (London: Macmillan, 1970).

FEYERABEND, P., *Against Method* (London: New Left Books, 1975).

FODOR, J., 'The Appeal to Tacit Knowledge in Psychological Explanation', *Journal of Philosophy*, vol. 65 (1968).

—, *The Language of Thought* (New York: Crowell, 1975).

—, *Psychological Explanation* (New York: Random House, 1968).

—, BEVER, T. and GARRETT, M., *The Psychology of Language* (New York: McGraw-Hill, 1974).

GARFINKEL, H., 'Remarks on Ethnomethodology', in J. Gumperz and D. Hymes, eds., *Directions in Sociolinguistics* (New York: Holt Rinehart & Winston, 1972).

GASSENDI, P., 'Fifth Set of Objections', in E. Haldane and G. Ross, eds., *The Philosophical Works of Descartes*, vol. 2 (Cambridge: Cambridge University Press, 1911).

GELLNER, E., 'Explanations in History', in J. O'Neill, ed., *Modes of Individualism and Collectivism* (London: Heinemann, 1973).

GETTIER, E., 'Is Justified True Belief Knowledge?', *Analysis*, vol. 23 (1963).

GOLDSTEIN, L., 'Two Theses of Methodological Individualism', in J. O'Neill, ed., *Modes of Individualism and Collectivism* (London: Heinemann, 1973).

GOODMAN, N., 'The Emperor's New Ideas', in S. Hook, ed., *Language and Philosophy* (New York: New York University Press, 1969).

218 *Bibliography*

GRAVES, C. *et al.*, 'Tacit Knowledge', *Journal of Philosophy*, vol. 70 (1973).

HARMAN, G., 'Psychological Aspects of the Theory of Syntax', *Journal of Philosophy*, vol. 64 (1967).

——, 'Reply to Arbini', *Synthese*, vol. 19 (1969).

——, 'Review of *Language and Mind*', in G. Harman, ed., *On Noam Chomsky* (Garden City: Doubleday, 1974).

HARRIS, Z., 'Distributional Structure', in J. Fodor and J. Katz, eds., *The Structure of Language* (Englewood Cliffs: Prentice-Hall, 1964).

——, *Methods in Structural Linguistics* (Chicago: University of Chicago Press, 1951).

HARRISON, A., *Making and Thinking* (Hassocks: Harvester, 1978).

HAUSMAN, C., *A Discourse on Novelty and Creativity* (The Hague: Martinus Nijhoff, 1975).

HOBBES, T., *Leviathan*, ed. C. B. Macpherson (Harmondsworth: Penguin, 1968).

HOCKETT, C., *A Course in Modern Linguistics* (New York: Macmillan, 1958).

HUME, D., *An Enquiry Concerning Human Understanding*, ed. L. A. Selby-Bigge and P. H. Nidditch (Oxford: Clarendon Press, 1975).

——, *A Treatise of Human Nature*, ed. L. A. Selby-Bigge (Oxford: Clarendon Press, 1888).

HUTCHINSON, L., 'Grammar as Theory', in D. Cohen, ed., *Explaining Linguistic Phenomena* (Washington: Hemisphere, 1974).

HYMES, D., 'Models of the Interaction of Language and Social Life', in J. Gumperz and D. Hymes, eds., *Directions in Sociolinguistics* (New York: Holt Rinehart & Winston, 1972).

——, 'Review of *Noam Chomsky*', in G. Harman, ed., *On Noam Chomsky* (Garden City: Doubleday, 1974).

JESPERSEN, O., *Language: Its Nature, Development and Origin* (London: Allen & Unwin, 1922).

KANT, I., *Critique of Judgment*, trans. J. H. Bernard (New York: Hafner Press, 1951).

——, *Critique of Practical Reason*, in *Kant's Critique of Practical Reason and Other Works on the Theory of Ethics*, ed. T. Abbott (London: Longmans, 1909).

——, *Prolegomena to Any Future Metaphysics*, trans. P. Lucas (Manchester: Manchester University Press, 1953).

KATZ, J., *Language and Other Abstract Objects* (Oxford: Basil Blackwell, 1981).

——, *The Philosophy of Language* (New York: Harper & Row, 1966).

——, *The Underlying Reality of Language and Its Philosophical Import* (New York: Harper & Row, 1971).

KIPARSKY, P., 'Linguistic Universals and Language Change', in E. Bach and R. Harms, eds., *Universals in Linguistic Theory* (New York: Holt Rinehart & Winston, 1968).

KOESTLER, A., *The Act of Creation* (London: Hutchinson, 1964).

KUHN, T., *The Structure of Scientific Revolutions* (Chicago: University of Chicago Press, 1970).

LABOV, W., 'Methodology', in W. Dingwall, ed., *A Survey of Linguistic Science* (College Park: University of Maryland Press, 1971).

——, *Sociolinguistic Patterns* (Philadelphia: University of Pennsylvania Press, 1972).

——, 'Where Do Grammars Stop?', in R. Shuy, ed., *Sociolinguistics: Current Trends and Prospects* (Washington: Georgetown University Press, 1973).

LAKATOS, I., 'Falsification and the Methodology of Scientific Research Programmes', in I. Lakatos and A. Musgrave, eds., *Criticism and the Growth of Knowledge* (Cambridge: Cambridge University Press, 1970).

LA METTRIE, J. DE, *Man a Machine*, trans. G. Buddey and M. Calkins (LaSalle: Open Court, 1912).

LEIBNIZ, G., *Discourse of Metaphysics*, in *Leibniz Selections*, ed. P. Wiener (New York: Scribner's, 1951).

——, *Monadology*, in *Leibniz Selections*, ed. P. Wiener (New York: Scribner's, 1951).

——, *New Essays Concerning Human Understanding*, trans. A. Langley (New York: Macmillan, 1896).

LEVELT, W., *Formal Grammars in Linguistics and Psycholinguistics* (The Hague: Mouton, 1974).

LOCKE, J., *An Essay Concerning Human Understanding*, ed. A. C. Fraser (New York: Dover, 1959).

LYONS, J., *Noam Chomsky* (London: Fontana, 1970).

MC NEILL, D.: 'Developmental Psycholinguistics', in F. Smith and G. Miller, eds., *The Genesis of Language* (Cambridge: MIT Press, 1966).

MALCOLM, N., 'The Myth of Cognitive Processes', in T. Mischel, ed., *Cognitive Development and Epistemology* (New York: Academic Press, 1971).

MANDELBAUM, M., 'Societal Facts', in J. O'Neill, ed., *Modes of Individualism and Collectivism* (London: Heinemann, 1973).

MARGOLIS, J., *Persons and Minds* (Dordrecht: Reidel, 1978).

MILL, J. S., *A System of Logic* (London: Longmans Green, 1947).

MINSKY, M., *Computation: Finite and Infinite Machines* (Englewood Cliffs: Prentice-Hall, 1967).

MISCHEL, T., 'Language Learning and Innate Knowledge', in S. Brown, ed., *Philosophy of Psychology* (London: Macmillan, 1974).

MORAVCSIK, J., 'Competence, Creativity, and Innateness', *Philosophical Forum*, vol. 1 (1969).

NAGEL, E., *The Structure of Science* (New York: Harcourt Brace & World, 1961).

NAGEL, T., 'The Boundaries of Inner Space', *Journal of Philosophy*, vol. 66 (1969).

NEWELL, A. *et al.*, *The Processes of Creative Thinking* (Santa Monica: The Rand Corporation, 1959).

NICKLES, T., 'Can Scientific Constraints be Violated Rationally?', in T. Nickles, ed., *Scientific Discovery, Logic, and Rationality* (Dordrecht: Reidel, 1980).

——, 'Scientific Discovery and the Future of Philosophy of Science', in T. Nickles, ed., *Scientific Discovery, Logic, and Rationality* (Dordrecht: Reidel, 1980).

O'NEILL, J., *Modes of Individualism and Collectivism* (London: Heinemann, 1973).

PETERS, R. S., 'Authority', in A. Quinton, ed., *Political Philosophy* (Oxford: Oxford University Press, 1967).

PLATO, *Phaedo*, in *The Dialogues of Plato*, vol. 2, trans. B. Jowett (Oxford: Clarendon Press, 1892).

POPPER, K. R., 'Autobiography of Karl Popper', in P. Schilpp, ed., *The Philosophy of Karl Popper* (LaSalle: Open Court, 1974).

——, *The Logic of Scientific Discovery* (London: Hutchinson, 1959).

——, *Objective Knowledge* (Oxford: Oxford University Press, 1972).

PUTNAM, H., 'The "Innateness Hypothesis" and Explanatory Models in Linguistics', *Synthese*, vol. 17 (1967).

——, 'What is Innate and Why?'.

QUINE, W. V., 'Linguistics and Philosophy', in S. Hook, ed., *Language and Philosophy* (New York: New York University Press, 1969).

——, 'Methodological Reflections on Current Linguistic Theory', in G. Harman, ed., *On Noam Chomsky* (Garden City: Doubleday, 1974).

——, 'Two Dogmas of Empiricism', in *From a Logical Point of View* (Cambridge: Harvard University Press, 1953).

——, *Word and Object* (Cambridge: MIT Press, 1960).

RESCHER, N., 'A New Look at the Problem of Innate Ideas', *British Journal for the Philosophy of Science*, vol. 17 (1966).

RITTER, A., *Anarchism* (Cambridge: Cambridge University Press, 1980).

ROOT, M., 'How to Simulate an Innate Idea', *Philosophical Forum*, vol. 3 (1971).

ROTHENBERG, A. & HAUSMAN, C., 'The Creativity Question', in A. Rothenberg and C. Hausman, eds., *The Creativity Quest* (Durham: Duke University Press, 1976).

RYLE, G., *The Concept of Mind* (Harmondsworth: Penguin, 1973).

SAMPSON, G., *The Form of Language* (London: Weidenfeld & Nicolson, 1975).

——, *Liberty and Language* (Oxford: Oxford University Press, 1979).

——, *Making Sense* (Oxford: Oxford University Press, 1980).

SANDERS, G., 'Issues of Explanation in Linguistics', in D. Cohen, ed., *Explaining Linguistic Phenomena* (Washington: Hemisphere, 1974).

SAPIR, E., *Language* (London: Rupert Hart-Davis, 1963).

SAUSSURE, F. DE, *Course in General Linguistics*, trans. W. Baskin (London: Fontana, 1959).

SCHLEICHER, F., *Darwinism Tested by the Science of Language*, trans. A. Bikkers (London: Hotten, 1869).

SCHWARTZ, R., 'On Knowing a Grammar', in S. Hook, ed., *Language and Philosophy* (New York: New York University Press, 1969).

SEARLE, J., 'Chomsky's Revolution in Linguistics', in G. Harman, ed., *On Noam Chomsky* (Garden City: Doubleday, 1974).

SIMON, H., 'The Architecture of Complexity' in *The Sciences of the Artificial* (Cambridge: MIT Press, 1969).

——, *Models of Discovery* (Dordrecht: Reidel, 1977).

SLOBIN, D., 'Data for the Symposium', in D. Slobin, ed., *The Ontogenesis of Grammar* (New York: Academic Press, 1971).

——, *Psycholinguistics* (London: Scott Foresman, 1974).

SPINOZA, B., *Ethics*, trans. R. Elwes (New York: Dover, 1969).

STERN, K., 'Neorationalism and Empiricism', in S. Hook, ed., *Language and Philosophy* (New York: New York University Press, 1969).

STICH, S., 'Competence and Indeterminacy', in D. Cohen and J. Wirth, eds., *Testing Linguistic Hypotheses* (Washington: Hemisphere, 1975).

——, 'What Every Grammar Does', *Philosophia*, vol. 3 (1973).

——, 'What Every Speaker Knows', *Philosophical Review*, vol. 80 (1971).

TAYLOR, C., 'The Explanation of Purposive Behaviour', in R. Borger and F. Cioffi, eds., *Explanation in the Behavioural Sciences* (Cambridge: Cambridge University Press, 1970).

222 *Bibliography*

TOMAS, V. 'Creativity in Art', in V. Tomas, ed., *Creativity in the Arts* (Englewood Cliffs: Prentice-Hall, 1964).

VIVAS, E., 'Naturalism and Creativity', in V. Tomas, ed., *Creativity in the Arts* (Englewood Cliffs: Prentice-Hall, 1964).

WATKINS, J., 'Confirmable and Influential Metaphysics', *Mind*, vol. 67 (1958).

——, 'Historical Explanations in the Social Sciences', in J. O'Neill, ed., *Modes of Individualism and Collectivism* (London: Heinemann, 1973).

——, 'The Human Condition', in R. Cohen *et al.*, eds., *Essays in Memory of Imre Lakatos* (Dordrecht: Reidel, 1976).

——, 'Ideal Types and Historical Explanation', in J. O'Neill, ed., *Modes of Individualism and Collectivism* (London: Heinemann, 1973).

——, 'Metaphysics and the Advancement of Science', *British Journal for the Philosophy of Science*, vol. 26 (1975).

WELLS, R., 'Innate Knowledge', in S. Hook, ed., *Language and Philosophy* (New York: New York University Press, 1969).

WHEWELL, W., *The Philosophy of the Inductive Sciences* (London: Frank Cass & Co., 1967).

WINCH, P., 'Authority', in A. Quinton, ed., *Political Philosophy* (Oxford: Oxford University Press, 1967).

WIRTH, J., 'Logical Considerations in the Testing of Linguistic Hypotheses', in D. Cohen and J. Wirth, eds., *Testing Linguistic Hypotheses* (Washington: Hemisphere, 1975).

INDEX